By the same author

Winners and Losers — Investment in New Zealand

A Guide to a Successful Retirement
(with Merren Parker)

Made in New Zealand

THE STORY OF

JIM FLETCHER

SELWYN PARKER

Hodder & Stoughton
A member of the Hodder Headline Group

Typeset by Egan-Reid Ltd.
Printed and bound by Wright and Carman, Wellington,
for Hodder & Stoughton, a division of
Hodder Headline PLC, 46 View Road, Glenfield,
Auckland, New Zealand.

Contents

Acknowledgments

Fletcher Holdings' decision many years ago to preserve its history has meant the company has kept archives going back to its early years. Without them, research for this book would have been much more difficult.

I am indebted to many people: Michael King, who not only wrote the foreword but did important early interviews; Malcolm McPhee, who disciplined a profusion of research material into some sense; Arthur Jewell, a diligent company historian and long-serving executive, for his invaluable advice and assistance; Bruce Wallace, until mid-1993 Fletcher Challenge's manager for corporate affairs, who nursed the project from its beginning; the many other Fletchers executives who made their time freely available; and my editor, Graham Adams, for polishing the manuscript.

Above all, I am beholden to Sir James for his help, and his astonishing memory for events that occurred half a century ago.

Selwyn Parker

Chapter 1

Young James Takes Over

J im Fletcher became the new managing director of Fletcher Holdings in 1942, aged only twenty-seven. He had been with the company for less than five years, a junior accountant who had done his papers at night school, yet here he was, head of one of the biggest, highest-profile, fastest-growing and controversial construction companies in New Zealand.

Jim, the second son of the shy Charlotte and the gregarious James snr, the company's founder, did not have his dad's presence nor did he seem a likely future captain of industry. Businesspeople remember him in his early twenties when he accompanied his father on his rounds of construction sites as a slightly built young man of below average height, with a deferential manner, not as someone likely to carve out his own style and strategy, let alone move out of his father's long shadow. Thus many talked privately of nepotism when young James moved into the managing director's office in Fletcher Holdings' new offices in Penrose.

Yet it was far from a pre-ordained succession. For many years, James had actively discouraged his two sons, John and James, from entering the business. Indeed, he felt manufacturing chemistry — in which one of his cousins had done well back in Scotland — would be a more appropriate pursuit for them. As their younger sister, Ella Phillips, recalls: 'Father didn't want either of them to go into the business. He said, "If you make a success of it, people will just say, 'Well, of course, it was only your father's. He made the business anyway.' And if you don't make a success of it, they'll just say, 'Well, you weren't as good a man as your father was.' So you are really better off on your own."'

Normally an obedient young man who addressed his dad as 'father', Jim joined the firm in spite of his father's advice, choosing to take on the risks his father had warned against.

If he had been looking for a quiet life in a sinecure, he couldn't have chosen a worse job at a worse time. It was wartime, and the job of managing director had become vacant only because his father had been unexpectedly co-opted by the Government into a crucial emergency job with special powers as commissioner of defence construction and wartime shipbuilding. Impressed by the company's extraordinarily fast rebuilding of the Social Security Building in Wellington after it had been razed by fire, Prime Minister Peter Fraser wanted to harness James Fletcher's unrivalled knowledge of the construction business for the enormous task of the wartime building programme. In practice, that meant a ragbag of big projects because New Zealand had become a forward base for the United States war effort — military camps and hospitals, landing barges for the Pacific offensive, huge stores, ammunition dumps, garrisons for the frontline forces in Guadalcanal, repair of war-damaged shipping.

There were plenty of precedents for the power that James Fletcher had been given. In Britain, for example, Winston Churchill had given the job of accelerating production of fighter planes to publishing magnate Lord Beaverbrook in the Second World War.

It was more than a full-time job, although Fletcher didn't take any payment for it. Thus the father didn't have time for the business he had spent thirty-three years building. Indeed, he felt obliged to sever all connections with it because, like other builders, Fletcher Construction would be in the running for some of the contracts.

Young Jim Fletcher inherited a company at the crossroads. Though still primarily a construction company, Fletcher Holdings had moved into manufacturing, primarily to ensure a regular and competitive source of materials for its building projects. Vulcan Steel Construction, which Fletcher Construction had with considerable foresight established in Auckland in 1923, and Wellington Structural and Reinforcing Steel, established in 1936, were two successful examples because they produced a lot of steelwork for the money-making construction side of the company.

The Government, which was urging Fletchers and other major companies to manufacture from local raw materials and cut down on imports to save foreign exchange, had also requested Fletchers to lead its house-building programme. James Fletcher felt, as he did about so many other projects, that it was 'good for New Zealand' if not necessarily for Fletcher Holdings.

Fletcher Holdings wasn't a big company at that time, and in 1942, in its second year as a public company, could boast a profit of only £17,477 before tax on a turnover of £2.2 million. It wasn't a great return on all the money tied up in the company, and a priority for the incoming managing director was to 'sweat the assets', in modern business parlance, or to produce increased turnover and profit from the machinery and other expensive equipment.

Then there were the highly sensitive family complications. Although it hadn't become public knowledge, the Fletcher family had fallen out quite badly in the previous few years over James's relentlessly expansionist style. He had launched the company, nurtured it, carried it through many crises, and dominated it, even though Andrew, who had come out from Scotland and joined Fletcher Bros in 1919, ran the Wellington division and William managed the Auckland office. Another brother, John, had managed the Dunedin office for a time but did not find business life to his taste. He had been a schoolteacher in Scotland and became a politician after leaving the company.

In 1942, the Fletcher family still dominated — overwhelmed, perhaps — the board of control. There were five of them: James, not yet knighted, as chairman, William, Andrew, Jim's elder brother John, and young Jim himself, who was widely known within the group as JC. In 1942, William was chairman while his younger brother looked after wartime construction, Andrew was also a director, Jim was managing director, John company secretary. This state of affairs wouldn't last much longer, and over the next few years most of the family would bow out of senior positions and it would become more clearly the company of James's own family.

The family tensions had begun before the public float of Fletcher Construction two years earlier, in 1940. None of the uncles had been enthusiastic about the float, but James had steamrolled it through. He could see that as the brothers moved towards retirement they might want to cash up their years of work by selling their share of the company. If that happened, James wanted to avoid an unseemly family scrap over valuing the shares. Going public was a way of establishing a fair market value for the company, a basis on which family members could establish the value of their respective holdings.

The state-housing contracts were another source of tension. They had proved at the start to be serious loss-makers, and the brothers blamed James, who had pushed the project in the late thirties. Even earlier, in 1937, the brothers had grown alarmed over yet another of his schemes — readymix concrete.

James Fletcher had always called the shots in the company, and inevitably young Jim inherited some of the resentment that usually attaches to the boss. There was also an element of jealousy at head office. A coterie of senior executives, working in Auckland under William, felt somewhat put out at a much younger man being promoted way over their heads and, some said privately, way over his.

Though most of them later came to support him, Jim Fletcher clearly had a lot to prove when he was installed as managing director in 1942.

Unless you tried to conduct business at that time, it's difficult to appreciate how commercial life operated in the early forties. Travel was tedious and time-consuming. A trip from Auckland to Wellington was an exhausting exercise — down on the Limited train with a poor night's sleep and tea in thick cups with a pie in place of a meal at Frankton or Taihape, a day's appointments with public servants, and then back again that night. Overseas trips typically occupied two or three months, and a company could fail in the boss's absence while he looked for overseas business. Communications from abroad were usually by letter, sometimes by cablegram, less commonly by the unreliable phone link.

All businesspeople were male and they wore suits. Respect for politicians was high. In the commercial world, bankers were practically venerated. 'You had to treat them with more respect than the politicians,' remembers Jim Fletcher now.

Public servants enjoyed enormous status and could make or break a business, so comprehensive was their control over the economy, which was very much a colonial one producing agricultural commodities for Britain.

The Industrial Efficiency Act of 1936 had been designed to make New Zealand more self-sufficient in manufactured goods by encouraging companies to make domestically what had previously been imported. Thus, in the forties, industries struggled to their feet under the protection of tariff barriers and the import licence policy that applied from 1938. Quite quickly, the Manufacturers Federation became a powerful lobby group.

Ordinary New Zealanders lived in ways that were dramatically different, much simpler, narrower than ours. They listened to crystal sets, queued to watch Shirley Temple movies, spent the summer holidays in fibro baches or in tents, rarely travelled outside New Zealand, hardly ever ate in restaurants, none of which were licensed. A few avant garde folk drank wine instead of beer. New Zealand was still a 'dominion' and when people talked of going 'home' it could only mean to Britain.

In 1942, war dominated the public's thoughts. So many of its sons, brothers and husbands were dying in countries few New Zealanders had visited, such as Crete, where the New Zealand force had been driven back by the Germans. After war had been declared on Japan in 1941, the territorial force had been mobilised and able-bodied young men were conscripted. There was rationing of food. The Americans were coming, too, as New Zealand became a staging post for the Pacific offensive.

Neither Jim Fletcher nor brother John went to war. Though thousands of others didn't, and especially builders because they were considered to hold jobs necessary to the domestic economy, the Fletchers' absence from the enlisted forces was flung in their faces over the years. In fact, Jim, aged twenty-four at the outbreak of war, volunteered but was turned down. He suffered at that time from migraines, and a severe attack of jaundice had weakened him. Brother John was also rejected on medical grounds because of his feet. As a boy, high insteps had meant that the tendons had to be cut and, after nine months in plaster, he had worn surgical boots.

Rejection was a blow for Jim because some of his friends had signed up and he had wanted to join them. Right until 1943 he wanted to enlist, but in that year he was 'manpowered', told to stay at home because he held a job deemed essential to the wartime economy, and he lost any chance of enlisting.

The young managing director would spend the next forty-two years in Fletchers, the first thirty-seven of them in the top job, where he was the turbine of its dramatic growth. He guided the company from a time of relative simplicity to one of complexity. In those days, a company didn't have to worry about managing currency risk, about shareholder relations, about corporate image, about third-party suits or sharemarket raids.

The numbers were much smaller, too. Jim Fletcher started business in a period when a £100,000 decision was a critical one that could make or break even a public company. In 1942, the company's total assets were just over the equivalent today of $600,000. He retired in December 1979, just before Fletcher Challenge, the large industrial company fashioned from Fletcher Holdings, Tasman Pulp and Paper, and Challenge Corporation, spent $400 million buying Crown Zeller-bach, one of British Columbia's oldest and proudest forest products operations.

This huge leap offshore could not have happened without Jim Fletcher's thirty-seven years in the driving seat.

James Muir Cameron Fletcher was born on Christmas Day 1914, in Dunedin, the city where the company had been founded just five years earlier. The second son of Charlotte, called 'Lottie', and James, he was fifteen months younger than his brother John. Given the scorching business career that lay ahead of him, the fact that the chimney caught fire on the day he was born could be seen as symbolic. Ella was born four years after her second brother, who was always known within the family — and still is — as Jim. Even now, when he introduces himself it's always 'Jim Fletcher', never 'James Fletcher' and certainly never 'Sir James Fletcher', as he later became. But in the company he was always 'JC'. (He had dropped the 'M' from his initials at his father's suggestion when he signed for his first cheque-book.)

The Fletcher family lived and breathed business. Long before Jim got his first job, he was receiving a business education by default. Even as a toddler, he would accompany his dad on visits to Fletcher Construction's joinery factory just off Andersons Bay Road, in Kensington, travelling in a horse and dray to the factory. As the boys grew up, they would visit construction sites, such as the one for the Dunedin Exhibition (where young Jim learned that the most profitable concession was for the toilets because they were guaranteed a healthy cashflow at a penny a visit).

The family often discussed business at dinner, even when the three children were young. 'Father discussed business so openly and so often in the house that we were conditioned to taking an interest in the family company,' Jim Fletcher recalls. Visiting businesspeople frequently dined with the family, and Jim and John would pick up, by osmosis, techniques of negotiation, financial planning, deal-making, character assessment and good commercial behaviour.

There were favourite dinner guests like little Willie Briscoe, an Englishman who owned a chain of merchant stores with branches all over New Zealand and Australia selling hardware and general goods. Jim and John would always cancel whatever they had organised for themselves when they learned that Willie Briscoe was coming to dinner.

'He was only about knee-high to a grasshopper, much shorter than I was,' Jim now recalls. 'He spoke with a lisp and sounded like a complete bloody fool, but he was absolutely the reverse. He used to tell the most marvellous stories.

'In those days, he travelled out to New Zealand by sea, and he drank a bottle of port every night. He was drinking the port his grandfather had laid down for him and he was laying down the port he expected his grandson to drink. He used to send out to New Zealand and Australia the port that he would consume while he was there, and then stock up on the ship enough port to see him through the voyage.'

The irrepressible Briscoe once told the Fletchers over dinner about one voyage from Britain when he took a berth on a cargo steamer, with a circus for company. Even now, Jim Fletcher can recall Briscoe's story almost word for word:

'I decided that at my age I just couldn't be bothered saying good morning to 200 or 300 people I had never met in my life and never really wanted to meet. So I thought I would come by cargo steamer. Unfortunately, when I got aboard I found that there was a circus aboard. What was worse, the elephants were outside my cabin, and tethered the wrong way round. I had to keep my portholes closed for the duration of the journey.'

Briscoe took ill in Christchurch, a long way from home, and his local manager, a man called Thompson, hurriedly got him into the Mater Hospital. As Jim Fletcher recalls: 'After a day or two, it was obvious, even to Briscoe, that he was dying. He called for Thompson and said,

"Look, Thompson, I would much sooner die in the spirituous atmosphere of the United Services hotel than the spiritual atmosphere of the Mater Hospital, so get me the hell out of here!"

'After a lot of persuading, Thompson ordered the ambulance. When it arrived at the door of the United Services hotel, the ambulance people were lifting him out on a stretcher and Briscoe addressed Thompson again: "Look, Thompson, one of the ambitions in my life is to be carried around a square of a foreign city in a litter, like a Roman senator. Tell these fellows to carry me around the Square." '

And so they did, one at each end of the stretcher. The dying Briscoe was borne at a stately and proconsular pace around Cathedral Square while the locals gazed in wonder at this cheerful but final procession. The circuit done, the ambulance men transported the delighted Briscoe to his room. He died the next day, as far from home as it was possible to be.

Another regular guest after the family moved to Auckland was Len Stevens, the dry and deeply conservative Auckland lawyer who managed much of the company's legal affairs for nearly fifty years and who later chaired Fletcher Holdings.

James Fletcher was often away on business, on average two weeks out of every month, driving around construction sites, taking the Limited train from Auckland, then the Lyttelton ferry, and finally the train to Dunedin. On the road, James spent a lot of time with architects to see what projects they were working on and for which Fletchers might bid. He was always chatting, listening, learning, winkling out opportunities, spotting potential danger.

It wasn't all business, however. When he was home, James dominated the household with his jokes, tales of experiences on the road, and story-telling from favourite authors such as Kipling and Mark Twain. He would recite from memory whole passages out of current bestsellers like Bulldog Drummond novels. 'There was always laughter and literature,' remembers Ella warmly of her growing-up.

James passed on two of his dominant personality traits to Jim: a congenital optimism and a capacity for thinking big. Having arrived in Dunedin in 1908, an immigrant from the village of Kirkintilloch, near Glasgow, who could boast not much more than a set of carpentry tools, he had set up his own company within a year and had survived crises that would have destroyed a man of less nerve and resourcefulness, eventually to hand over a business that owned brickyards, engineering works, joinery factories, quarries, structural steel plants and ship-building works.

With partner Albert Morris, an Englishman, his father had built a fine wooden house for a local storekeeper, one Herbert Green, at Broad Bay, Dunedin. The net profit on this first building contract was three shillings and sixpence on a total price of £375. Within three years, the young business was boldly tackling much more ambitious projects than houses: a local town hall, municipal baths, a three-storey office block for Whitcombe and Tombs, and Auckland city markets after the Dunedinite lodged a brash bid on his first trip north.

He had survived frightful ups and downs. Apparent in frequent references to the rise of Fletcher Construction is an assumption that economic conditions somehow made the development of the company an inevitable process, that the economy was a locomotive onto which a company had only to hitch itself. Social historian Bruce Jesson, for example, has regularly written about the company as though it couldn't help but make money given the country's thirst for big construction projects, its tariff walls, import licensing and so on. In fact, a fair reading of commercial history shows that it was often touch and go for the emerging company. Indeed, it has always been like that for young commercial ventures and probably always will be.

In Australia — and there's no reason to think it's not true in New Zealand too — just 37 percent of family businesses survive into the second generation. And only 13 percent — an 87 percent failure rate — last through to the third generation. The history of Fletcher Holdings shows that on any one of a score of major construction projects it could have gone under and only James's stubbornness and ingenuity brought it through.

'Father saved the company in the Depression,' Jim Fletcher says. 'Business was drying up. He went looking for it everywhere. But he went to the National Bank and pledged all his personal assets and the company's assets as collateral.' This reassured the bank, as it felt confident it could always call in Fletchers' assets if the company were to topple over.

Sometimes Fletcher could be rash, plunging into projects with more enthusiasm than caution. He was a construction man, a doer, and this of course was exactly the quality necessary to take on what he did. One of his strengths as a businessman was to see the opportunities rather than the difficulties, and his second son inherited that too.

'Father and I, we tended to act on more of an instinct under the old flier's syndrome — "seat of the pants", the feel of the thing — and I think both of us had an ability to see an opportunity perhaps a bit quicker than other people and be prepared to take a few chances on it,' Jim Fletcher argues. 'We minimised the difficulties and maximised the opportunities.' Like father, like second son.

James Fletcher didn't run the company from a desk but from on the road. Indeed, Jim can't recall his father ever carrying a briefcase. These days he would be called a hands-on manager.

In an insular commercial climate, Fletcher looked outwards. He believed in the opportunities created by travel. He had contacts around the world — Britain, Scandinavia, Europe, North America — and he often dropped in on them. Jim's business career would illustrate the same willingness to pick up ideas and expertise from abroad.

James Fletcher was a hearty, joke-loving and gregarious individual. But he could be bossy and argumentative as well. Associates keenly remember being chewed out by him. He could be pretty tough on his own elder brothers, too, and some of their dislike for him was deserved. On three different occasions, he sent letters to Andrew in Wellington that outlined his faults as a manager and concluded by telling his brother he'd been fired. The letters never seemed to faze Andrew — he just kept on turning up for work. He refused to be sacked, even by his brother.

The sons remember how their father's nose would turn pale if they incurred his wrath. Contradict him at a bad moment and he could turn angry. As Jim grew older, he contradicted his father more and more often, usually prefacing his dissent with 'Pardon me, Father'. The expression became a family joke. Perhaps more than anything else, Jim's willingness to take him on might have convinced his father that the second son could be the man to run the company.

Fletcher was a cheerful risk-taker. Early in the company's career, he took on the construction of municipal baths in Dunedin and then discovered to his horror that the water leaked out as fast as it was poured in. After opening day, the baths were shut for three months while he figured out how to seal the concrete walls of the pool. He did so by grouting them, using a technique later widely copied. It was the same confidence that won him the contract to build Milne and Choyce's department store in Auckland after barely a decade in the construction business.

Fletcher Construction grew through a reputation for reliability and advanced techniques. James was always looking for a better way of doing things. He could be inventive, sometimes copying or adapting ideas he picked up abroad, and he was an omnivorous reader of technical literature. It was Fletcher Construction, for example, that pioneered the electric winch to convey bricks and other materials to the upper storeys of buildings, saving an enormous number of man-hours. For the Milne and Choyce contract, James studied the construction of the largest American chain stores, such as Sears Roebuck.

In early 1937, he and George Winstone introduced to New Zealand the readymix concrete system years before it became available in Australia. He also introduced tubular steel scaffolding to New Zealand, a boon to the construction industry.

Innovative, yes. But probably above all, James Fletcher was his own man, confident of his expertise, firm in his opinions, dogged in the defence of his actions, candid in the admission of his mistakes. And, perhaps oddly for a businessman, he never worried much about making money for himself. He was project-oriented rather than profit-oriented, and his second son inherited that trait, too.

Jim and John Fletcher had a spartan schooling. Jim's pre-school years were spent in the house in which he was born in Albert Street, St Clair. With the company's business axis shifting northwards, the family moved in 1919 to Roseneath, in Wellington, where the boys attended the local primary school for five years. Guests, usually relatives like Uncle Andrew or businessmen and their wives, used to come at weekends for croquet parties on the lawn in front of the fine old house overlooking Evans Bay.

In 1925, the family moved back to Dunedin, to a new house in High Street, mainly for the major project of building the Dunedin Exhibition buildings. Jim attended High Street Primary School for two years and then the boys boarded at Waitaki Boys' High School, which included a junior section. This was an experimental school — the only other junior high school at the time being Kowhai at Kingsland, Auckland.

Waitaki had a warm atmosphere but a cold environment. The headmaster was Frank Milner, an innovative teacher who used to talk to his pupils, who came from all over New Zealand, about world affairs for five or ten minutes each morning at assembly. In some ways, the school's philosophy paralleled Scotland's Gordonstoun. The dormitories were deliberately only half finished, with timber walls that came up to the top of the bed. A canvas screen finished the walls and corrugated iron provided the roof. Every morning, the boys could, as Jim Fletcher now remembers, 'take their pick — a cold bath, a cold shower, or a dip in the school baths'. Twelve-year-old Jim opted for the cold bath. He would take a flying dive into the bath at one end and haul himself out the other, all in one practically continuous movement.

The routine was said to be character-building. After the swim, the boys went for a run in the school lane and out onto the main road, often splashing through frozen puddles. Any transgression of school discipline resulted in 'slushy' — gardening, sweeping up leaves or other chores.

The Fletcher household was always a warm and, in a relaxed and catholic way, an intellectual one. 'You were wrapped in love,' Ella recalls. 'That was pervading over everything else. There was always laughter and literature.' They regularly attended Sunday school and the Presbyterian church, where James Fletcher would launch into the hymns in a flat voice. While their father was a voracious but undisciplined reader who picked up practically anything lying around, John subscribed from his teenage years to such British intellectual periodicals as the *New Statesman*.

Ella, now living on the Whangaparaoa Peninsula, north of Auckland, remembers how different the two boys were. 'There was a lovely balance because brother John had this beautiful brain . . . he educated me to read. He would direct my reading without my ever realising what he was doing.' She remembers her other brother, however, as somebody who was exciting and entertaining.

Ella had isolated the two qualities in James that would characterise

the chief clerk (it was long before time-clock machines appeared), ran myriad errands and did a lot of filing.

Still, the office boys had fun. In their few idle moments, one of them, Dick Sharp, used to ring other South British branches and drive them mad with bizarre insurance requirements, such as demanding immediate cover on all his chickens because their coop was burning down. It was Sharp who once felled the leading soprano of an opera at His Majesty's Theatre with a large swede because he believed he had been cruelly deprived of a major role.

Jim Fletcher studied accountancy at night school, usually running straight from the office to private coaching at Banks Commercial College, and later to Seddon Technical Institute. If there wasn't time to put the ledgers away because the ledger-keepers hadn't finished with them, he usually had to skip classes. Sometimes he had to return after classes to tidy up at the office. In those days, employment was job- rather than hour-oriented. You did what you had to do and then you left, not before.

In 1935, the Labour Government of Michael Savage came to power and passed laws establishing a minimum wage, which shocked the management of South British. For years they had extracted maximum performance from Jim Fletcher and the rest of the staff. For a fixed wage, they worked at least three extra evenings a week as well as Saturday morning. It wasn't unusual for twenty or thirty staff to come in after playing rugby or some other sport on Saturdays to do another two or three hours' work. When he could, Jim played rugby for the Grammar Old Boys club, but often Saturday work would intervene and he would have to drop out of the team. Only Sunday could be guaranteed to be free.

Suddenly this overtime stopped when the management had to pay for it under the minimum wage legislation, which laid down maximum hours to be worked before overtime was owing. Small perks were cancelled, such as the half a crown tea money of which the office boys spent only part at the Cottage tearooms and pocketed the balance. Additionally, the office boys were allowed to cash in their vouchers in only two places — the Cottage and a little basement tearooms, the Mecca, in nearby Yorkshire House. Management had discovered that employees were buying cigarettes with the balance of the cash issued, so they stopped giving out cash. Perhaps it wasn't surprising that the

Auckland office was, after Johannesburg, the most profitable of all of the company's branches.

Productivity was impressive. But the management didn't reduce the workload or hire more workers with the new maximum forty hours, which meant there weren't enough hours to get the job done. So Jim Fletcher and the others would simply come in but not sign the attendance book, catching up with their work in their own time.

He recalls, 'They were harsh taskmasters but it was a wonderfully good working atmosphere. Quite good business training actually.' By 1937, he had moved on from office boy to the job of endorsements — reviewing and endorsing new policies, and then to ledgers as a bookkeeper. But a break with South British was imminent.

In 1937, his mother and father were travelling to Europe on a business trip and asked Jim if he would like to come. Jobs being scarce, an employee was not allowed to take leave of absence, so Jim Fletcher resigned from his job in April. South British, however, in an unusual display of magnanimity (probably a result of their desire to retain a hard-working employee and to keep a valued client onside), told young Jim he could come back to the job when he returned to New Zealand. In short, the company didn't accept his resignation and, to boot, intimated that a posting overseas might soon become available.

The family left on the *Monterey* for Sydney and then boarded a P&O ship, the *Orford*, for Britain via the Suez Canal. The trip turned out to be an extensive tour of big businesses. The party visited Karlstad Mekaniska Werkstad in Sweden, which had been contracted to manufacture the paper machine for the Whakatane Board Mills, the huge Brown Boveri company, which manufactured diverse types of heavy machinery including the turbines in which Whakatane Board Mills was interested, Bovings, which was providing the power units, Jonsereds, manufacturers of woodworking machinery, pulp and paper mills in both Sweden and Finland, a reverted superphosphate plant in the little Finnish town of Kotka, near the Russian border, and big building and manufacturing sites all over Britain. As the months went on, Jim Fletcher formed a resolution. Life, he decided, would be much more interesting in the construction and manufacturing business than at South British as a bookkeeper.

In America, Britain and Canada, they studied readymix concrete plants while James Fletcher received increasingly lugubrious mail from his brother Andrew about the planned contract with Winstones to launch the Fletchers into so risky a venture as mixing concrete off-site. There was no way, Andrew insisted, that concrete could be mixed more cheaply or reliably than on-site. Andrew had even put the wind up George Winstone, who would later profit massively from the venture, to the extent that he had mothballed some of the imported machinery and was considering sending it back to the manufacturers in the United States.

The readymix story makes an interesting interlude. James Fletcher returned with detailed and enthusiastic accounts of how readymix concrete worked in Britain and North America. He hadn't taken notes, and rarely did, but he had an astonishing memory. George Winstone recovered from his fears and agreed to build a first plant at Grant Road, just by the Wadestown Hill in Wellington, and a second one at Madeira Place in Symonds Street, Auckland. The first concrete from the company, Certified Concrete, went out in hastily improvised Ford and GMC trucks, each batch being guaranteed as to quality and strength, and quickly gained acceptance.

Fifty-five years later, the Grant Road plant is still turning out readymix concrete, though now carried by Japanese trucks, and has done well out of contracts including the Wellington motorway, Terrace tunnel, Wellington airport, the Beehive, many a Wellington high-rise building and countless driveways and floor slabs in Wellington homes.

Not everything went smoothly on the trip. To alleviate a chronic shortage of roofing materials for the state-housing project, James Fletcher had ordered a large consignment of roofing tiles, but the tiles were smashed to bits in rough seas on the voyage to New Zealand and the wharfies had to shovel them out of the hold in thousands of small pieces.

An early port of call was Glasgow, where they arranged for the company's buying agents there to hire carpenters at a rate of two and sixpence plus one halfpenny an hour to come to New Zealand and build the thousands of houses contracted under the state-housing scheme. When they heard of these advertisements, the Carpenters' Union in New Zealand complained bitterly, though it became clear once state-housing construction got into full swing that there was a serious shortage of carpenters of any nationality. In fact, the shortage was so great that many of the carpenters were headhunted from Fletchers when they came to New Zealand, and one of Jim Fletcher's first jobs was to tour building sites all over Auckland and remind them of their contracts.

The visit to Kotka produced a deal that had better results than those for the tiles and carpenters. The Finnish plant produced a new type of phosphate, which was released slowly through the soil, prolonging its grass-growing effect. Fletchers immediately introduced it to New Zealand farms under the name 'Reverted Super' through a company it established in Dunedin, Dominion Fertiliser, which challenged the local Kempthorne Prosser monopoly.

This was a lot more fun than organising lunches at South British. Until the trip Jim had been almost teetotal, but the travelling party enjoyed drinks before dinner aboard ship. The Scandinavian and Swedish businesspeople were hosts with a heavy hand for schnapps with beer chasers. (Jim's Aunt Min, the chairwoman for West Scotland of the British Women's Temperance Union, was not pleased.)

It was heady stuff in more ways than one and it turned young Fletcher's career around. On that six-month trip, he effectively became a Fletchers man. It was like a conversion. His father had asked him towards the end of the trip, probably after keeping a weather eye on his interest in the visits to industrial sites, if he wanted to join the family firm after all. The break with South British had become inevitable.

When he returned to New Zealand in November on the *Niagara*, after having crisscrossed North America by train, Jim Fletcher immediately resigned from South British and joined Fletcher Construction as a junior accountant. He wouldn't go back to South British except as a director and finally chairman of the board.

It wasn't a senior job that he walked into at Fletchers. He was third and last in the hierarchy of the accountancy sector, behind the company secretary, Cecil Batley, and accountant Mark Death.

Fletcher Holdings didn't throw out the welcome mat for the son of the founder. The uncles were far from pleased when James Fletcher wrote to tell them that his son would be joining the company. During the trip, James had received a reply from Andrew in which the elder brother told him that young Jim wasn't going 'to have any exalted position, that he'd be under Batley and Death and he'd have to like it'.

Wisely, James Fletcher didn't insist on a higher posting, nor did he tell his son about the letter.

Jim Fletcher started at the company the day after coming ashore. He found the books in a mess, despite Batley's supposed superior merits, and tried to tidy them up. This effrontery didn't endear him to the team that had developed around William and quite quickly he became an outsider, somewhat adrift in much the same way as at Auckland Grammar in form IIIB.

As he now cheerfully admits, his own manner didn't help. 'I was hot-headed,' he says bluntly. In one memorable outburst, he shouted at a quantity surveyor with whom he could not establish any sort of working relationship: 'Look, Nelson, you'd better wake up to one thing in this company and that is that there's only one man who can't be fired. It's not you. It's my father!'

The offended surveyor reported the incident to William, and Jim was hauled over the coals. The surveyor concerned was Nelson Carlton, who later left the company to form Carlton Construction and subsequently Carlton Cranes.

The untidiness of the accounts, however, continued to irritate the insurance-trained bookkeeper, and the row with Carlton wasn't the only one he would have with his uncle's staff. The tensions grew when Jim acquired sole responsibility for the Auckland office's accountancy operations when the revered Batley left for private practice and Mark Death was transferred to the housing division.

State housing had caused a lot of ill-will, so much so that a new subsidiary, Residential Construction, was formed in 1938 to head off complaints by the elder brothers and to satisfy the Government's conditions before it would issue a guaranteed overdraft. Many of the letters James Fletcher had received from his brothers during the six-month trip were full of the state-housing problems, and he would open them gloomily. Andrew's letters were studded with paragraphs starting 'I regret to say . . .' and 'It grieves me to report . . .' before launching into a recital of the difficulties with the contracts. The brothers wanted him to separate the problems of state housing from the company, and then solve them himself.

With his father so heavily preoccupied with state housing, Jim

21

Fletcher developed more and more independence. Though he still lived at home, he usually came to the office on the tram before his father and started work before the rest of the staff arrived. He was as keen as mustard, too keen for some of his older colleagues. Though only a night-school accountant, his natural candour and sense of honesty required that the books be what would be called today 'thoroughly transparent'.

He had discovered that William's contracts never showed a loss because inappropriate credits would be shovelled into the profit and loss statements to brighten up the figures a little. His nephew objected to this on the grounds that the contracts weren't true and fair indications of the outcome of a job. He told his uncle: 'If we have a loss, we should recognise we've had it, ask how the hell it's happened and see what should be done.'

Thereupon Jim started breaking out separate accounts for all the Auckland departments — the joinery factory, transport department, plant and boxing yards and so on — to see how they were performing individually. 'They have to stand on their own two feet,' he told William. Until then, the office had never factored overheads or other fixed costs such as interest on overdrafts into the figures, and still wouldn't. 'Your figures are wrong,' William would advise this brash young relative who was causing so many problems. James Fletcher, however, took his son's side because of earlier incidents involving his other son, John.

John had joined the company two years earlier. He had started under Andrew in Wellington Structural Steel and Reinforcing and transferred to the housing division in 1937. But when the problems with state housing arose, the uncle had given the young man a particularly hard time. William in Auckland had not intervened on his nephew's behalf, as James had expected that he would — and should. Never mind disputes over readymix concrete and state housing, this was family and it's doubtful if James ever fully forgave his elder brothers for their treatment of John. James Fletcher expected his children to fend for themselves, but he hadn't bargained on his own brothers picking on them.

Jim's insistence on extra detail, on separating out the accounts, has been standard practice for decades now. Company secretaries of public corporations are now required to report the independent income streams of the company's various subsidiaries so shareholders can see which divisions are making or losing money.

Despite the battles, Jim was enjoying himself. He had autonomy and he was winning most of his battles. Then he got his first taste of big, urgent construction.

Two months before it was due to open in 1939, the Social Security Building in Wellington burned down and indirectly caused one of the more famous incidents in domestic construction history. Happening to bump into the Prime Minister, Peter Fraser, the morning after the fire, James Fletcher took him by the arm and promised to put the building back up, better than new, inside the two months. The astonished Prime Minister agreed, particularly as social welfare policies were a major part of Labour's manifesto and some of the Government's credibility depended on their success.

Jim Fletcher was taken off the job of reconciling the company's books and given the task of office manager (in those days it was called office clerk). Though green, he played his part conscientiously, working all hours, and the four-storeyed, timber-framed structure with stucco cladding opened on time. The men had worked twenty-four hours a day under floodlights (but not on Sundays at the Prime Minister's request) to create a legend in New Zealand's construction history.

It was one of those dazzling exhibitions of his father's energetic style that created such admiration among the public and matching resentment among some civil servants. They had said the job couldn't be done and had even tried to render the miracle impossible by adding to the replacement plans a basement below tidewater level that hadn't been included in the original specifications. It wouldn't be the last brush Jim Fletcher would have with bureaucracy.

Fletcher Construction had become a public company, Fletcher Holdings, in 1940, with twenty-five-year-old Jim Fletcher taking the job of company secretary. The company, with a turnover of £602,000, was only a fraction of the size it would become, and the flotation had hardly riveted public attention. Though the 50,000 £1 preference shares had been snapped up because they guaranteed a 6 percent rate of interest — a top return at that time — less than 2,000 of the 50,000 £1 ordinary shares had been sold.

Things were happening, however, within the company. By 1942, Fletcher Holdings was acquiring the commercial logic that would propel almost all its future growth, although the logic might not have been immediately apparent. Its main sectors would be backed by manufacturing companies that would ensure its materials, its essential feedstock.

There was the commercial and industrial division, which handled the big projects, supported by Vulcan Steel in Auckland and Andrew's Wellington Structural and Reinforcing Steel, and by joinery factories, and marble- and stone-working yards in Auckland and Wellington.

Then there was the house-building company, Residential Construction, backed by the joinery factories, by the malthoid-roofing company Pabco, in Onehunga, Auckland, by New Zealand Plywood in Auckland and by Residential Construction's own door and corestock factory in Wellington.

Soon to start up were two new manufacturing operations, the asbestos-cement and linseed-oil plants, which were placed under the umbrella of Dominion Industries, formed in 1942 as the vehicle for all of Fletchers' future industrial developments.

There was also Dominion Sales Corporation under the dynamic and hard-nosed leadership of Woolf Fisher, who would become Jim's best mate and, much later, recognised by the public as the father of the steel industry in New Zealand. (Others would claim that mantle for Jim Fletcher.) Dominion Sales distributed the building products, from doors and veneers to roofing and the asbestos products that would later come out of the new plant.

Finally there was Fletcher Trust and Investment, then mainly a property-owning company but one that would later have a large part in the expanding company's operations.

Thus there was a grand plan at work. General construction and housing — both backed by their own plants — and the new and challenging areas of manufacturing from indigenous materials.

Indeed, by 1942 Fletcher Holdings had easily topped the magic million mark that had been an ambition of its founder. Its annual turnover had almost quadrupled since 1940 to £2.2 million.

The company was poised for big things, as was Jim Fletcher.

ment could not buy any more than a fraction of what it needed from the United States. The essential reserves of iron and steel, which were the raw material of munitions, had not been stockpiled. Nor had suitable manufacturing equipment and other materials been purchased.

Rubber, for instance, was so much in demand that gumboots were strictly rationed to deserving persons. Unless an applicant could prove he owned at least twelve cows, and was therefore judged to be a farmer, he wore leather boots instead. But the rubber industry became an example of how New Zealand could turn somersaults to adapt. It soon started turning out everything from tyre retreads and fruit-jar rings to lifebelts, gas masks, aeroplane matting, pram tyres and hundreds of parts for aircraft.

To get things under way, the Government began belatedly to take some tough measures. One of these was the appointment of Fletcher senior as commissioner of defence construction and, from November 1942, controller of shipbuilding as well. He was by no means the only controller. The Forestry Service's Pat Entrican, later to become a bitter foe of James Fletcher and of the company, was appointed controller of timber.

For Fletcher, it was a case of Mr Fixit coming to Wellington with a mandate to ride roughshod, if he had to, over government departments. Sparks were bound to fly and they did. The country quickly got a taste of the decisiveness and shrewdness that had shaped the Fletcher company and kept it alive.

Immediately, James ordered a fifty-four-hour working week for contractors. Next he handed out contracts with just the briefest references to government departments. With the Americans assuming that New Zealand could achieve the impossible, troops having to be trained for the 1943 Solomon Islands campaign by the Third Division, and Prime Minister Peter Fraser making impossible daily demands, the niceties could be observed only in the breach.

Fletcher senior set up a new method of writing contracts to replace the existing crude cost-plus system. Originally designed to account for armament expenditure in the First World War, cost-plus meant the contractor was reimbursed for proved expenditure, plus a standard $7^{1}/_{2}$ percent to cover overheads such as office and other costs including profit. The Government's audit office was supposed to check all the claims before settling them, but its staff was often too rushed to do so. Inevitably, some exorbitant charges were passed on. A lot of contractors did much better than 7½ percent, as government records show.

This was taxpayers' money and, whatever the pressures, it had to be accounted for. James Fletcher's solution to this contracting chaos was typically resourceful. The master schedule he introduced in March 1942 essentially broke down all jobs into common components. An initial contract price was arrived at by multiplying these component parts by unit prices for labour and materials agreed in the master schedule. It was reasonably flexible — a few extras could be factored in for country work and other non-routine items. On top of all this came 5 percent for profit and 2½ percent for overheads. The result was the total contract price. Thus contractors couldn't, to describe just one flaw in the previous arrangements, overman a job and charge for it. The massive and urgent work load required something much faster than the leisurely pre-war methods, and the master schedule did the job well, if not quite perfectly.

Though the master schedule meant the contractor could no longer present the Government with a bill including profit without prior agreement, there were some flaws. Manpower was the problem. There weren't enough quantity surveyors to prepare schedules to cover the hundreds of jobs going through their hands each week. However, Fletcher's system provided a reasonably weatherproof pricing structure compared with the leaky one that had been there before. Probably no system of tendering, however ingenious, could have withstood the pressure on it. The job had to be done first, and the tidying-up could come later.

All available resources — human and material — went into wartime construction. Building materials, even nails, were severely restricted in their use, and practically all private construction, including housing, stopped. From 1941, as shortages grew, a lot of goods were rationed including rubber tyres, flour, sugar, butter and tea.

Equipment of all kinds was lacking, and emergency was the mother of desperate solutions. Refrigeration, for example, was critical for preserving meat that couldn't be shipped because of the expected disruption to shipping. So two government departments — public works and railways — stripped refrigerating plant from a wrecked cargo vessel, the *Port Bowen,* which had run aground off the port of Wanganui in September 1939. They even purloined the bronze from the propellers and steel from the bulkheads and hull. Desperate for materials, the Navy then descended on the wreck and took what gear it could salvage including the winches.

Engines were ripped out of condemned vessels in Auckland Harbour, were repaired and then installed in minesweepers. Known as 'Rotten Row' engines, they chugged away for the duration of the war.

Never was the resourcefulness of New Zealanders better illustrated. For the first time they produced a dazzling range of previously imported goods — iodised table salt, nails, paint (in which Fletcher Holdings had a major role through its linseed-oil mill producing paint's raw material), electrical appliances, washing machines, carpets, plastics, tobacco and cigarettes, cosmetics, concentrated foods, even raincoats and pot mitts. Emergency was also the mother of invention — Jim Fletcher drove a car partly powered by a gas cylinder mounted on the roof feeding fuel to the motor.

The war effort involved almost everybody. Workers stayed on for compulsory overtime. Retired schoolteachers dusted off their old notes and poured into the schools to replace enlisted teachers. Women joined the armed services, worked as farm hands, drivers, mechanics, radio operators, railway porters, drove trams, took over jobs in banks and repaired tramlines.

New Zealand became a sort of giant larder. The American forces ate so much food that locals ran short of potatoes and onions, and the Department of Agriculture entered the vegetable-growing business on a grand scale. Dehydrated-vegetable factories couldn't keep up with demand.

By good luck, Fletchers was in a strong position to win its share of wartime contracts. When the emergency measures were introduced, the size of the contracts awarded was based on each bidding company's manpower capacity to do the job. Because it had increased its workforce for the state-housing contracts, now sidelined along with other private work, Fletchers had a big payroll and thus qualified for major work.

The action was fast and furious. Projects such as the reconstruction of the Social Security Building had given Fletchers a national reputation for swift completion of projects and it carried that through the war. There were scores of rushed jobs; in fact, all of them were rushed. Although wartime censorship prevented Fletcher Holdings from noting these contracts in its annual reports, the company joined with Cole Bros to build extensions to the Horotiu and Westfield freezing works to help feed the soldiers pouring into New Zealand almost daily, the Sylvia Park stores for military supplies in Auckland, ammunition magazines all over New Zealand, a hospital at Avondale, and the Burnham and Papakura military camps for training troops.

The last was typical of how quickly Fletchers could move. The contracts were let on 18 September 1939, almost as soon as war broke out, and the troops moved in less than two months later. The rain poured down for the first few weeks of the job, drenching the men and equipment and turning parts of the site into small lakes. But the graders, rollers, bulldozers, mechanical shovels, draglines, trench diggers, mechanical loaders, compressors and other equipment kept on working. Over 1,200 men were on the job at its peak in October, working twelve hours a day, six days a week. On 6 November, the camp was ready. The next day, the battalion moved in.

Fletchers soon became experts at building military camps in a hurry. The Department of Public Works regarded the construction of a camp for United States forces at McKays Crossing, Paekakariki, as 'the most noteworthy achievement in the Wellington district'. It took Fletchers six weeks, even faster than its performance at Papakura, to build this camp for 20,000 Marines.

Fletchers' shipbuilding subsidiary, Stevenson and Cook, did a considerable amount of critical work building minesweepers to protect the coastline and barges. James Fletcher also organised house carpenters to build Fairmiles — submarine-chasers that would later be converted by private owners such as Auckland's Mayor Sir Dove Myer-Robinson into cruising launches. Most of the parts were imported from the Fairmile company in England and the yards finished them with New Zealand kauri and other domestic timbers.

There's a simple way of describing the extent of this furious wartime productivity. Without counting all the other construction work on gun emplacements, tank traps, stores and magazines, Fletchers and other major contractors put together, by the estimate of the Department of

Public Works, the equivalent of seventeen new towns of 10,000 people each, all in a period of five years.

The latest American equipment, hitherto unseen in New Zealand, helped speed things up, and construction companies like Fletchers learned a lot from the Americans that would stand them in good stead in peacetime. The Yanks, as they were widely called, brought mobile cranes that made the old Scotch derrick, a fixed-leg crane which was then standard equipment for lifting materials up floors, seem pretty silly. New Zealand builders also looked in wonder at compressors, man-hoists instead of ladders or temporary stairs, and other labour-saving, time-saving mechanisation. Fletchers never forgot the lesson that there just might be somewhere out there a better way of doing something. After the war, it regularly sent its top people abroad to trade shows, such as machinery exhibitions. Timber man Lou Hahn, for example, used to travel all over Eastern Europe, even into the Soviet Union, looking at the latest logging equipment.

For New Zealand manufacturing in general, the war represented a coming-of-age. It was able to achieve things it never knew were possible and that confidence spilled over into peacetime.

The war had interrupted the state-housing contracts, but Fletchers resumed building low-cost housing later. One of the most persistent myths about Fletcher Holdings is that it made an easy fortune from state housing. In fact, it looked for a time as though the company might founder because of this. As recently as 1992, Ken Douglas, president of the Council of Trade Unions, told an investment conference of overseas bankers in Auckland that it was state-housing construction that had 'given Fletcher Challenge its start'. That is incorrect and the real story is worth telling, even though JC wasn't closely involved.

As John Fletcher, the first company historian, notes in his diaries: 'The genesis of the state-housing scheme goes back to father's advocacy in the early thirties of state-assisted [rental] housing as a means of lessening unemployment as well as being a less costly form of unemployment relief.'

James Fletcher was determined to help pull New Zealand by its bootstraps out of the Depression and, although not a speechmaker by inclination, he delivered at Rotary clubs a few rousing calls to arms on the subject with his 'running board' speeches. Their general theme was that the Depression-ravaged economy was stuck in the mud and the business community should remove their driving gloves, get off the running board and start pushing. The speeches found the right audience there, especially coming from a man recognised as New Zealand's most dynamic builder.

The existing Coalition Government was not as impressed, however, with the idea of state-subsidised housing, but politicians from the opposition Labour Party, who often shared a carriage with James Fletcher on the Limited down to Wellington and back, liked it. Labour's finance spokesman, Walter Nash, who had seen state-built accommodation in his native Britain, was particularly enthusiastic.

Labour then wanted to go a step further. It suggested to James Fletcher that the Government buy Fletchers lock, stock and barrel, nationalise it and get it to do all its public works schemes including schools, hydro schemes, bridges and, of course, houses. In effect, Fletchers would be a ministry of works. James Fletcher thought about the offer seriously but, concluding that he wasn't cut out to be a public servant, argued for the rental-housing scheme as an alternative. James Fletcher felt passionately about the country he had adopted, and he was quite prepared for Fletchers to build all the houses.

After endless bureaucratic delays, caused in part by resentment from the Department of Housing at outside architects and contractors usurping some of its functions, the first house was opened in September 1937 in Miramar, Wellington, and a tram conductor, David McGregor, and his family moved in.

At the suggestion of James Fletcher, who wanted to break the various bureaucratic deadlocks, the contracts had been let at a guaranteed price that Fletchers and other contractors, some of which did better out of state housing than Fletchers, considered generally acceptable. Money could be made on the agreed rates and charges. But hardly had the contracts started than Labour ordered a 10 percent jump in the minimum wage and made the payment of travelling time and tea money compulsory.

Overnight, the profit margins on the houses, already cut to the bone, disappeared. As the major contractor, Fletchers saw its cash reserves start to diminish rapidly. Only a Government-guaranteed £200,000 overdraft saved the company, even though it was never drawn on. It faced annualised losses in 1937 of £100,000 on the contracts, about $6.4 million in today's dollars.

Fletchers took a lot of unfair criticism from other contractors, who believed that its founder had contrived to get the company into Labour's inner circle. Indeed, over the years Fletchers became known as a 'Labour' company. The other contractors' resentment became obvious in a lot of ways. For example, many of the preliminary pricing calculations were done in an upstairs room at Brandon House in Wellington, but feelings towards Fletchers were so intense that John A. Lee, at that time in charge of the Department of Housing, advised John Fletcher that he and other senior Fletchers people should stay away from Brandon House.

An absurd situation then developed, as John Fletcher describes in his diaries. Although Fletchers had fathered the housing scheme, John and other staff had to meet Housing Department staff in secret locations around Wellington to iron out hundreds of problems before tenders could be called.

The company's highly ironic position of being *persona non grata* in the scheme James Fletcher had proposed contributed to an unfortunate result. Fletcher's original concept called for 400 different designs to avoid all the houses looking depressingly uniform, like a Soviet housing project. In fact, that's pretty much how they did look because, as John had tried to point out to officials in the newly established Housing Department, all the roof pitches were 32 degrees. 'Until the vegetation grew, many streets had a monotonous and institutional look,' he notes.

Fletchers' housing division in Wellington had a disastrous start, which the rival Auckland division noted with some satisfaction. (The family rift was widening at that time.) It started the contracts with a serious shortage of labour, largely because the company was completing the Wellington Railway Station and Joe Craig was fully occupied with that project. Within weeks, Fletchers was losing £200–300 a house, or $16,000–24,000 in today's dollars.

The bureaucracy developed nit-picking tactics that delayed jobs, with serious consequences for profit. Because the project had a high political profile — practically the entire Cabinet had turned up to the opening of the first one at Miramar — the bureaucrats were omnipresent and Fletchers staff felt that Housing Department inspectors were more than zealous. Fletchers old-timers maintain to this day that the inspectors had it in for the company.

Jim Fletcher remembers one inspector all too clearly. 'He had a mirror attached to the end of a walking stick. He would use the mirror to inspect the back of every bit of framing. If he found a piece of unprimed timber as big as a thumbnail, it all had to be redone.'

Housing Department officials subjected the pricing schedules to minute analysis. If they found any discrepancy, the department would claim thousands of pounds off the total price for a particular run of houses. They had done just this after an inspection turned up a discrepancy in plumbing and drainage that had, in fact, been the department's own fault. There were also delays in providing materials — 'too much of, say, stoves and too little of tiles', wrote brother John. For some reason, Wellington officials were far more obstinate than their counterparts in Auckland, where the housing contracts had gone smoothly from the day the first nail was driven.

After a while things bedded down and Jim Fletcher is philosophical about these events now. 'The pin-pricking only went on in the early days of the contracts, and only in Wellington,' he recalls. 'After things settled down, we formed lasting friendships with the senior executives in the department.' He points out that the Housing Department was itself a new one and was finding its feet.

State housing was an experiment in private and public co-operation, with inevitable tensions. In a contract with the Government, Fletchers had built joinery factories in Auckland and Wellington purely for the housing scheme and leased them from the Government. The factories' purpose, in a country chronically short of trained joiners, was to provide machined, mass-produced, standard joinery for the houses. Kiln-drying equipment for the timber had been installed because the huge scale of house building required much more timber than the usual yard-stacked, air-drying method, which takes months, could hope to provide in sufficient quantities and at sufficient speed.

Kiln-drying local high-resin timbers was a process new to New Zealand and it was months before anybody could master it, with consequent delays and losses. A lot of timber had to be discarded and the price of the wastage was devastating.

John Fletcher, flung in at the deep end, also had problems with inadequate financing and cashflow. The financial arrangements made by his father had proved typically optimistic, and the overdraft of £25,000 he had negotiated with the Wellington branch of the National Bank before he went overseas in 1937 came up hopelessly short as creditors clamoured for payment. John hastily negotiated a doubling of the overdraft, but that wasn't enough either.

James Fletcher wasn't a man to be easily alarmed but Andrew's 'you will be shocked to hear . . .' volley of letters about the state-housing contracts left him disquieted. He cabled John in Wellington to ask if things were really that bad. Though deep in problems, John replied as encouragingly as he could. He told his father: 'We are having difficulties but are coping. I see no good reason why you should cut short your trip.' Andrew wasn't giving his nephew much support, if any, and the Auckland office of the housing division, which was making good profits, left John to his own devices.

Wellington posed special problems. Skilled and unskilled labour was scarce and the city's difficult terrain added enormously to the fixed-cost contracts. Some of the foundations cost more than the rest of the house.

When James Fletcher returned in late 1937, he immediately saw the severity of the problem and it gave him some uncharacteristically sleepless nights. The company was now building roughly half of all the houses and losing heavily. He tackled the problem quickly and a £200,000 Government-backed overdraft was the result. He soon sorted out the other problems and the scheme in Wellington got back onto a profitable footing.

By then, however, the months of anxiety and overwork had taken their toll on young John Fletcher. Never very robust, he took ill and went to hospital in late January 1938, and couldn't return to work until the spring. He had done a fire-fighting job in the opening months of the contracts and, in his absence, Alec Craig and another Fletchers executive, Noel Burnett, who later left to join a rival construction company, fine-tuned the contracts and the house-construction methods.

John pays due tribute to his colleagues in his diaries: 'While Noel was making these sorts of innovations to make the administration easier, Alec was able to perfect the gang system, to reduce costs by significantly improving productivity, to achieve better co-ordinated progress with a new set of subcontractors, and above all to begin to develop a working relationship with the housing department from which all sorts of benefits flowed.'

The Auckland division of Residential Construction had fine-tuned house-building, putting up a four-bedroom, six-room house in five weeks. Perhaps it's a comment on the dearth of alternative recreation at the time, but by then the houses had become part of Auckland's entertainment. It was a Sunday outing for Aucklanders to drive down and see Fletchers houses taking shape in Orakei.

Then war broke out. From 1942 onwards, as the Americans poured in, Residential's key staff was plundered for other more urgent jobs. State housing did not start up again in volume until after 1945, when the soldiers returned and Fletcher Residential was given the job of finishing off some of the frozen contracts. Materials were desperately scarce and the Housing Department ordered the old nine-foot stud height reduced to eight feet, the overall size of the house cut back, and finishing touches such as architraves abandoned. But Fletchers had forgotten some of its skills and new tradesmen had to be trained.

Jim Fletcher, who was now in charge, put unflappable Alec Craig back on the job with the message: 'Make money or else.' He did, touring every house site one by one to check on each building gang's efficiency. Within a few months, the houses were going up as fast as in the glory days of the early forties. Alec Craig appointed a site man, Lloyd Parker, who 'shared Alec's enthusiasm and penchant for innovation,' according to John's notes.

The post-war team could have written the manual on efficient house assembly. It was based on the gang system — a foundation gang, a framing gang that put up pre-cut and pre-nailed frames, a cladding gang and a finishing gang of tradesmen who fitted out the interior. Residential Construction was in the forefront of low-cost house-building once again. As Alec Craig told his boss, Jim Fletcher: 'We were consistently 10 percent cheaper than other builders.'

Then, in 1949, the new National Government of Sid Holland, which had been sceptical of Labour's housing scheme, changed the rules. As John puts it: 'The beauty from our point of view was that we had had one client [the Housing Department], who paid us monthly, who provided the land and who sold or owned the finished product.' Instead,

The methods of producing asbestos cement were a closely guarded secret, and Fletchers found it difficult to acquire the necessary knowledge. As the Christchurch plant was being finished in 1943, John found himself looking at a lot of machinery but having little idea how to make it function. Just before Japan entered the war, James had sent Andrew, and later Sandy Cormack, then general manager of Certified Concrete, to study asbestos-cement production and, with expert input, several decisions had been made.

The so-called Hatschek method of production was judged best. 'Far ahead of the methods used by Hardies,' noted John. All the raw material, asbestos fibre, would be ordered through the Newark, New Jersey, company called Asbestos Ltd Inc, of international asbestos broker N. E. Newman. In return for the contract to supply asbestos fibre, Colonel Newman would provide technical information and/or key operators for Fletchers and allow company people to be trained at his plant, which was something of a coup for Fletchers.

Next, Fletchers hired through Sparrows, its London agents, a British engineer called Eustace (later nicknamed 'Useless') Pulbrook, whom James Fletcher had met on his overseas trip in 1937. Pulbrook had negotiated the high salary for the time of £1,000 a year.

Together with a Fletchers tradesman, Pulbrook had been despatched to Newmans' plant in Newark with a full set of instructions from JC. Pulbrook's brief was to find out how to install the machinery when it arrived in New Zealand, and the tradesman's job was to make sure he knew what all the equipment did and how to run it. Between them, they were expected to produce a layout to suit the building under construction, plus details of the process, steam requirements, handling gear, likely production levels for different products, cost of manufacture, cost of equipment and a lot of other data. Much of this was necessary to obtain the import licences and foreign currency required. As Minister Extraordinary in Washington during the war, Walter Nash helped greatly in securing much of the plant by processing the paperwork through the War Production Board and other United States authorities.

Back home, John's aim was to be good and ready when all the equipment arrived in company with Pulbrook and the tradesman. 'When the United States equipment arrived, we could get off to a good start,' he noted cheerfully at the time. By early 1943, the building was going ahead rapidly, but the Fletchers man and Pulbrook had, it later transpired, fallen out in the States and the job wasn't being done. The information filtering back to Christchurch was usually incomplete, often wrong and always late.

Then Pulbrook, bearing thirty suitcases filled with goods rationed in Britain, arrived back from America in May 1943, but 'did not know very much about the plans and details he had brought', an anxious John Fletcher noted. In itself, this was serious because Fletchers had put a lot of money into the enterprise. It was a classic greenfields manufacturing project.

The first experimental runs started in November with a complex mix of cement, silica sand and shingle scrap. They were disasters. After each run, practically all the moving parts had to be replaced because the sand was so coarse that it chewed them up. It could take a full week to prepare the equipment for another run.

Some of the dummy runs worked, after a fashion. John's team was able to produce some asbestos boards, but they turned out to be expensive because of problems with the equipment. The motor of the sludge pump overheated, losses were high, and all the sheets of fibreboard had to be trimmed by hand. But at least the quality of early board was judged superior to Hardies', and John had every reason to expect that the plant would steadily improve.

Instead, things deteriorated once John launched into what he hoped would be regular production. This proved to be slow, prone to constant stoppage while the tradesman fiddled with the machinery, and high in waste.

The delays were infuriating because the market was favourable. A dramatic shortage of steel because of the war had created a demand for asbestos roofing, sidings and tiles, and John had organised a three-shift, round-the-clock roster to fulfil the anticipated demand. By this time, Pulbrook had gone back to Auckland and the engineer was the only one on site who had seen these expensive and erratic machines actually produce high-quality asbestos board in New York. They would often clog up so badly that the midnight shift would clean the equipment and knock off until the engineer turned up at eight o'clock to get things started again. Thus there were huge wastages of labour as well as of materials. Some shifts produced thirty to forty boards, others none.

There were midnight-to-dawn emergency sessions, rows, frustration, continuing losses.

'The operators were manfully trying to operate the machine as we were foolishly trying to carry on full-scale production with three shifts,' wrote John. A pile of dry scrap began to accumulate and soon became known as Mount Misery. It was becoming clear to the increasingly distracted John, who often went back to the plant at midnight, that this experience was even worse than the difficulties of the housing contracts.

The money was pouring out. It was essential that Fletchers get its plant into profit as soon as possible because a new plant in Wellington, planned by Hardies, would decimate the Christchurch factory's market.

Several times John Fletcher suggested the company import an expert from Newmans' New Jersey plant but the tradesman, offended by the implication, argued against it. In his diaries, John Fletcher recognised that he should have been tougher much earlier.

In Auckland, Jim Fletcher became increasingly impatient with the endless production problems and overrode his brother. He decided the company had to hire an expert from America. He turned out to be an Italian-American called Bill Andreiorio; it was an unfortunate heritage because it meant long delays in getting him to New Zealand, since the Allies were at war with Italy.

As was his polite habit, JC met Andreiorio at Auckland airport. 'He got to the plant at ten the next morning. By one o'clock he had it going,' JC recalls. Technically, the plant was about ten years ahead of its competitors in Australia and New Zealand. The asbestos sheets were not air-cured, as was the usual practice, but baked in an autoclave, an industrial oven, and could therefore be sold immediately without a long curing process.

Fletchers' asbestos venture made satisfactory profits once Andreiorio had got to work, but demand fell away with the increasing availability of steel after the war. Fifteen years after it opened, the plant was producing less asbestos yardage than it had at the outset. From its North Island vantage point, Hardies now comfortably dominated the market and was producing over four times the asbestos of its competitors. The Christchurch plant struggled on until its closure in March 1974.

Although the asbestos-cement venture couldn't be called a success, it did provide Fletchers with a lot of experience that would help the company in the future, increasing its knowledge of America, from where it would draw some of its best ideas, friends and expertise. And it had broken new ground in New Zealand manufacturing. Indirectly, it also proved a blessing. Alarmed by the losses that kept on piling up with the mounds of discarded roofing, JC had set up a system of weekly financial reporting for all manufacturing units. In future years, this system became a boon to the company.

If the asbestos-cement plant proved an object lesson in the difficulties of manufacturing, the linseed-oil plant illustrated the reverse. It was a raging success from day one.

In the forties, New Zealand already had a linen flax industry, the flax being used in the manufacture of parachute canopies. But that left the immature seeds as the unwanted residue of the manufacturing process, and it was felt that these should be utilised and turned into a product that replaced imports. The seeds would be used primarily for the production of raw linseed oil, which was the basis of paint, as well as for the manufacture of linseed meal, a prized stock food. The industry was licensed and Fletchers, having won a public tender against stiff competition, moved into the processing of linen flax seeds.

The company already owned the plant and equipment. It had bought for the bargain basement price of £3,000 (about $156,000 in today's dollars) some old plant that had been stored at Westfield, near Auckland, ever since the Oil and Cattle Cake Company had closed down in the twenties. It was shifted down to Christchurch, where it was overhauled by Stevenson and Cook's engineers and set up in the factory in Dunedin and opened in April 1933.

Jim Fletcher, who was involved from the outset, says, 'The factory was a dream. From the day we started up, it ran at over its rated capacity.'

It was almost too successful. The plant quickly processed the stockpiles of seeds and Fletchers had to hunt worldwide for more raw material. Fletchers staff showed a lot of ingenuity in bringing the raw material to New Zealand in wartime: a consignment of linseed even arrived from India in the hold of an old square-rigger, the *Pamir.*

After the war, one of Jim's first calls was to the Archer Daniels head office in Minneapolis, where he was introduced to a new variety of seed called Golden Viking. By then, New Zealand's notoriously conservative farmers had seen the excellent returns from the crop and overcome their initial scepticism that it would plunder the soil of its nutrients.

The plant's first manager was 'Stitch' Hemming, a chemist who was convinced that the once-unwanted seeds could have yet another commercial life. They could be processed into biscuits fit for human, not just animal, consumption. On one of Jim Fletcher's and his colleague Woolf Fisher's many visits to the plant, Hemming plied the pair with what he was convinced was a breakthrough — a linseed and bran biscuit. The two of them had serious misgivings about the unappetising-looking biscuits but they obliged Hemming by munching their way through a few of them over morning tea. Almost immediately, they were attacked by violent diarrhoea and were hardly able to venture far from a toilet for a week.

Although it was all too clear that Hemming would have to do some extra work on his precious biscuits, Jim Fletcher also saw the possibility for a return, even if it wasn't a commercial one. His Uncle William had been troubling ('riding' is probably the right word) the young managing director, who had at that time not been long in the job, and he saw an innocent opportunity for revenge. 'Next time Uncle William comes down, give him a few of these biscuits,' he advised Hemming. The plant manager duly did so, and with the same result. JC heard the news about the riot in his uncle's bowels without regret.

A s Fletchers moved into manufacturing, Woolf Fisher became Jim Fletcher's closest associate. Outwardly, it seemed an unusual appointment. Fisher was the entrepreneurial partner with the publicity-shy Maurice Paykel in a newly established whiteware-manufacturing industry, and used to being the boss. Yet he threw it all in to work for Fletchers in a junior capacity to Jim Fletcher. In fact, Fisher and Paykel, then an assembler of imported and local components, didn't need its managing director and marketer. The Government had requisitioned almost the entire output of Fisher and Paykel, and Woolf Fisher had little to do.

JC and Fisher had met at the Pakuranga Hunt — 'He wasn't a good horseman, but he was better than me,' notes Jim Fletcher now. So Jim said over one of their frequent dinners together: 'Why not come over and help me? We're manufacturing and we need a marketing man to look after sales.' Thus Woolf Fisher, suave, assertive and gregarious, a natural glad-hander and salesman, became managing director of Fletchers' selling arm, Dominion Sales. It was the start of a deep, if short, friendship.

Fisher was many things that Jim Fletcher wasn't, and the boss acknowledges that he learned a lot from him. One of these was the art of 'cold-calling'. Fisher would breeze up to offices, announce himself airily and virtually demand an appointment with the boss, civil servants or whoever he wanted to see. Whether in New Zealand or overseas, he demonstrated the same confidence and energy.

'He couldn't sit still for a moment,' remembers Jim Fletcher. 'He'd jump up and say, "Let's go and see so and so."' Together they cold-called on people all over the world, introducing themselves, developing valuable relationships and promoting New Zealand manufacturing.

Fisher had a reputation for using people, too, and it's not unfair to say he would later use Jim Fletcher during the attempts to set up a steel industry. He was tough in business, unusually quick to spot an opportunity, and a brilliant marketer with a passionate belief in New Zealand's ability to produce world-class products. 'For Woolf, New Zealand-made was the best, no question about it,' recalls JC. In this, Fisher was far ahead of his time. In New Zealand in the forties and fifties, the word 'imported' was used as a sales plus; 'New Zealand-made' was a minus. Later, Fisher would be knighted for his work in the steel industry.

Together the pair travelled throughout New Zealand, Australia and Britain. Even twenty years later, after Fisher had died, his erstwhile boss would be greeted in Sydney hotels with, 'How are you, Mr Fisher?'

The relationship finished at the end of the war when Fisher went back to Fisher and Paykel. As a parting gift, JC got Fletchers' board to sell to Fisher and Paykel at a knockdown price — at least two times below book value — an office the company owned in Rutland Street, Auckland. Later, Fisher sold it to the State Advances Corporation for a killing.

Jim Fletcher was out-negotiated early in his commercial life by, of all people, his future wife. He had first met Vaughan Gunthorp in 1939 when he was looking for a personal assistant to relieve him

would worry about the pace at which Jim Fletcher drove the company. They would discover that CSR had bought into a company that thrived on action.

The logic of the deal was that, with CSR developing its building materials side rapidly, it made sense for Fletchers to protect its New Zealand market by forming a partnership with a powerful potential competitor. As Sir James Vernon, then a senior executive in CSR and later its chief executive, put it in a 1986 interview: '[We could] proceed without trauma, without throat-cutting.' Fletchers agreed to keep out of the building materials business in Australia and CSR agreed to employ Fletchers to develop its interest in the same products in New Zealand.

This was only the start of CSR's long involvement in Fletchers, but for the Australian company it was a relatively minor investment. The appointment of its local staff, the Auckland branch manager and the manager of its sugar refinery at Chelsea, Auckland, both relatively junior executives, recognised the size of that early investment. CSR would eventually appoint its Australian heavyweights to the board after lifting its shareholding in Fletchers.

The injection of Australian dollars helped Fletchers speed up the development of the sector where Jim Fletcher felt its brightest future lay — manufacturing. By the end of the forties, he was impressing his style deeper and deeper in the company, albeit anonymously. To the public, Fletchers was still the company of Sir James, who had been knighted in 1944. But it was his second son who was dictating the pace and direction.

Jim Fletcher's restless vision was beginning to rapidly form alliances. A new plywood mill, which started production in 1949, was jointly owned with Kauri Timber Company (New Zealand), a subsidiary of the Australian timber giant of the same name and, of course, indirectly financed with CSR money as a new shareholder. He would see links develop with the giant American builders like Bechtels, Kaiser and form relationships with the United States banks. These were connections that would open his eyes, expand Fletchers' horizons and deliver projects for New Zealand that had not previously been thought possible.

Heavy construction, manufacturing and offshore alliances combined to provide a strong platform for Fletchers to launch into the fifties.

Chapter 3

The Tasman Gamble

I f they had thought about it at all, the general public would have assumed that Jim Fletcher was only babysitting his father's company during the war and would give it back at the end of hostilities. He had, in fact, quietly taken over and started to move the company in a different, more manufacturing-based direction. Soon after the war, his father moved upstairs to the chairmanship.

The balance sheet alone told Sir James that the company was in good hands. Fletcher Holdings had grown steadily under his son's direction. Since JC had taken over in 1942, turnover had jumped from £2.2 million to 1950's £6.7 million. Those figures may not sound impressive, but £6.7 million is equivalent to over $280 million in today's dollars. Profit before tax had more than matched the increase in turnover, having risen by four and a half times to £76,600, equivalent to $3.2 million. The direction was certainly right.

Sir James had smoothed the transition of power with a wise decision that his son would remember when it was his turn to pass on the mantle. He moved out of the Penrose headquarters and took an office in Auckland. Then, as now, business relied on relationships and trust, and Sir James had found that business colleagues of long acquaintance routinely sought him out when they came to Penrose, rather than his son or other senior executives. In doing so, they were cutting across lines of responsibility and undermining the executives' authority. In some cases, they didn't realise that personnel changes had been made.

Removing himself from the seat of decision-making must have been a wrenching decision for Sir James, but it was a selfless and sensible one. Far from hanging blindly onto power, as many self-made men do, the company's founder had taken practical steps to ensure an orderly transfer of the torch of responsibility.

Having made the decision, Sir James stuck to it. Old Fletcher hands recall how Sir James would often travel down to the South Island to help his other son, John, with the manufacturing enterprises. But he never took a decision without first consulting his second son, back in Auckland. 'We'll have to ask Jim first,' said the man who had for four decades been accustomed to giving the orders.

The enduring difference between the two Fletcher brothers was evident in the fact that John subscribed to English magazines and Jim to American ones. JC was a keen reader of *Fortune* magazine, launched by Henry Luce, the China missionaries' son who founded the Time-Life group. Jim read every issue of *Fortune* from cover to cover and often extracted ideas from its features, principally those about the giant United States corporations. At Penrose, *Fortune* was practically mandatory reading, and each issue became increasingly dog-eared as it made the rounds. It was from *Fortune* that Jim Fletcher borrowed the idea for his first major innovation at Fletchers — the establishment of a universal superannuation scheme for men and women (at that time, very unusual), and for wage- and salary-earners alike.

Jim Fletcher had met a lot of Americans during the war, many of them captains of industry who had been drafted into wartime management jobs. He liked them for their openness — 'you were on first-name terms within half an hour' — and their sense of adventure, their willingness to crash through difficulties, their hunger for new techniques that would enable them to build better, faster, stronger.

It was hardly surprising, therefore, that Jim Fletcher's first trip outside New Zealand after the war should be to America. He travelled with Vaughan, who fulfilled the job of unpaid secretary. They bought a blue Lincoln at Niagara Falls and called on companies on both eastern and western seaboards and many other towns and cities in between. Their routine was standard. They would check out of the hotel at about 7.30 a.m. and JC would make his first cold-call to factory managers or anyone else on his list.

His reception was unpredictable. 'You didn't know if you were going to get fired out on your neck or be welcomed and stay for hours,' he recalls. Most often, he was greeted warmly — in those days visitors from New Zealand had a novelty value.

He would take full notes as he went and dictate to Vaughan, who had excellent shorthand, as he drove on to the next appointment. Then, after covering hundreds of kilometres and attending perhaps half a dozen meetings before nightfall, the couple would book into the next hotel. Vaughan would type up the notes on a mechanical portable typewriter, stick them in an envelope and mail them back to New Zealand. On that 1947 trip, the couple called on grain merchants, resin-glue-makers like Monsanto, with whom Fletchers had commercial links, Chase Bank and factories making plywood, linseed-oil and asbestos-cement products.

After 16,000 kilometres of driving and dictating notes, Jim Fletcher sold the Lincoln back to the marque's dealer in San Francisco, and happily remembers pocketing $US500 more than he had paid three months earlier.

Jim Fletcher found he liked the Americans and their way of doing things. When he began working with them, the benefits went far beyond anything he could have envisaged.

His first major venture with the Americans had its origins in a letter to his father from one of the naval top brass Sir James had met in Wellington during the war. Sir James had received a note five years after the war from Admiral Cotter, then president of United States contractors Merritt-Chapman Scott and earlier a key member of Admiral 'Bull' Halsey's Pacific staff. The letter would turn out to be a seminal one for Fletchers.

In it, Admiral Cotter expressed Merritt-Chapman Scott's interest in any joint venture in New Zealand on projects of marine works, tunnels or submarine pipelines. Merritt-Chapman Scott was then one of the biggest contractors on the east coast of the United States and a dominant company in the sector of marine works, where it was known for brilliant and innovative engineering. It also owned and ran a fleet of tugs, barges and heavy lifting equipment in New York.

Cotter had clearly been impressed by Sir James's ability to get things done during the war — and by the trout fishing. The letter, which Sir James quickly passed on to his son, also expressed a desire to come down to New Zealand to try for a few rainbow trout.

Fortunately, the letter arrived a few months before the Auckland Harbour Board called tenders in 1950 for a new wharf. Jim Fletcher showed he could move when an opportunity presented itself. Joe Craig was soon despatched to New York to meet Cotter and discuss the possibilities of a joint venture for the wharf. Next, Cotter called in George Ferris, a legend in American construction who was president of Raymond Concrete Pile, later Raymond International. This company was a major United States sub-contractor in piling, and particularly in the sort of foundation work required by the Auckland Harbour Board.

An engineer, Ferris had been seconded from Turner Construction, which had built skyscrapers in New York, to the United States Navy to head the operating committee of the entire building programme for naval and air bases in the Pacific. These were the bases in Guam, the Philippines, Hawaii and other Pacific launching points for the battles against Japan in the Far East.

According to *Builders for Battle,* an account by David Woodbury of that epic feat of construction under pressure, Ferris was practically one of America's secret weapons: 'He was a master at getting things done in the field, as well as a good solid engineer. George's specialty was red-tape cutting, which he did with a fine glint in his Scot's eye and an unholy ingenuity in bypassing obstacles. George could have talked Carrie Nation [a popular American evangelist and teetotaller] into setting up a round of drinks.'

When the wartime job was done, Ferris had left Turner Construction for Raymond Pile. He wasn't your average leatherneck construction guy. Urbane, socially well connected, Ferris moved easily across many strata of society and became another important bridge to American expertise for Jim Fletcher.

In turn, Ferris introduced Jim Fletcher to 'Mac' Gilmore, a spectacularly wealthy American manufacturer and steelmaker who owned with his brother a mini-mill in Portland, Oregon. He also owned a steel fabrication shop, a ship chandlery and a builders' supply business. What Gilmore didn't know about the marketing of steel was either unknowable or irrelevant. The firm price and delivery date for reinforcing steel that Fletchers won from Gilmore Steel was crucial in the tender for the wharf job. Reinforcing steel was in short supply and extremely expensive. Yet Fletchers secured a highly favourable steel contract, which enabled the consortium to enter a firm bid with guaranteed and prompt delivery of the critical steel supplies.

The New Zealand-United States consortium was called Fletcher Merritt Raymond, and it won the £1.8 million contract in early 1951. It was Fletchers' first joint venture with major overseas contractors and a coup for JC. Once again, 1951 figures are deceptive — the wharf cost over $66 million. The project turned out to be profitable, on time and on budget. The American contractors had deployed a range of construction methods and equipment new to the country, and the public used to congregate on the waterfront to watch the wharf taking shape as it jutted further and further into the harbour with the aid of one of Raymond's advanced pieces of technology, a patented pile-driving rig.

The wharf was also a symbol of Auckland's dominance of commercial life and of Fletchers' role in that dominance. Two years earlier, in 1949, the port of Auckland had become the largest in the country. Twenty-six percent of all trade crossed its wharves, although it is worth noting that the majority of that trade was from the rural and not the manufacturing sector — the chief exports being butter, frozen meat, milk products, tallow, hides and skins.

Jim Fletcher gained much confidence in himself and his company from the project because it showed that Fletchers could work with the best. Fletchers' own work force had learned a lot from the Americans, and between them Jim Fletcher and Fletcher Holdings felt they could take on much bigger jobs.

JC's American trips became quite frequent, at least twice a year. Some were planned well in advance, others hastily arranged to respond to sudden opportunities. He found inspiration as well as business opportunities in the United States, and correspondingly less in the United Kingdom. After 1946, his trips to Britain became increasingly rare.

In 1950, he and Alec Craig, then head of Fletchers' housing division, bought a Cadillac in New York and toured sawmills and plywood companies, taking notes as usual all the way, building up contacts, developing their knowledge. JC never threw these notebooks away and he still has many of them, forty-year-old mines of scribbled information decipherable only by the writer. On that trip, Jim Fletcher maintained his reputation for driving good bargains when he sold the car for the original purchase price to another Cadillac dealer in San Francisco.

By the early fifties, he was on first-name terms with some of the biggest people in United States business. They talked business over dinner parties and JC quickly absorbed their uninhibited enthusiasm.

At one New York dinner party hosted by Ferris in his own apartment, Jim Fletcher found himself discussing commerce and architecture with a who's who of American construction names — architect Frank Lloyd Wright, Robert Moses, the New York parks commissioner who masterminded the New York Expo, and another architect, Louis Skidmore, of Skidmore, Owings and Merrill, renowned for the new Lever Building in Park Avenue, New York, with its total absence of a ground floor. In this milieu, JC couldn't help but have his eyes opened to what his relatively small company could aspire to.

He quickly developed the skills of networking, though the word wasn't in use then. Whenever he was in San Francisco, Jim Fletcher would breakfast with Mac Gilmore in the Palace Hotel, an unofficial club of America's biggest downtown contractors. Since the fifties, much of the Palace's splendour has faded, but then it was a grand old hotel with an entrance large enough to accommodate carriages.

Jim Fletcher met the men who had built the Boulder and Hoover Dams, the Empire State and Chrysler Buildings and other landmark American projects, and who would do the same for much of Europe by employing advances in materials and techniques developed during the war.

The wharf job wouldn't be the end of the American connection if Jim Fletcher could help it. Indeed, even before the wharf was finished, he picked up two more big contracts in Australia. He had taken the flying boat to Sydney to check on Fletchers' burgeoning Australian construction company, only to find his local manager, Lyall Young, anxious about an appointment that very afternoon with the American contractors for the big Kurnell refinery project in Botany Bay. Young had been trying to get some work out of the project but hadn't had any luck, and asked JC to come with him.

On paper, Fletchers' position looked hopeless. The Caltex-led consortium regarded Fletchers as 'a two-bit construction outfit from New Zealand', as the managing director put it. The Americans didn't even know where New Zealand was.

The pair arrived at the city office to talk with the project manager, a hard-negotiating American construction man called Rocky Rochester, who worked for general contractors E. B. Badger.

The appointment proceeded politely but without any discernible hope of a contract coming from it. Until, that is, Jim Fletcher dropped onto the desk a copy of Fletchers' annual report, opened at a page with an illustration of a Raymond rig. The American sat up with a start. 'God! A Raymond rig! In New Zealand!'

Jim Fletcher told him about the consortium and the wharf project. As he did, he could see Rocky Rochester's estimation of the New Zealanders rising. If this company was working with Merritt-Chapman Scott and Raymond, perhaps it wasn't such small fry after all.

'Could you get one of those rigs over here?' the American asked. 'Or could we come and see it?'

Fletcher said he thought both might be possible. The Americans immediately came to New Zealand. Though it was an eight- to ten-hour trip by flying boat, they had thought they could hop across the Tasman and back in an afternoon. They came, saw and were conquered. The Raymond rig duly came to Sydney.

That was how Fletcher Merritt Raymond came to build the Kurnell refinery pier and, later, the submarine pipeline across Botany Bay, two of Australia's biggest civil engineering projects at that time. The American connection was paying off handsomely.

Even so, not even Jim Fletcher envisaged that a project so huge and complex, so pioneering and so financially dangerous as the Tasman pulp and paper project would later emerge from the contract for the Auckland wharf.

Mac Gilmore would become a firm friend of Jim Fletcher and important to the company's success. For example, he later steered Fletchers into its profitable steel-making plan while New Zealand Steel adopted the risky and hugely expensive route of converting ironsands into steel. Gilmore's own career was already a reflection of the American dream: he was a multi-millionaire from steel, steel-merchandising and envelope-manufacturing among various business ventures in which he was involved with his numerous brothers.

He took a liking to the younger New Zealander and introduced JC to Henry J. Kaiser and his son, Edgar, principals of the Kaiser construction family, which built the Hoover Dam, and owned Kaiser Steel, Kaiser Aluminium, Kaiser Engineers and a host of other companies. He brought him into the circle of Steve Bechtel senior and junior of the huge Bechtel construction company. Gilmore would regularly drive the New Zealanders around San Francisco to inspect shopping malls, hotels, bridges and other construction projects.

A man about town, Gilmore cut a dash in San Francisco. Every doorman of every nightclub knew him. So did the hotel receptionists, who were under strict instructions not to let the New Zealander pay for his accommodation or food. A sort of game developed between them: who would pay for the hotel first? Jim Fletcher even took to running down to reception with payment minutes after checking in. But Gilmore had that covered — he started paying before the New Zealander got off the plane.

The local police also knew Gilmore. Once, after Gilmore was stopped for running two red lights, the policeman peered through the window at him and said hastily, 'Sorry, I thought it was somebody else,' and waved the car on.

Gilmore was an assiduous party-goer and when Jim Fletcher and other business acquaintances got together with him on the American mainland, Gilmore would usually sweep them along on a round of nightclubs and bars. His sense of humour was pure varsity fraternity. One night, he insisted on taking Jim Fletcher to 'a nightclub you've never seen before'. A policeman was on duty at the door, which puzzled Jim Fletcher, but a few dollars changed hands and he admitted the pair after the American had explained, presumably with a wink behind the New Zealander's back, that he had promised he couldn't let him go back to his home country without having sampled the nightclub's pleasures.

Inside, JC was startled to see in the first room an assortment of dangerous weapons, and in the next room trolleys covered with bodies with cardboard tags tied to their toes. The penny dropped — it was the local morgue. Gilmore enjoyed the joke, even if JC didn't.

It was Jim Fletcher who introduced Gilmore to New Zealand, and he found the country lovable though quaint in some of its practices. Whenever he travelled here in the fifties and sixties, Gilmore was startled by the habit hotels had of serving a cup of tea at 7 a.m., whether the guests liked it or not. So, to get his own back, after one riotous night at The Hermitage, Gilmore took over the kitchen at 3 a.m. and insisted on serving tea to every guest and every member of the staff including the manager. Next day the party was farewelled, probably with some relief, by all of them waving from the front steps.

Gilmore 'could charm the birds off the trees', Fletcher has said many times about this persuasive American. There are countless examples of the results of Gilmore's winning manner, but one he remembers with special affection happened in Central Otago within a few hours of the impromptu tea-serving party at The Hermitage. The carload of Fletchers people, including Gilmore, Ferris and Jim Fletcher, arrived at a wooden bridge miles from anywhere to find workmen in the process of lifting the decking for replacement. There would be a three-hour delay, the roadmen explained, and the car would have to wait.

The others despatched Gilmore to see what his powers of persuasion could achieve. Within a few minutes, by which time the workmen had already started to put back the old decking, Gilmore returned to the car with the good news and they drove across. 'However, there's a price to pay for everything,' he told them. In this case, the price was morning tea in the roadman's shack.

His wife served them girdle scones that had enjoyed only the briefest acquaintance with a stove and tasted like raw dough. They were all but inedible and the party grimly munched through one each, but Gilmore clearly felt he owed the roadman more.

'That's delightful,' he said after swallowing his first scone. 'Can I please have another?' He later sent the couple a gift from America.

Certainly an opportunist who could bend the law to get things done, Gilmore was a businessman who excelled at marketing because he had a genuine warmth for people, not because he had read some textbook on how to fake sincerity. He knew everybody's name, and made a point of doing so. This warm, shrewd and likeable American died in 1974. Jim Fletcher's face invariably breaks out in a happy grin when he recounts stories about Gilmore.

It was the American connection that first alerted Jim Fletcher to the possibilities for New Zealand and Fletchers in the manufacture of newsprint. One day, soon after the signing of the Auckland wharf contract, he walked into the foyer of the New York offices of Merritt-Chapman Scott to keep an appointment with Admiral Cotter, president of the company.

Jim Fletcher was travelling with Alec Craig, and they had a few minutes to wait before being ushered in to see Cotter. They spent the time well. Jim Fletcher noticed that the entire reception area had an unusual decor — huge photographs of Merritt-Chapman Scott's major projects, some of them occupying a complete wall.

'A big proportion of these were of paper mills,' he recalls. An idea came to him, and when the pair were ushered into the handsome wood-panelled office overlooking the Hudson River, he told Cotter they had been very interested in seeing the photographs.

Cotter explained that the company had been at the forefront of a dramatic change in the pulp and paper scene in America. The trend in the industry was moving rapidly away from old-fashioned sulphite hardwood pulp mills, using slow-growing timbers of finite supply, to kraft pulp mills based on softwoods. The bulk of these softwoods grew in the southern states, Cotter said, and Merritts had built a lot of pulp and paper mills in the South for the giants of the industry — St Regis, which had invented the Bates heavy-duty multiwall bag, and other paper-makers like Union Bag and Paper. But what made Jim Fletcher's ears prick up was Cotter's reference to a mill that Merritts had built in a little place called Lufkin, Texas.

This was for the Southland Paper Mills company, and for New Zealand it would have tremendous significance. The Lufkin paper mill was the first in the world to make newsprint from southern pine. As it happens, southern pine is not unlike some New Zealand-grown varieties of radiata, which are notably 'sappy', with a high resin content.

Jim Fletcher then explained to Cotter the New Zealand Government's long-gestating scheme to build a pulp and paper mill based on this country's fast-growing timbers and to produce newsprint from them. It had been an on-again, off-again scheme, but this time it looked as though the Government was determined to implement it. Cotter was interested and asked if there might be something in it for Merritts.

Fletcher suggested another job for the New Zealand–American consortium then building the wharf. 'Why shouldn't Fletchers represent the consortium and promote it to the New Zealand Government?' he asked. 'We are the logical people to build the mill.' Admiral Cotter agreed. Work was starting to slow down in America in any case. And thus began Fletchers' involvement in the biggest industrial project ever undertaken in New Zealand.

Ignorance was probably bliss for Jim Fletcher. He had only a nodding acquaintance with the pulp and paper industry, though he had seen it in operation during the 1937 trip with his father. But Fletchers was a construction company and construction companies built things. A pulp and paper complex was merely bigger than other things the company had attempted.

When the Green Book appeared in New Zealand on 1 April 1951, plans for the pulp and paper plant speeded up. The book with the green cover was the Government's opening shot in a grand plan to make money from the forests. It was just twenty-eight pages long, ironically made from imported paper because the quality of New Zealand-made paper wasn't good enough at the time, and it contained the Government's offer to sell 23 million cubic feet of logs a year from its central North Island forests for the manufacture of pulp and paper, including newsprint. The area concerned was known initially as the Murupara Working Circle, which referred to the area of logging operations in the Kaingaroa Forest. The book's pitch was that anybody who built an integrated sawmill and pulp and paper plant would, by paying a minimum stumpage price for the timber of threepence a cubic foot, be able to manufacture pulp and paper at a cost that would launch the manufacturing company into world markets on an equal footing with the overseas giants, as well as earning 'an attractive profit before provision for tax'.

According to the report's assumptions, the successful tenderer could process the 23 million cubic feet of timber harvested annually into 70 million board feet of sawn timber, 50,000 tons of newsprint, 10,000 tons of printing and writing papers and 25,000 tons of sulphate pulp, of which about half would go into the manufacture of newsprint.

The Government wanted £200,000 worth of free shares in the company that won the tender in exchange for a multiplicity of technical reports it had garnered over the years and would make available to the winning consortium. The main reports had been prepared by American companies, notably Rust Engineering, from Pittsburgh, Pennsylvania, and sawmill consultant W. H. Rambo, from Portland, Oregon.

The driving force behind the Murupara Scheme, as it was originally called, was Pat Entrican, Director of the Forest Service. He was a knowledgeable and tireless propagandist for the forests who had first envisaged an integrated mill at Murupara in what he called 'a blinding flash of vision'. He had written about it eloquently in his book *The Romance of Murupara* and had promoted it in numerous trips abroad to the world's paper-making companies (and especially the British company Bowaters), sought much overseas technical advice on the suitability of making newsprint from radiata pine and tawa, and lobbied for it tirelessly to Labour and National governments.

For better or worse, Entrican regarded himself as the guardian of the entire grand plan and was deeply sensitive to any criticism of it, genuine or imagined. In knocking the Forestry Service into a blue-riband department of government, Entrican had made a lot of enemies among Wellington's senior public servants. As Arthur Jewell, one of Entrican's bright young men and later Fletchers' timber man, put it: 'He had trampled on a lot of fingers.'

The Green Book's prognosis of profits waiting to be plucked like so many leaves from the trees would prove to be highly optimistic. The forest had also not been properly managed and much of the planting had been haphazard, with inefficient wide spacings between trees in some areas. Frost was a problem on the flat land. Successive Governments and Entrican had also left the development a bit late. By 1951, the scheme was already nearly twenty-five years old and sections of the Kaingaroa Forest were rapidly approaching maturity. Indeed, much of it was already too mature for conversion into newsprint, which would become a controversial issue later.

As long ago as 1913, our foresters, recognising that trees grew exceptionally quickly on the pumice soil of the Kaingaroa Plains, ordered a tree-planting programme. This was mostly in radiata pine, also variously known then as *Pinus insignis*, Californian pine or Monterey pine. The seeds of this tree, which has since become so crucial to the economy, may have arrived by happenstance — in the rucksacks of the goldminers who flooded into New Zealand in the 1860s — though there are several alternative theories about how the tree came to be growing here. It is, however, accepted that the tree originated in the Monterey peninsula in California.

Even by the 1940s, not a lot was known about the merits and properties of radiata pine. The timber retail trade didn't regard it highly and the wood was used mainly for secondary purposes such as boxing. No self-respecting builder would dream of using it for a house. However, radiata pine did grow like Topsy in New Zealand. Radiata planted in the central North Island plateau matures up to three times faster than in Monterey and, incredibly, 'something like seven or eight times faster than radiata grown in the colder northern latitudes of Scandinavia', according to Brian Healy's densely researched *A Hundred Million Trees*.

Pat Entrican, then rising through the Forest Service ranks, saw more than a fast-growing species of tree, however. He saw a renewable source for pulp and paper that would establish an entirely new industry for New Zealand, to be run by the state, not by private enterprise. It was a vision he would seek to implement almost messianically.

There were certainly a lot of trees. By 1925, 10,400 hectares of Kaingaroa Forest had been planted. By 1929, there were 41,600 hectares. In the Depression, the Government had put the unemployed to work on the forests, and plantings accelerated rapidly again. (It is not, however, true, as is often claimed, that during the Depression the unemployed singlehandedly planted the forest.) By 1939, the plantings had doubled to 100,000 hectares, and by the late forties the Forestry Service was boasting that Kaingaroa was the largest man-made forest in the world. The claim was never substantiated, but Entrican frequently used it anyway.

Among the radiata grew ponderosa, Corsican, contorta (which was highly unsuitable), strobus, muricata, patula and larch. The Murupara Scheme was to be based on these enormous unused and unproven hectares of forests.

The idea of using these 'exotic' forests for making newsprint dates back to the early 1920s. But the Labour Government of Peter Fraser, with Walter Nash as its powerful Finance Minister, took up the task by formally recognising in 1946 that it was time to establish a national pulp and paper industry as a great saver of precious foreign currency.

A British expert, William Adamson, had visited New Zealand in 1925 for a preliminary survey of the possibilities of making pulp and paper and was struck by the immensity of the Kaingaroa Plain and its possibilities. Even sappy radiata pine could make satisfactory newsprint, he declared. Fired by Adamson's opinions, the Forest Service — and especially Entrican — immediately started working with American and Australian scientists to establish the relative pulp- and paper-making potential of various exotics growing in New Zealand.

Some of those early laboratory tests looked promising. By the mid-thirties, Entrican was well ahead of the rest of the world, including the United States, in research into using pine for newsprint. And when some editions of Auckland and Wellington papers were published in 1950 on paper made from radiata pine, Entrican thought his optimism had been vindicated. But it shouldn't be forgotten that the paper had been made in the United States, not in New Zealand, and from carefully selected trees.

There were certainly compelling reasons for New Zealand to make its own pulp and paper. Most of our newsprint came from Canada, and even our ordinary brown-paper shopping bags and brown wrapping paper were made from kraft pulp imported from Canada, Scandinavia and Britain. We couldn't even produce the bleached white paper used for lolly bags.

The loss in foreign-exchange dollars because of this enormous gap in New Zealand's manufacturing capability was serious for the beleaguered economy. The dollar shortage was so acute that the Government assumed that all the equipment for the pulp and paper project, if it ever got off the ground, would have to come from Britain, simply because the country couldn't buy enough American dollars.

No progress was made on the scheme during the war, and after it Labour lost office. The new National Government fully understood the virtues of exports. Instead of merely trying to stem the flow out of the country of dollars and British pounds, the new Government saw an industry that could earn these currencies. As Sid Holland, the Prime Minister, noted in a 1952 Budget speech shortly before the Tasman project was under construction: 'The project . . . will produce sufficient newsprint and pulp to supply the needs of New Zealand and some of the needs of Australia.' The Australians, in fact, were very interested in the prospect of newsprint from New Zealand and had put up their own proposals.

Sir Keith Murdoch, father of the world media magnate Rupert, had spent one evening in Wellington in September 1948 talking with the Labour Government's top ministers, including Arnold Nordmeyer and Nash. Murdoch was managing director of the powerful Melbourne Herald group and a director of Australian Newsprint Mills. He articulated ANM's desire to build a newsprint mill in New Zealand. All it needed, he said, was a thorough investigation by ANM and the Government's willingness to grant the necessary licence. The mill would be sited beside the kraft pulpmills of NZ Forest Products.

These revelations alarmed Entrican. It was, he told the Government, an Australian plot to stop the development of the Murupara project. For the next few years, he would fight tooth and nail for his version of the vision, and continue to regard Australian press barons with deep suspicion.

Not everybody accepted Entrican's conviction that the Kaingaroa Forest could produce high-quality paper and newsprint for fat profits. Nordmeyer, Minister of Industries and Commerce in the Labour Government, and one of its keenest intellects, was highly sceptical of the rosy financial information presented in some of the reports commissioned by Entrican. He clearly regarded some of them as propaganda.

'Has Pat got the answer he needs or would another more favourable report be required?' he asked innocently at one Cabinet discussion on the subject of pulp and paper.

Certainly, Entrican's language in memoranda to his seniors was decidedly fulsome. Consultants engaged were 'world famous'; the Forest Service's investigations over the years had been 'searching'; the scheme was 'the most promising industrial investment ever promoted in the Dominion'; it would save immense sums in foreign exchange, up to $US16 million over the first twenty years of operation.

Entrican knew what he wanted. All of his correspondence shows that he wanted Bowaters in and the Australians out. Bowaters 'should be accorded the first opportunity of considering co-operation with the Government'. The Australians' main objective was 'securing cheap newsprint from New Zealand'.

Entrican's notes of later discussions with Holland are equally revealing. They show his strong bias against the Australians. He didn't want them to have consultants' reports, he told the Prime Minister, because 'we were really concerned that the Australian interests [the press barons] would try to use the reports for their own interests'. He was also anxious that the Australians, whom Sid Holland characterised in discussions as 'hard businessmen', might try and drive down the stumpage prices, which were the Government's main source of revenue from the scheme.

Entrican was an excitable and mercurial man, and his zeal could make him enemies. During the war he had a couple of run-ins with Sir James Fletcher to whom, as controller of timber, he had been junior. He blamed Sir James, for example, for stopping the Forestry Service's wartime scheme for a state-owned mill at Reporoa in the Kaingaroa Forest. Sir James had, in fact, argued only that a proposal for a privately owned enterprise should be examined before a final decision was made on the publicly owned one, which was surely sensible business advice. It was probably, however, the vociferous and well-funded opposition of the Sawmillers Federation, which saw a state-owned mill cutting 25 million board feet of timber a year as a serious threat to their livelihood, that killed the scheme. But Entrican continued to blame Sir James.

Entrican, devoted to state ownership, even felt threatened by other companies' expressing an interest in the grand plan. Fletchers shouldn't have worried that Entrican was hostile to it alone. He fought NZ Forest Products in the same way when that company applied to produce newsprint, and he opposed Whakatane Board Mills when it sought permission to use its exotic forests. He had heavyweight opposition from within the ranks of civil servants, notably from Bernie Ashwin, who was the head of Treasury. All along, Ashwin believed a state-owned scheme was the wrong path to take.

But things were moving and the Green Book invited tenders worldwide for the 'utilisation of not only the largest man-made forest in New Zealand but also one of the largest concentrations of annual wood growth in the world . . .' Proposals had to be submitted by 1 November 1951, with a deposit of £10,000. The invitation went to United States, British, Swedish, Australian and New Zealand companies.

It was huge money by New Zealand's standards. The Government's costings estimated that about £17 million, the equivalent of $680 million today, including working capital, would do the job, plus another £14 million for public facilities such as harbour development, railways, transmission of hydro-electric power, housing and community facilities. The problem was that nobody outside New Zealand seemed to want to put up the money. And the Government certainly wasn't prepared to do so.

Until the Tasman project (JC had coined the name) the history of New Zealand investment in big projects was a saga of dependency on overseas investment. As Bill Sutch, a theoretically minded head of the Department of Industries and Commerce, put it in a 1966 book, *The Quest for Security in New Zealand,* we had made ourselves 'a colonial preserve' by allowing outsiders to control and direct the shape of the economy. Sutch contrasted this with the more independent path that Sweden, for instance, had taken. Until the fifties, there was hardly an industry in New Zealand that wasn't foreign-controlled and Sutch lists them all — banking, insurance, shipping, meat freezing, soap-making, motor-vehicle assembly, rubber manufacture, sugar (through Fletchers' minority partners, CSR, which had established the local sugar-processing industry), cosmetics, tobacco, petrol and oil distribution and refining. Even through to the mid-sixties, overseas money called the tune in the new industries — carpets, radio, television, electrical appliances, plastics, paint, glass, chemicals, pharmaceuticals, biscuits, confectionery, soft drinks, building materials, textiles, metals and many engineering products.

JC knew Sutch and used to discuss commerce with him. Sutch was professedly a believer in self-development and, inevitably, in protection for native industries. Jim Fletcher used to get on well with Sutch, and he and Woolf Fisher often dropped in on him unannounced in Wellington and took him out to lunch. Later, when he became permanent head of the Department of Trade and Industries, Sutch wasn't available any more. After two or three fruitless calls, finding Sutch's door shut, Jim Fletcher left a pointed message with Sutch's secretary: 'Please tell Dr Sutch that my door is always open and I would be very pleased to see him whenever he is in Auckland.' Fletcher never called on him again.

Trees are, of course, the raw material of paper, and the history of paper-making from locally grown trees was up to that time significant for its failures. It wasn't that paper hadn't already been produced in New Zealand. In 1876, Otago Paper Mills at Woodhaugh, on Dunedin's River Leith, started making paper, beating by one month the Mataura Falls Paper Mill Company fifty kilometres north of Invercargill. What emerged from an unpromising raw material of a mixture of rags, sacks and native grass, processed by primitive machinery, would hardly be called paper today though. Twenty-three years later, in the last year of the century, a consortium of Aucklanders produced paper from the Riverhead Paper Mills, north-west of Auckland, this time from an equally unlikely compound of waste paper and cotton waste. All but one of these mills had closed before the outbreak of the Second World War. The point, however, is that the paper-making capabilities of New Zealand's pines — the 'exotics' — were still unknown and a matter of considerable scientific debate in the early fifties.

Whakatane Board Mills had started making cardboard, which is a form of paper, for boxes and cartons from 1939 out of exotic timbers. Fletchers had taken a close interest in the process, having built the plant at Whakatane. Sir James and young Jim had also toured the Scandinavian engineering companies that supplied the machinery. Still, there had been no serious suggestion that Whakatane Board Mills could produce newsprint, which was much more difficult.

In the late forties, NZ Forest Products sought a licence to produce newsprint for its new pulp and paper plant at Kinleith. The application was refused through the intervention of Entrican, who saw it as a threat to his own scheme. At that time, the state was still reserving for itself ownership of the newsprint industry.

David Henry, NZ Forest Products' long-serving chairman, had long sought a newsprint licence. He had lobbied the Government vigorously not to put Murupara out to international tender. But he was a spiky character and 'enjoyed the worst of relationships with Entrican', in the words of George Fraser, the Fletchers staffer who worked closely with the Tasman project. Anyway, NZ Forest Products was already fully occupied in building a kraft pulp and paper plant and sawmill at Kinleith, which opened in 1954.

Henry had a stormy but durable career at the top of NZ Forest

Products, quixotically promoting and demoting favourites. It was widely said that staffers were promoted if they did not constitute a threat to Henry and demoted when they did. Some staff, including Reginald (later Sir Reginald) Smythe, who took over as chairman after Henry's death, found him impossible to work with on several occasions.

Henry also managed to preserve an astonishing private business arrangement with NZ Forest Products throughout his long career there, an arrangement that became a running sore between Henry and the directors. This was the royalty his own firm of tinsmiths and plumbers' suppliers, D. Henry and Sons, collected on NZ Forest Products sales. It was an extremely lucrative and unusual arrangement, to say the least. D. Henry and Sons picked up 2.5 percent commission on all sales of Pinex insulating board, underlay, cases and timber, and 5 percent on refrigeration board. It wasn't until after the death in 1963 of Sir David, who had hung on to power almost until his final weeks, that NZ Forest Products ended this highly irregular arrangement by buying the company.

Given the absence of previous newsprint production in New Zealand, it was clear in the early 1950s that any successful bidder under the Green Book's terms would be a pioneer conducting a large-scale experiment in the continuous production of newsprint from radiata pine and other even less well-known exotic species. 'People had great doubts about it,' recalls Jim Fletcher. 'Particularly about whether it could make a paper of quality like those produced from Canadian spruce and other traditional fibres. Pine was still a despised timber, used for boxing, dunnage and packaging. We were using it only in fairly small ways. Our Wellington factory was making door frames out of radiata.'

Even for a risk-taker like Fletcher, owning and operating an unfamiliar operation like a pulp and paper plant would be a huge punt for the company. Indeed, for quite a long time he had no plans of doing anything other than a construction job, albeit a massive one. After Fletchers had finished building the associated town, the mill and the plant, it would leave and it would be up to the pulp and paper company, whichever it might be, to worry about the manufacturing process.

Over the next few months ensued a fascinating process of diplomacy in international commerce, which had started in early 1950 when

Colonel Ian Bowater, scion of the Bowater family (whose males all carried the middle name of Vansittart), arrived in New Zealand to talk about pulp and paper.

Colonel (later Sir) Ian Bowater was the cousin of the autocratic Sir Eric, head of the Bowater paper-making company. Eric could be extremely lordly and once commandeered one of the company's new freighters for a Caribbean cruise. He and his brother, Noel, who each became Lord Mayor of London, were friends of the royal family and captains of industry, wealthy through business as well as inheritance. That's probably why Ian was put up on later business visits to New Zealand as a guest at Government House, the Governor-General's residence.

The Bowaters looked like the frontrunners in the bid to own and operate the plant. Labour's Minister of Works, Jerry Skinner, had invited Bowaters' participation at an overseas meeting with Sir Eric in 1949, so Bowaters already knew a lot about the Murupara project. On his visit to Wellington, Ian, who was Bowaters' international sales director, would have met the inner circle in Government that had the say-so on the forthcoming massive investment. Including Sid (later Sir Sidney) Holland, a stout supporter of the scheme, they were a bluff group of men comprising racehorse owner Stan Goosman, who was sometimes known as 'the colossus of roads' because he had the highways portfolio, Whakatane builder 'Big Bill' Sullivan, and the more serious Ted Corbett, a Taranaki dairy farmer who was Minister of Forests and an Entrican acolyte.

Arthur Jewell, then a junior staffer in the Forest Service but later Fletchers' chief timber man, remembers one Saturday morning discussion in Parliament Buildings over the Green Book, just before its release. In the middle of the talks, Goosman broke off to tune his radio to a race commentary. Nobody seemed to mind.

Behind the ministers were three mandarins of exceptional ability — Treasury Secretary Bernie Ashwin, Commissioner of Works Mac McKillop, and the Director of the Forest Service, Pat Entrican. Jim Fletcher knew them all and got on well with most of them all the time, and with Entrican most of the time.

The Australians were watching developments closely. The Australian newspaper-owners, rumbustious characters like Ezra Norton, Sir Lloyd Dumas of the *Adelaide Advertiser*, Sir Keith Murdoch and Sir Frank

Packer, were exceedingly interested in the proposed newsprint mill. And Rupert ('Rags') Henderson, the power behind the Fairfax-owned *Sydney Morning Herald,* later became Tasman's most consistent Australian advocate.

The Australians' interest stemmed from the fact they were buying substantial tonnages of newsprint from overseas, most of it from Bowaters. They jointly owned a mill at Boyer, Tasmania, which made newsprint from eucalyptus, but not very satisfactorily. The paper emerged with a pinkish tint, which was highly unsatisfactory for a newspaper, not only for reasons of legibility but also because the Australian press barons, and especially Packer, were fiercely anti-communist. They could see that newsprint from New Zealand would give them the alternative source of supply they could use to drive down the price of Bowaters' and other overseas manufacturers' paper. The New Zealand scheme offered bargaining leverage, provided the paper was of international standard. This point was, of course, not lost on Bowaters. Thus the Australians were determined to take part in the Murupara project, if at all possible, to protect their Australasian sales.

For the Australian and New Zealand publishers, more was at stake than the price of newsprint. A local manufacturer of newsprint could offer them stability of supply. For years they had been sold newsprint almost as an afterthought by the North Americans and Europeans, who naturally looked after their main markets first. If newsprint could be produced locally, publishers could get by with smaller stocks, which would mean huge savings in cost. Later, these savings would become part of the negotiations over price, but initially the publishers agreed to pay a premium above the cost of overseas-supplied newsprint for the guarantee of local supply.

The Australians continued to flirt with the possibility of operating the plant themselves. But if it wasn't going to be them, they were certainly interested in a local alternative to Bowaters. Every now and again, the press barons descended on Wellington seeking the Rust Report and other technical data prepared by the overseas consultants at Entrican's behest. In most cases and possibly in all of them, Entrican, who distrusted the Australians intensely, found reasons not to hand over the information they sought.

Overhanging all the tendering parties was the tight deadline of

1 November 1951. As the months wore on, it became increasingly plain that the rest of the pulp and paper world was not stampeding to avail itself of the opportunities contained in Entrican's Green Book. The big developments in pulp and paper were occurring in Canada and America, and New Zealand's grand plan was something of a sideshow for the other international players. Entrican was well aware of that, and of Bowaters' preoccupation with its expansion into North America, but he still hoped to interest the British company, despite growing doubts about its commitment. The Scandinavians, who had a paper-making tradition and sold newsprint all over the world, weren't interested, though they later hustled to sell machinery. Canada had substantial resources of softwoods such as hemlock and spruce and were equally uninterested. America had bought most of its newsprint from Canada but was now moving its industry into the soft, quick-growing pines, and a similar New Zealand resource held no attraction for them.

It was then that Jim Fletcher moved. Observing the lack of interest from overseas, Bowaters and ANM excepted, he conceived his own grand plan. Why not build the plant *and* operate it? Fletchers would enter the pulp and paper field as a manufacturer, taking a giant leap into the big league.

Aside from the external diplomacy required, Jim Fletcher had to argue his case within the company. Both his father and long-time legal associate Len ('LJ') Stevens, had thought the construction job sufficiently ambitious and believed, almost until the day the bid went in, that this would be the extent of the company's involvement in the Murupara Scheme. Jim Fletcher admits with a chuckle that he kept his real intentions from the board until the full proposal was ready. 'I acted first and sought permission afterwards,' he says.

Long-term business acquaintances of Jim Fletcher have sometimes said that he regarded boards as 'a necessary evil'. Most of them found this a rather endearing quality, since the plans he hatched from inside the executive suite and later revealed to the board usually worked out so successfully. A reading of the minutes of board meetings right through 1951 and 1952 show that the entire board, Sir James included, believed that Dr Karl Karlson, the United States pulp and paper expert hired by Merritt-Chapman Scott, was in New Zealand solely to investigate the construction option, not ownership and management. As a minute of a board meeting as late as September 1951 shows, it wasn't until then that the directors knew that Fletchers was also planning to bid to operate the plant. A minute of that board meeting shows that Fletcher Merritt Raymond proposed to 'tender for the proposed Murupara scheme covering the erection and operation of a pulp and paper mill in and around Murupara'. That was less than four months before Fletchers got the job. But there still wasn't any mention of the size of the financial commitment involved.

Had it not been for Sir James's prestige, however, Fletchers would probably not have been allowed even to submit a bid. During the war years, still very fresh in New Zealanders' minds, Sir James had worked well with the civil service mandarins like Ashwin and McKillop, who had been his deputy. After the bid went in, Jim Fletcher argued his case persuasively and gradually Sir James was won over. Once convinced, he became as enthusiastic as his son, but Stephens was a conservative lawyer and had much more difficulty in accepting the risk. After all, Fletchers' initial investment in Tasman represented 44 percent of shareholders' funds.

It's been widely assumed that because Sir James became the first chairman of Tasman, and because his entire commercial life had been that of a risk-taker, he was the protagonist in the plan to own and operate the plant. That view is incorrect, as everybody within the company acknowledges. It was definitely his son's idea to tender. It wasn't his first big independent step within Fletchers — the wharf contract was that — but it was certainly his biggest so far.

By this stage, Fletcher Merritt Raymond had found a way around Entrican and gained access to all the technical reports. Indeed, this seemed essential whether they were bidders merely to build the mill or to own and operate it. Entrican had firmly refused several overtures, 'clearly reluctant to accept that a local organisation might well take a leading role in his precious Murupara Scheme', as George Fraser notes. 'All Entrican's contacts were from the British, North American and Scandinavian and Australian industries and Fletchers, the local outfit, looked small fry to him.'

Civil servants were powerful then, and Entrican kept Fletchers out by maintaining that the company didn't qualify for any access to information because it had no pulp and paper experience. His view is perhaps understandable; he didn't want the scheme being compromised by the involvement of companies that were out of their depth.

In early 1951, Jim Fletcher cabled George Fraser in London, where he had been busy hiring Dutch workers for the wharf project. He asked if George could try to get a copy from English Electric, a British company that had been involved in early talks for the project. JC suggested he approach chairman Sir George (later Lord) Nelson, a business acquaintance of his father and, unknown to Fletchers, soon to be a competitor for the pulp and paper bid.

After several fruitless attempts to see Sir George, Fraser procured an interview with a lesser light of the company, a certain Paul de Lazlo, who airily informed the New Zealander that the scheme was 'too big and ambitious for New Zealand, let alone Fletchers, and further, the New Zealand Government's undertakings to provide road and rail access, housing and a deep-water port were unreal and unattainable'. Fraser sat through this lecture but still didn't obtain a copy of the technical reports Fletchers urgently needed. That was eventually obtained through the charm of Mac Gilmore, who successfully buttonholed Entrican at Jim Fletcher's request on one of his many overseas trips. The American connection had proved its worth again.

By this time — April 1951 — Jim Fletcher was firmly resolved, as he cabled George Fraser in London requesting his urgent return, to go the whole hog. 'The position is, George,' he said, 'we are definitely going on with Murupara on our own from a financing and operating as well as from a construction standpoint.' It was a landmark decision, but there was a mountain of work to get through between April and September before he broke the news to the board.

As the months slipped by in 1951, Entrican wasn't happy. It was by now acutely clear to him that his scheme would not interest overseas investors. But he was even less pleased that a mere New Zealand company would assume responsibility for it, and he sought Cabinet's approval for yet another world trip to market the grand plan once again. To his credit, Sid Holland refused.

Meantime, Fletchers was engaged in a fury of activity. It was hiring architects, engineers, estimators and town planners to work on plans for the pulp and paper complex, a whole town, a port, roads, power and railway lines. The architects were Christchurch's McKenzie and Hall.

Dr Karl Karlson, seconded to Merritts by Perkins Goodwin of America, was the technical pulp and paper adviser.

George Fraser was right in the thick of all this. He was Jim Fletcher's right-hand man, his personal assistant, PR person, wise counsel, conscience, bridge to the unions, spirited editor of the company magazine *Arrowhead,* which became the widely read public face of Fletchers, and the self-appointed company humorist. A noisy maverick in the corridors of capitalism, Fraser would come into the office each morning bellowing out some song or other. His choice of clothes was religiously anti-suit. He would often wear a favourite cardigan with holes in the elbows, and trousers with violently coloured socks underneath.

Fraser was an unlikely person to spend thirty-five years at the elbow of Jim Fletcher. How could a former communist, somebody whose political past made it difficult for him to enter the United States even in his fifties, have walked into a senior appointment at Fletchers? Even now, JC seems surprised that he hired Fraser, though he adds he is immensely glad that he did.

Woolf Fisher, by now back in his own company, had rung Jim Fletcher suggesting that he interview Fraser, who was at that moment in his office looking for a job. This was in mid-1950, and JC saw Fraser immediately. The top team at Fletchers was composed of rough-handed practical men who had come up through the ranks, having begun as carpenters, surveyors or foremen. They were construction men, not intellectuals. Fraser was an anti-establishment literary sort, an agnostic who could quote the Bible freely, a former member of the Communist Party in Britain, an espouser of left-wing causes who had distributed the *Daily Worker* on street corners in London, the former editor of *This Week,* a tabloid in competition with the *Eight O'Clock.*

No, Jim Fletcher told Fraser. Fletchers just didn't have a job for him. Other executives who had met Fraser had thought him 'too pink'.

But later, Jim Fletcher thought it over. Now that his father had withdrawn from daily contact with the company, Fletchers was weak in its political relations. Sir James had kept up contact with politicians, but the company had become too big for his son to put in the time that good relations with Wellington demanded. Fraser, who had worked for Peter Fraser's Labour Government, was on first-name terms with

many of the bureaucrats and most of the politicians. After some reflection, Jim Fletcher called Fraser back and proposed a six-month trial.

In 1950, Fraser was thirty-four, a year younger than his new boss.
He had taken a hard road to a good salary at Fletchers. He was grateful
for it, for the way that the Fletchers, father and son, stood by him over
the initial misgivings of some directors and executives. He would do
brilliant work for the company.

Oddly enough, there were parallels between the outwardly different
careers of Jim Fletcher and George Fraser, although Fraser had grown
up in very different circumstances. Born into a poor family near
Wellington, he had had a tough early life. After leaving school early, he
had, like Jim Fletcher, worked at accountancy, though he hated it —
'dreary lectures and second-hand, smudged, cyclostyled notes'. He had
also briefly worked for an insurance company, North British and
Mercantile, and had gone to Britain a year after young Jim — in 1938,
when he found a job at New Zealand House. But instead of having his
own cabin, as young James had, Fraser worked his passage as a steward
in third-class dining. Instead of staying in hotels in Britain, he booked
into youth hostels. Whereas the Fletchers bought a Lincoln Zephyr for
transport, Fraser acquired a pushbike and toured Britain in the saddle.
When the war started, Fraser was thrown onto the dole of seventeen
shillings a week, of which board and lodging consumed fourteen shillings. He signed up as a gunner and seaman for the duration of the war.

Both of them soon forgot about the six-month trial. Fraser had
unusual vigour and quickly became indispensable. He was extraordinarily versatile. He smartened up the company stationery, organised
what would now be called power lunches, wrote lively annual reports,
had different logos designed for the various divisions and gave them
their own colours (orange for steel, for example), invented parties like
the famous 'Back to the Grindstone Party' on the first working Friday
in January, for which the principal decoration was a giant grindstone
in the foyer, checked JC's spelling and grammar, set up a labour relations
department, which maintained a constant dialogue with the unions and
persuaded the executives to have the union secretaries in for cocktail
parties, formed a bridge to the bureaucrats and politicians in Wellington
and introduced visits by lecturers from Stanford University. Intensely
interested in people, highly gregarious (a CSR director once described

him as 'everybody's friend'), Fraser set up intercompany sports, picnics and other activities. And he constantly prodded the company to be better — 'not just big, but good,' as he reminded JC.

'We had become a bit preoccupied with our own affairs,' Jim Fletcher recalls. 'George taught us to be more outgoing and open.' JC often travelled with the extrovert Fraser, who once entertained the president of Mitsubishi in Japan with a Maori song during a get-together of the huge Japanese company's senior staff. The normally undemonstrative president surprised his own executives by responding in kind.

George Fraser was just what the company needed, even though some directors didn't know it at the time. Founding director J. T. Martin was nearly apoplectic when he learned that a socialist had been appointed to the staff. 'You must sack him immediately,' Martin demanded of Jim Fletcher. If Martin had known the new staffer had also been a card-carrying communist, he might not have survived the knowledge. Fraser stayed for thirty-five years. He died in 1986.

Finance was Fletchers' main worry in the months before the Tasman tender. At that time, Fletcher Holdings' total shareholders' funds were only £1.6 million. Thus the company was committing £700,000 to the project, or 44 percent of shareholders' funds. If the project didn't work, Fletchers would probably go bust. It was high-risk financing, and Jim Fletcher fully understood this. So did his father.

Sir James knew that a business had to take risks in order to grow. In any event, his entire career had been motivated by the desire to do big things, and Tasman was the biggest yet. He was genuinely excited by the scheme, even if others were sceptical.

Entrican told the Cabinet that Fletchers could not possibly meet its £700,000 commitment. It is true that, under normal commercial lending standards of the time, the company was much too small to carry the loans necessary for the job. However, Jim Fletcher knew from earlier talks that finance was available. He had held discussions in Washington with the Export Import Bank, an institution funded by the United States Government that made loans to big projects, provided they were spent by the borrower on United States-provided services and equipment. He had also formed a friendship with John Snyder, President Truman's Secretary of Treasury. In principle, the bank's lenders had said they would loan up to $US20 million.

The noon deadline for the delivery of the tender on 1 November, what Entrican called 'the fateful day', was zero hour for Fletchers, in part because Entrican had made it clear to Jim Fletcher a few months earlier that even an hour's lateness could mean the tenders would be reopened. Jim Fletcher had also insisted that the proposal documents should 'look good as well as read well', and be at least up to the standards of an overseas company.

The document was finally delivered on time — illustrated and bound, wrapped in black leather with a gold-blocked cover and a logo designed by printer and typographer Bob Lowry, an old friend of George Fraser and the man responsible for producing the landmark literary journal *Phoenix*.

JC had come up with the name Tasman in a session with Karl Karlson, Fraser and John Watt as they drove back from Rotorua one afternoon in his Packard. (At that time he favoured American cars.) Later, he learned to his surprise that Berridge Spencer, the Caxton printing magnate, had nearly challenged the use of 'Tasman' through the courts, having registered a similar name much earlier.

The prose in the tender was fulsome. One paragraph read: 'The history of civilisation can well be measured by the history of the pulp and paper industry, and its establishment on a scale and in a form comparable with the most modern overseas units will mark a new era in the Dominion's history.'

Normally, the tender would have been opened and read along with any others. But Tasman's document went straight into a safe in Parliament Buildings, unopened. The reason for this divergence from accepted practice was a last-minute request for a six-month postponement from the powerful Anglo-Australian Corporation, the company that had been trying for over a year to put a bid together. Just two days before tenders closed, Sid Holland had received a cable from English Electric's Sir George Nelson informing him of a startling turn of events — namely, the formation of a 'British-Australian group of which the English Electric company is a part', which would put up 'certain proposals in relation to Murupara'. The request came in the name of ANM as well.

Holland had also received at the same time a cable from Sir Eric Speed, the managing director of Anglo-Australian in Melbourne. Clearly, the two companies had linked strategies. The most riveting news was that Bowaters, of all companies, would come in with this British-Australian bid as the technical experts.

The telegram was a bombshell for Jim Fletcher and his father but they knew that for years the Australians, in the form of ANM, had looked for a slice of Murupara. Eventually, Anglo-Australian Corporation, a company representing British and Australian heavy industrial and financial forces, became involved to help them mount some form of bid. Anglo-Australian had powerful parentage — London merchant bankers Lazards, which also had links with Sir George Nelson's English Electric, merchant bankers Morgan Grenfell and a Melbourne sharebroking firm, whose principal partner was Ian Potter, later Sir Ian. A lot of British suppliers, some of the biggest names in the United Kingdom's heavy industry, were backing Sir George Nelson.

Sir George had already been to New Zealand to sniff out business opportunities. Indeed, Entrican had given him an advance copy of the Green Book, as Jim Fletcher knew when he had asked George Fraser to try to procure one by stealth. Entrican had, on his own initiative, sounded out Anglo-Australian in an interview with Sir Eric Speed in Melbourne, but had been furious that Speed had leaked what they had talked about to the Australians. Sir George's English Electric obviously hoped to sell some of the big electrical equipment to a pulp and paper mill and was co-ordinating British heavy industrial interests to maximise British involvement in the project. Whenever they met, Sir George would warn Jim Fletcher or his father of how disastrous North American involvement in the project would be. Lazards, advisors to English Electric, were in the business of financing any British exports and were working on the bid too.

Jim Fletcher had got wind of what was afoot only in early 1951 after he had visited Anglo-Australian's man in Melbourne, Sir Eric Speed, who had put a fatherly hand on Jim Fletcher's shoulder and said, 'I wouldn't like you to think you don't have some competition, young man.' What Jim Fletcher didn't know was that Anglo-Australian had by that stage joined forces with ANM.

At that meeting, Jim Fletcher had given notice to Sir Eric of Fletcher Merritt Raymond's intention to mount a bid to design, build and operate the plant. Sir Eric had immediately cabled Sir George Nelson in London to inform him that this upstart consortium was a serious contender.

Telegrams were now flying. Having received the cable from Melbourne, Sir George quickly cabled Auckland to enquire of Sir James exactly what Fletchers' intentions were. The pair had been talking, though not too seriously, about some form of financial involvement. When Sir George got the bad news from Sir James that Fletchers wanted to operate the plant, he withdrew from any negotiations with Fletchers and looked to his own Anglo-Australian friends.

JC knew all about these interests. At one point in the extended preliminaries, in September 1951, Jim Fletcher had got together with the British-Australian group. He had attended a meeting in London with English Electric and the British interests where he received more warnings about the foolishness of a partnership with the North American pulp and paper industry. He gave back as good as he got. 'I'd been to a long lunch at Thomas de la Rue [which printed banknotes],' he recalls, 'and I wasn't taking any cheek from them.'

Thus the last-minute request for a postponement arrived and the unread Tasman tender duly ended up in a safe.

There had been one other tender, which should have received an award for impudence. It came from a wealthy American called Ed Ball, who had married into the Du Pont chemical family and controlled the St Joe Paper Company. He had called into Wellington after a visit to Australia and met Stan Goosman, with Entrican present. If the Tasman bid should fail for some reason, Ball, with the arrogance of the seriously rich, wanted to buy the entire forest, provided he could do what he liked with it. It wasn't, of course, a bid at all, because it completely ignored the terms of the tender documents and he wanted an extension of the deadline. Ball's offer was rejected out of hand.

Prime Minister Sid Holland, his resolve stiffened by the Fletchers, who argued that their American partners could not wait a further six months while the British made up their mind about something they had known about for years, stuck by the local bid. Having listened to a deputation from Anglo-Australian arguing their case for a postponement, Holland then asked them point blank: could they guarantee that a firm bid was imminent or at least definite? No, Sir Eric Speed admitted, they couldn't. He was quite frank in accepting that Anglo-Australian had been dilatory. Sir Eric left town, putting Entrican out somewhat: 'He was discourteous enough to leave without calling on me.'

Obviously, this was yet another British delaying tactic and it bore the mark of the Bowater hand, for it was clear that Bowaters wanted control of the project. The Australians would not countenance this and they thereupon fled the brief 'British-Australian' consortium.

The Holland Government then rejected the request for a delay and opened the safe. It was certainly the right decision. Had the Government agreed to a six-month extension, it would have left itself open to an embarrassing and possibly damning refusal by the British-Australian group to bid after all. If Bowaters had said no after another half-year's investigation of Entrican's Murupara Scheme, it would have amounted to a highly public condemnation of the project's viability. Bankers and suppliers all around the world would have noted this, and thus Fletchers, as the surviving bidder, would have faced a tough job in getting the necessary loans and endorsements.

Entrican's profound and understandable disappointment at the complete absence of the British commitment he had wooed so assiduously for years was in marked contrast to Fletchers' relief. The local company had, or thought it had, the field to itself. Jim Fletcher had even posted a man outside the offices of the Forestry Service in Fitzherbert Terrace, Wellington, to make sure that an emissary from some other bidder didn't rush in at the last minute with a rival tender.

Mindful of the urgency of the project, Holland's Government moved quickly. By 7 December 1951, the Prime Minister had a five-centimetre-thick report on Fletchers' offer. And fourteen days after that, Holland handed a letter of intent to Sir James Fletcher. By any standards, this was a remarkably quick decision.

The letter of intent — a non-binding agreement in principle to go ahead with a project — was another idea imported from America. Jim Fletcher had urged the Government to make this commitment, and the Tasman letter of intent was a first for New Zealand.

That should have been the end of it, but the British hadn't finished. Bowaters worked on Sid Holland when he went to London in early 1952.

Sir Eric made an appointment to see Holland for afternoon tea at the Savoy Hotel in The Strand, the usual accommodation for visiting New Zealand Prime Ministers because it was close to the old New Zealand House. Sir Eric quickly got down to business and urged yet another postponement on the grounds that his technical people were so heavily involved in work on a new mill in the southern United States that they could not travel to New Zealand. Also, he said, Fletchers was far too inexperienced and small a company to take on a project of such magnitude as a construction project, let alone as a mill-operator, and the project could not really proceed without Bowaters' expertise.

By this stage, as Sir Eric knew, the Fletchers had in their hands the all-important letter of intent from the Government. (The Government had even provided a plane for Jim Fletcher and his father to fly down to Wellington to pick it up on Christmas Eve.)

What Holland must do, Sir Eric went on, was to urge Sir James to fly immediately to London and see the British group, but he musn't tell the Australian press barons. It was obviously a divide-and-rule ploy intended to delay the entire project for Bowaters' convenience.

The Australians, through Australian Newsprint Mills, had by now signalled their intention to back the Fletchers bid with a £1 million investment of one newsprint machine in return for a contracted supply for the newsprint. The price would be around £NZ3 15s per ton (or £A5, since the New Zealand currency was higher than Australia's) above prevailing world prices. There were two reasons for the premium: one was for a guaranteed supply of newsprint on their doorstep, the other was as encouragement to get the project off the ground.

At that time, New Zealand publishers were buying 75 percent of their newsprint from Canada and about 25 percent from Britain. They agreed to pay £2 a ton premium.

These pricing negotiations had been conducted primarily by Rupert 'Rags' Henderson, a combative former journalist who had become all-powerful within the Fairfax-owned publishing group. For Fletchers, this was a tremendous boost because it guaranteed a substantial export market from start-up. And Bowaters, of course, understood its implications, hence Sir Eric's anxiety that the Australians shouldn't know what was going on.

Sir Eric was clearly trying to sideline the Australians and protect Bowaters' Australian sales. At first, Holland fell for it and immediately cabled New Zealand for Sir James, then aged sixty-five and clearly considered by Bowaters to be a softer touch than his son, to come to London on the next plane. Henderson happened to be in London and was able to contact Holland and explain how Machiavellian big business could be. But the telegram had already been sent.

It was now 27 January and Fletchers had already done a lot of work on the project. Jim Fletcher and his father didn't budge after receiving the cable. Instead, they drew up a reply that in hindsight was a lesson in the realities of international commerce to the provincial Holland. This cabled response, which is now in the Fletcher archives, pointed out several things politely and firmly in abbreviated English.

First, while Sir James 'was willing to make the journey', it was his duty to point out that the company 'had already taken certain steps which make it difficult to envisage workable agreement with these British interests'. Also, further delays were inadvisable because the forest was maturing rapidly and required 'earliest possible utilisation'. Negotiations with the Australian press barons were 'proceeding very satisfactorily and provide for disposal entire output [of] mills with substantial capital contribution by Australian consumers'. The Australians would not work with Bowater 'and hostile such proposal'. Fletchers' advisor, Dick Sandwell, was arriving shortly. It was 'absolutely imperative in New Zealand's interest [that] control of company remain in New Zealand hands'. Fletchers had 'completed satisfactory selling agreement with [paper merchant] B. J. Ball Ltd covering all pulp and paper products'. Sir James could not 'imagine Bowater Group making substantial capital available unless control of company and disposal of products is in their hands'. He finished by pointing out that Bowaters hadn't taken an earlier opportunity to come and argue its case and anyway if the British came in, the Australians would depart.

Sprinkled with duly deferential remarks that Sir James would do as Holland wished *but* . . ., the cable was a model of firm diplomacy. Holland saw it New Zealand's way, especially when Australian Newsprint Mills cabled him confirming it wouldn't have anything to do with a consortium that included the British group. The Prime Minister dropped the request for Sir James to hotfoot it to London.

Once again, that should have been the end of the matter, but the British, who had clearly underestimated Fletchers' combativeness, tried one more shot. Having failed to bring Sir James to London on their terms, the British came to New Zealand in late February 1952. This time they came at Fletchers' invitation, JC arguing that New Zealand was the logical place to talk things through. At that stage, it was probably the most significant commercial deputation, aside from the American civilian generals who came to Wellington during the war, to have made the journey to the capital.

Colonel Ian Bowater led the group, which included Thomas Brand (later Lord Hampden) of blue-chip merchant bankers Lazards, a former senior Treasury official named Sir John Henry Woods, who represented Sir George Nelson's English Electric, Ernest Hughes, who was Bowaters' top man in Australia, and another English Electric executive, called A. E. Carnegie. The party made a diplomatic gaffe in not dropping in to see Fletchers; instead, they passed straight through Auckland en route to Wellington.

The Australians were invited, and Rags Henderson and Sir Lloyd Dumas attended the discussions, which Bowaters clearly thought would involve only themselves, Fletchers and the Government. The New Zealand publishers were there as well. To Entrican's chagrin, Holland had very properly forbidden government officials from taking part, and thus Entrican was barred from the talks. He had asked to be allowed to attend, even as an observer, but Holland was adamant. Entrican even telephoned to be allowed to turn up, 'lest any deadlock be allowed to develop'. Entrican later blamed Sir James, who as chairman of Fletchers was naturally present at the talks, for the deadlock that did develop, though the truth is that Sir James and other Fletchers staff had tried to keep the peace. A deadlock was probably inevitable anyway, given Bowaters' insistence on almost complete control of the operation of the plant, marketing of the product and, of course, its request for a further postponement.

The British were put out by the Australasian publishers' presence and the talks got off to an unhappy start. Negotiations were, according to George Fraser, who was Fletchers' executive co-ordinator of the project, 'acrimonious, lively and often amusing'. Henderson had a larrikin streak and pretended to confuse Lazards of London with 'Lizards of London'.

In any event, Bowaters did not gain the stay of execution it sought

— they wanted to count every tree, leaf and sirex beetle in the forests, Fletchers joked among themselves — and the party returned home via Australia. Fletchers had wanted British involvement, but not as the controlling shareholder, and Holland's Government had come to espouse the New Zealand-controlled option. Thus Fletchers was now pretty much in an impregnable position as the confirmed bidder. But it still had plenty of worries, including a serious shortage of permanent capital, no technical partner that would see them through the project (because, as Jim Fletcher said, 'we knew damn-all about pulp and paper plants') and a lack of reliable overseas markets for the newsprint. The Government had, however, agreed to provide bridging finance.

Fletchers and Holland still had to fend off one more rather lordly overseas captain of industry. He was Marcus Wallenberg, a legendary industrialist from Sweden, who was immensely wealthy and equally influential. The Wallenberg family owned the Enskilda Bank and had interests in the emerging SAS airline and a very old company, reputedly the world's oldest, called Stora Kopperbergs, that operated pulp and paper mills in Sweden. Wallenberg had also buttonholed Holland in Paris in early 1952 and filled his ear with doubts. The Murupara Scheme, with its plans for a large, American-style plant, was too big, too ambitious, too rushed. His Swedish interests could sort it out, he added. The smaller Swedish plants were better suited to New Zealand.

Wallenberg later came to New Zealand with his manager of the Stora Kopperbergs pulp and paper plant, at the Government's invitation, and was amply provided with technical reports and site inspections. At the conclusion of the visit, the pair produced a brief report, comprising just five foolscap pages, that primarily urged caution, the importance of cheap power, noted their enthusiasm for the project and urged the employment of a Scandinavian partner. Tasman paid their expenses.

With Wallenberg gone, Fletchers was finally able to carry on with the job without having to look over its shoulder. As things turned out, in the ensuing years Sweden and the rest of Scandinavia moved towards the American-sized operations. Had Fletchers and New Zealand followed Wallenberg's advice, it would have been a grave mistake.

Fletchers' tender argued for two major departures from the Entrican scheme. The tender proposed that the sawmill, a big and complex plant designed by an American consultant, 'Hub' Rambo, an old friend of Entrican, should be halved in scale (and for this Fletcher submitted an alternative set of plans). More importantly from a social viewpoint, it also argued for a different site than the one at Murupara espoused in the Green Book.

Murupara was on the Rangitaiki River on the eastern edge of the Kaingaroa Forest, but Fletchers' own studies indicated that the project should be based eight or nine kilometres upstream, at the bottom of a triangle that had Tauranga, Te Puke and the seaside village of Matata at its corners. The Murupara site was too far from the established towns of Rotorua, Whakatane and Mount Maunganui. The company also feared that Murupara's isolation might breed the condition called 'bush-happy', a 'what-the-hell' attitude among employees. Most importantly though, the risk of pollution there was too great in the event of the plant being expanded. Fletchers' own preferred choice was a coastal site near Maketu, but Mount Maunganui and sites in Te Puke were also seriously considered.

George Fraser pointed out that there wouldn't have been any problem in acquiring land at Mount Maunganui, even though there were considerable anxieties about pollution from the waste material. Fletchers' consultant described the smell of the emissions from the manufacture of kraft pulp as roughly equivalent to the odour of a giant can of salted cabbage being opened every day. But the Mount Maunganui Maori landowners' lawyer told the consortium that his clients weren't worried about this: 'Stink or no stink, if there's a bob in it for my Maori owners, we are all for it. We'll sell.' As Fraser, an early conservationist, drily notes, 'Fortunately for this attractive resort, it did not come to anything.'

Why did Kawerau get approval? It had proven geothermal steam for power, and the Ministry of Works argued strongly for the potential of this still largely untried form of energy. It was flat. It was beside the Tarawera River, which was essential for the clean water the plant would need for processing. It was reasonably central to other townships such as Edgecumbe and about halfway between the forest and the port of Mount Maunganui. And McKillop had visited Italian geothermal plants and come away a convert.

Kawerau wasn't, in fact, the name of the settlement. For half a century, the proposed location of the pulp and paper plant had been called Onepu. This site was near Te Teko, now known for its livestock sales, and indeed, before the new name stuck, Kawerau was sometimes called Te Teko. Inviting his members to consider looking for jobs on the site, Pat Potter, secretary of the Labourers Union at that time, suggested in the union's monthly magazine that they 'take a dekko at Te Teko'. A labour force of 2,000 was soon swarming over the district.

There wasn't an existing rail link, but the Government built one between Murupara, Kawerau and Mount Maunganui. The Department of Railways was persuaded, albeit reluctantly, to forgo its usual rail tariffs and accept a discounted rate in view of the high volume of business it would attract on the line. If Railways negotiators had held out for the standard rates, Kawerau would not have been a viable site. But the department saw sense and, over the next thirty years, the line proved to be the most profitable in the entire railway system.

And the export port? Whakatane was nearer but Mount Maunganui won the vote, provided it was dredged near the entrance.

A pool of senior executives started to form with the appointment of Englishman Maurice Hobday as chief executive after a worldwide advertising campaign. He came from a family that had been in paper-making for generations. New Zealander Geoff Schmitt, a civil servant from Treasury who had worked closely with Ashwin, became company secretary. A Canadian company, Abitibi, was signed to train technical staff and to commission the mill. A sales team was under recruitment.

The Government had promised bridging finance, but Jim Fletcher knew the company was obliged to raise the debt and equity capital itself. He also felt it was important for managerial independence — 'the sooner we got out from under the Government, the better'. Perhaps faith makes things happen or, to put it another way, fortune favours the bold, for the money came from an unexpected source.

By now, Colonel Ian Bowater had left the family company after a row over strategy with his cousin Sir Eric and had joined a well-known firm of paper merchants called Spicers, which was an agent for a rival of Bowaters, Albert E. Reed and Co. In turn, Reed had been dominated, Bowater-style, by a certain Colonel Sheldon. After his death, he had been succeeded by an ambitious chartered accountant named Philip

Walker. Reed didn't make a lot of newsprint, but it had a solid reputation in Britain for its paper-making operations of various types, especially of high-quality letter paper.

Now, Colonel Ian Bowater had interested Reed's managing director in the New Zealand project. Walker promptly wrote to Sir James in Auckland. By great good luck, Jim Fletcher and George Fraser were in London on business, and Sir James cabled his son about Walker's letter. JC immediately contacted Walker, who invited Fletcher and Fraser over to see them in elegant offices in Piccadilly.

Suffice to say that Reed and Co, later known as Reed International, made it clear it wanted to take part, subject to due inspection. And, moreover, it could bring in debt and equity finance through the Commonwealth Development Finance Corporation, a quasi-government agency that had full vaults available to lend to suitable enterprises in the 'colonies'. Fortunately, Walker happened to be a director of the CDFC. Thus at one stroke it looked as though Jim Fletcher had solved his two most pressing problems — a shortage of paper-making expertise and of money. The project was now internationally 'bankable'.

Their new partners looked ideal. Not only was Reed a cash-rich operation (unlike the perennially stretched Bowater group), its presence would be important in satisfying foreign bankers, who would be far more inclined to lend money to a pulp and paper plant at the bottom of the world if it had a well-known partner such as Reed. Also, the British company was prepared to cede its newsprint contracts Down Under to Tasman and would underwrite Tasman's production with extra newsprint tonnage.

Jubilantly, JC and Fraser went back home, to discover that their powers of persuasion had been perhaps too effective. Having been prised from the clutches of the British after the original Bowater overtures, Sid Holland was now all too completely converted to the notion that New Zealanders could do it and do it better than anybody else. He didn't want *any* foreign partners. 'I'd sold the New Zealand thing too well,' Jim Fletcher remembers ruefully. 'We were hoist by our own petard.'

Aware that this heaven-sent solution might be slipping from his grasp, he tackled Sid Holland at the seaside bach of Mac McKillop at Raumati, near Wellington. McKillop, head of the Ministry of Works, and Bernie Ashwin, the head of Treasury, were both there. JC went into the debate aggressively and nearly blew it. 'I was angry, and a young man,' he confesses. 'But we had this golden opportunity under our nose and Holland couldn't see it.' Holland bridled at the young managing director's tone, but Ashwin, the professional public servant, intervened and patiently explained to the Prime Minister the necessity of having international expertise and involvement, as distinct from control.

'I pulled my horns in a bit,' JC recalls. Holland finally accepted that Reed's involvement was acceptable provided the company reduced its equity and didn't have majority control. This was achieved by Fletchers and the Government taking a higher stake in the project.

The Prime Minister's sense of patriotism was now in full bloom. Holland wanted a New Zealander to lead the company. Thus the Reed appointee would have the title of director of operations, but not of managing director. JC agreed and the deal was struck in the bach, Kiwi-style, and celebrated with a round of whisky.

Sid Holland made a public statement in which he recognised the need for outside expertise: 'We have to look overseas for the knowledge and skill required to organise and operate the industry successfully.' And he acknowledged that Reed would provide a continuing 'stake in the welfare of the Tasman company'. However, the stake would be a minority one and 'the control of the company would remain firmly in New Zealand hands'.

Thus Reed bought 25 percent of the company for £1.5 million, or some $60 million if the deal had been struck today. The deal sounded straightforward enough, but the financial arrangements required some manoeuvring behind the scenes. The Government, the major shareholder, doubled its stake to £2 million. Suddenly it seemed that the Government wanted to dominate the board. This was quite different from the indicative terms outlined in the Green Book, which had assumed a 15 percent shareholding by the Government. Yet the new investment would give it a 33 percent stake.

'The Government wasn't the reluctant debutante any more,' Jim Fletcher notes. To maintain its strength on the board, which JC felt was important to protect Fletchers' majority ownership and to compensate for its lack of executive authority, Fletchers increased its equity in Tasman from £700,000 to £1 million, but only after overcoming Government resistance to its enlarged stake. It suddenly seemed that the Government was reluctant to allow Fletchers to maintain a dominant financial position. This was a first sign of future tensions.

There are several myths about Tasman and the way the huge project was financed is one of them. It's quite incorrect, as political scientist Bruce Jesson claims in *Behind the Mirror Glass*, that 'the Government provided the total financial backing for Tasman'. In fact, it was just one of several major investors.

Tasman's public funding came through a huge and highly successful issue of shares. The success of the issue of the accompanying debentures owed a lot to the Wellington-based Anglophile sharebroker Frank Renouf, whose company, Daysh, Renouf and Frethey, underwrote them. They were the first major issue of debentures since the Depression, and Renouf had shrewdly structured them around the appointment of a trustee for the debenture holders. Thus they provided a security for the investors, removing some of the anxieties that had surrounded earlier issues of debentures. Renouf also did a good job of selling the share issue — it was oversubscribed by five times. Renouf would later claim that he had 'made' Tasman, but that is a considerable exaggeration.

The pool of senior executives increased by one. Reed agreed to appoint somebody of outstanding abilities who would work alongside the English general manager, Hobday. Thus a Reed executive named Leslie S. Dougal was appointed director of operations, the title having been carefully selected in order to leave space for the prospective New Zealand managing director. As it happened, relations between Hobday, the veteran paper-manufacturing man, and Dougal were hostile. Dougal, Fletchers later found out, had no experience of a new operation like Tasman and had not even previously seen the type of fast-running newsprint machine that the operation installed. It later puzzled Fletchers and infuriated Jim Fletcher that Reed had not seconded one of its managers from a North American mill with its compatible equipment. When the shareholding changed later, the board headhunted an experienced Bowaters mill manager, John Franklin, from North America, and the mill's performance jumped sharply.

After a lot of executive friction, which did the new operation no good, an unhappy 'Hobbie' resigned to form a company that successfully imported paper-making supplies and equipment and then became chief executive of Whakatane Board Mills. He eventually rejoined Fletchers as the executive responsible for all non-Tasman paper-making activities, a senior job because Fletchers by then half owned the Caxton Paper Mills, established by the wealthy and highly private Spencer family. Hobday later ran the New Zealand Paper Mills at Mataura for Fletchers before he retired to Folkestone. In 1993, then in his nineties, he was still writing regularly to his former boss.

But in Tasman's critical early years, Dougal was never comfortable with Fletchers executives. Jim Fletcher grew increasingly frustrated with Tasman's mediocre results, and relations between Fletchers and Reed became strained. JC, seeking to maximise the company's and the Government's investment in Tasman, would fruitlessly badger Phillip Walker, Reed's chief executive, about it on every possible occasion, which was usually at board meetings. By 1957, Fletchers and Reed were at such loggerheads over Reed's performance that the latter offered to buy out Fletchers at £1 5s 7d a share. After some half-hearted negotiations, nothing came of this proposal.

The expression 'learning curve' wasn't in use in the early fifties. But it expresses the situation with the Tasman project perfectly — for everybody it was a steep learning curve, and especially so for Reed. It was a huge plant even by world standards, the fourth biggest ever built at that time, and inevitably there were teething troubles to match.

Construction contracts were signed on 12 March 1953, preliminary work began 1 July, the heavy work started on 1 September. Fletcher Merritt Raymond had the main contract, the one to build the mill, and it approached the job with the same attitudes of the wartime construction days. A notice on the mill site read: 'The impossible we do at once; miracles take a little longer.'

Fletchers' key men were its long-serving construction chiefs like Joe Craig, the carpenter who had joined Fletchers in 1928 and become managing director of Fletcher Construction. From the air, the site looked like a jigsaw puzzle that had suffered a direct hit from a bomb. In fact, the job was a triumph of timing, as exquisite as a perfectly executed dance involving hundreds of people. Yes, sometimes they got out of step, but in general they maintained formation. As *Arrowhead* noted, employing a different metaphor, the construction job's complexity approximated to 'six Davis Cup singles matches being played at once'. Excavation for the footings started on 1 September after some early minor disputes with the Maori landowners, disputes the team later referred to as the 'Maori wars'. In quick and syncopated succession, the administration building, newsprint machine room, the paper storage and general stores took shape. Silos, chemical storage, water-filtration plant and grinder house went ahead simultaneously. Employing American continuous concrete-pouring techniques on a scale new to New Zealand, four silos, each of them twenty-five metres high and twelve metres in diameter, went up in an astonishing eleven days, rising at the rate of eleven centimetres an hour. Five sulphate pulp digesters, each of them weighing fifty-four tonnes, were wrestled into place.

Timing was often hairsbreadth. To hurry things up, FMR had opted to start before full plans were available and sometimes the next blueprint would arrive on the plane from Vancouver just hours before the gangs were ready to start working on it. A new category of employee, the expeditors, was hired to ensure that the many items of foreign-made heavy machinery were completed on time and to specification, and were freighted to Kawerau by special rigs when they were needed. The expeditors landed equipment from Britain, USA, Canada, Norway, Sweden, Switzerland, Holland, Australia and Germany.

Huge construction sites daily illustrate the dictum that if something can go wrong, it will. Hundreds of things went wrong at Kawerau, but most of them were minor: FMR ran into shortages of skilled staff, there were labour disputes. But construction people *expect* problems. And because they expect them, they treat them as routine and solve them in the same spirit. Recalling it all, Jim Fletcher often quotes George Ferris: 'Nothing is impossible, but it might just cost too much.'

FMR nearly did achieve the impossible. Government-commissioned consultants such as Pittsburgh's Rust Engineering and Portland sawmill consultants W. H. Rambo had estimated a four-year construction job with a commensurately higher capital cost under the original proposal, which was for a sterling-based contract — that is, using British equipment bought with English pounds. A revised dollar-based contract with United States machinery brought the completion date down to two and a half years. Instead, FMR did it in just under two years. Far from being beyond New Zealanders, albeit using American and British skills, the project had been accomplished much faster than overseas consultants had estimated.

Sixty-hour working weeks were standard. Some projects, such as the fourteen-day-and-night battle against the Tarawera River to build an underwater pumping station, required round-the-clock work under arc lights. At its peak, Fletcher Merritt Raymond's construction force alone numbered 1,800 men. They all lived in a camp of huts — Dutch, Canadians, Australians and New Zealanders who drank together, played housie together, and competed against each other in soccer, cricket, rugby, indoor bowls, darts, archery and even judo. Each was issued with basic home comforts — mattress and wire-sprung bed, clean blankets, a kapok pillow and covers for both pillow and mattress. It wasn't quite like home, but 5,000 workers passed through the camp happily enough and discipline was remarkably good. Only once did one of the men 'wantonly destroy' camp property, as the records recall, and have to be reprimanded.

This diverse workforce built all the complex infrastructure of the mill — water-treatment plant, warehouses, digesters, boilers, chlorine plant, lime kiln, precipitators, storage for petrol, chemicals, chips and logs. They built the kilns, sawmill, shipping outlets, the bleach plant. They erected the paper machine and the grinders.

The Government was as committed to the job as was FMR. The Ministry of Works built new highways and repaired old roads, constructed a new port at Mount Maunganui in a huge reclamation job. Railways staff laid new lines from the forest to the mill, from the mill to the main line and then on to the new port. For this job, New Zealand Railways adopted prefabrication techniques for the first time. They made the rail sections in advance, driving the 'dogs' into the iron and sleepers in the factory and then laying the length as a unit.

Fletchers built most of the town of Kawerau to Ministry of Works design. Where sheep had grazed and lucerne had grown abundantly, there emerged a completely integrated settlement of company hostel, 550 houses with shops, schools, post office, police station, hotel and administration block, sealed streets and footpaths, sewage and storm water drainage. A smaller town of 200 houses went up at Murupara.

One ambition went unachieved. Fletchers and the town architects wanted to put all the power and telephone lines underground, but the Ministry of Works dismissed the idea as a waste of money.

The job was unprecedented in New Zealand, a huge act of faith in the country's ability to do it, to pay for it and to make it work. It was an exciting partnership of public and private enterprise.

When it was all done, Sir James Fletcher buried the hatchet by paying a magnanimous tribute to Pat Entrican in a commemorative edition of *Arrowhead*: 'My good friend, A. R. Entrican, Director of Forestry, who has devoted a great part of his life to the pulp and paper project. I look upon Pat Entrican as the symbol and representative of the many servants of the public who have contributed so much to Kawerau.'

A paper machine is a huge and intimidating piece of machinery. And Tasman's No. 1 machine was at that time the third biggest in the world — a behemoth one hundred metres long, fourteen metres wide and fourteen metres, or roughly four storeys, high. Designed to run at 650 metres a minute, no other paper machine was faster.

In pulp and paper parlance, it was known as a jumbo machine. When it was first switched on — at 10.30 a.m., 29 October 1955 — it produced the deafening roar that became familiar to anybody within hundreds of metres of the plant. It could produce 870 kilometres of seven-metre-wide paper per day, enough to carpet State Highway One from Wellington to Kaitaia.

Or rather, that was what it was *capable* of doing. Reduced to its essentials, the manufacture of paper sounds absurdly simple. And it is, provided very small amounts of paper are made. But huge rolls of newsprint are complex to produce. They require first of all the essential ingredients — ample supplies of wood of the right maturity and quality, plenty of clean water, and chemicals.

The first, and easier, part of the process produces mechanical pulp. Half of the wood, now cut into 'bolts' over a metre long, is attacked by rows of giant grindstones. It's a process that consumes huge amounts of power because the motors required to crunch up logs of wood are so massive. The result of the process is a bulky and short-fibred stuff called groundwood pulp, which looks like a particularly unappetising form of porridge.

What is done with the rest of the wood is much more complicated.

It is chipped, pressure-cooked in chemicals in massive digesters, and 'blown' into a tank where the chips shatter into millions of cellulose fibres against a steel plate. The next stage produces unbleached kraft pulp by washing the fibres in revolving drums and slurring off the residue of the process, called black liquor. Hot water sluices the stuff down to leave unbleached kraft or long-fibred pulp, 'kraft' being a German word meaning strong.

In its natural brown colour, kraft pulp is used for making brown-paper wrappings, corrugated and liner board. But when semi-bleached, its colour changes sufficiently for kraft pulp to be mixed with ground-wood pulp to make newsprint and magazine paper. When fully bleached, it produces high-quality printing, writing, blotting and other refined papers. Expensive letter paper is made from fully bleached kraft pulp.

For newsprint — the semi-bleached stage — the two pulps, kraft and groundwood, are screened, refined and blended together. The mix in those days was three-quarters groundwood pulp to a quarter kraft pulp. The latter has already been slightly roughened, rather like sandpapering a top coat of varnish or paint, so that the fibres cling together better when the newsprint is formed. (If you examine your newspaper closely with a magnifying glass, you will see a mat of short and hairlike fibres.) Dye is added for whiteness. This mixture, called stock, is the last stage before the manufacture of full newsprint.

The stock is then spread evenly over a fine synthetic mesh and drained of some water. This delicate, still-wet sheet rolls onto a series of presses that squeeze out more water. Finally, a giant dryer burns up the last of the moisture, the now more robust sheet roars through to the dry end of the machine, where it is rolled up, and you have a sheet of newsprint. The entire process from wire screen to rolled and dried newsprint takes less than forty-five seconds.

But in the continuous and high-speed manufacture of newsprint something, somewhere, is waiting to snarl up the process.

The experience of Barry Ashwin, later to become technical director of Fletchers' forest industries group, was fairly typical. He arrived in Kawerau as a young engineer in 1956, a few months after the pulp and paper mill had started up, and walked straight into crisis after crisis.

'Most of the people employed by Tasman lacked the expertise or experience to perform their duties correctly,' he recalls. 'The whole organisation was involved in a learning curve.'

Jim Fletcher, who was now sometimes working right through the night to stay on top of the company's giddy pace, had expected it would take time to train the workforce. Indeed, this was implicit in the original proposal, which called for the employment of predominantly New Zealanders for all except the critical positions. Of the thousand-strong labour force, only forty were hired from overseas.

It turned out that even the imported workers — supervisors and operatives for the pulp mill from Finland and for the newsprint machine from England — were initially out of their depth. The Tasman newsprint machine was, as Ashwin remembers, 'larger, faster and more sophisticated' than the ones they were used to.

Everything about Tasman was big. Apart from the mill, there was the essential supporting infrastructure — power and steam, water and effluent, laboratories, workshops, stores, warehouses. All were new operations and had to be integrated with each other by their inexperienced personnel.

Kawerau was a young town and couldn't keep a lot of the young men, who, in those days of shortages of skilled labour, might stay just a few months and move on to more entertaining locations. Staff turnover was thus exceptionally high. To arrest the problem and stabilise the drain of expertise, the company built whole streets of new houses and let them at peppercorn rentals to young married couples.

With giant-sized capital projects like Tasman, huge losses or huge profits can be made. To ensure the latter, it's essential that the plant reaches its design capacity as quickly as possible. The target date for Tasman's mill to reach capacity was within a year of being commissioned. But the teething troubles and continuing problems with senior management pegged back to 1958 the achievement of the full capacity of 75,000 tonnes of newsprint a year, two years behind schedule. Tasman didn't post a profit until the financial year ending 31 October 1958. By then, accumulated losses had climbed to $6.6 million, or around $175 million today, and it wasn't until 1962 that those losses were wiped off by profits.

Jim Fletcher's frustration with the Englishman Dougal grew almost daily. JC had no executive power, but he was furious at some of Dougal's actions. One of the most damaging, in his view, was the way the Englishman had quickly paid off the more experienced North American companies Abitibi and Sandwell. JC saw that as endangering the whole project.

But the delays arose from multifarious causes. Almost daily, electrical and mechanical faults, each one having effects on other plant, kept repair gangs busy. Many replacement parts had to be airfreighted from overseas — provided, that is, the necessary import licences were available; they often weren't. Specialised technicians had to come from overseas, too, since New Zealand didn't have a pool of skilled staff.

Nature often worked against the project. The water supply, whose purity is critical to the manufacturing process, was often contaminated. If there are any impurities in the huge volumes of water used by a newsprint mill, the newsprint quality suffers. In heavy rain the Tarawera River regularly filled with a fine pumice. The water-filtration plant couldn't cope with the impurities, and the plant was often shut down until the water became sufficiently clear again. Eventually the problem was solved when large settling basins were installed and the treatment plant expanded.

The supply of electricity was infuriatingly unreliable. Tasman generated about a quarter of its power needs internally but still relied heavily on the state grid, which came in through a single power line from the nearby town of Edgecumbe. Lightning strikes, among other problems, could black out the mill and cause a chain reaction of disruptions — blocked pulp pipelines, spilt chemicals, damaged paper-making fabrics on the newsprint machine. Often it would take a day to get things back to normal.

Perhaps the major problem was that Tasman was conducting an experiment in newsprint production. In the fifties, newsprint had not been made from radiata pine, except for one experiment of limited value. Pat Entrican had organised the shipping of carefully selected, high-quality, small-diameter young radiata pine to Southland Paper Mills of Lufkin, Texas, which had then produced good quality newsprint. But this was one isolated and far-from-conclusive trial and Tasman quickly discovered that Lufkin had not had to deal with the uneven and unknown nature of the nine species of timber in the Murupara Forest.

Radiata pine has a different chemistry to the northern spruce that had formed the basis until then of global newsprint production. It is a sappy wood: about 2 percent of it by weight is composed of resinous substances. The problem was that the resins were not removed in the normal groundwood pulping process, and thus the challenge was to find ways to bind the material to the pulp fibres. Anything that doesn't bind, even in small amounts, turns into the newsprint worker's enemy, a rogue by-product called pitch.

Pitch breaks off and deposits itself everywhere it can find a home and progressively blocks up the paper-making fabric. Pitch not only blocked up the fabric, it blocked up production. It took some thirty years to reduce the problem of pitch to a mere nuisance. But in the early days it was a nightmare.

The wood quality, quite apart from its natural sappiness, proved to be another formidable and daily difficulty. It's not possible to produce high-quality newsprint without suitable groundwood pulp, and the contracts Tasman wrote for the supply of newsprint promised it would be at least of overseas quality.

In the early days, the Canadian-made grinders, huge flywheels powered by 5,500-horsepower motors, shook themselves into pieces on the large deformed bolts of wood that the mill staff were obliged to feed into them because of the erratic quality of the forest. Worse, the quality of the pulp produced was also uneven, and this was what nearly broke Tasman.

It quickly turned out that some of the forest was quite unusable. Tasman had bought trees on the basis of a fixed price per cubic foot, the stumpage rate, but found it couldn't do anything with a lot of them. Consequently, they had a negative stumpage value.

It's a myth that Fletchers bought the trees at a subsidised value. Sir Robert Muldoon perpetuated this myth in his book *The New Zealand Economy, a Personal View*: '. . . stumpage from state-owned exotic forests, the principal source of Tasman's wood, has always had a subsidy element to it . . .' In fact, the trees were overvalued.

Entrican's own research assumed that the state would get a tidy return from the stumpage. In August 1949, just before his long-slumbering project came alive, he had produced a confidential memorandum for the new Commissioner of State Forests clearly stating the stumpage position. Entrican, then Director of Forestry, estimated that a stumpage price of twopence per cubic foot paid from 1953 would work out at 9.2 percent compound, a very handy return for the Crown at a time of nearly nil inflation. Even a rate of a penny per cubic foot would produce a 6.5 percent rate, according to Entrican. The memorandum went on: '. . . a stumpage price lower than 2d per cubic foot in the initial stages should still yield the forest a highly satisfactory monetary return.'

Fletchers had grave doubts about the forest quite early on. It had already committed itself to the project when it received some devastating information from Entrican, who himself sat rather unhappily on the project committee, frustrated at having a non-executive role in the project he had nursed for so long. In complete contradiction to his own Green Book, he told the project committee in February 1952 that sirex beetles had destroyed so many trees that the forest probably didn't contain enough suitable logs to permit newsprint production to reach the guaranteed 90,000 tonnes a year. The Green Book, which had been circulated around the world, had appeared only ten months before with contradictory information.

Entrican's revelations also followed by just one month an earlier meeting of the committee in the Treasury offices, when Entrican had talked very positively about the availability of enough trees for a second newsprint machine.

The first bit of news astounded and worried Jim Fletcher. Had the entire newsprint project been based on a low-grade forest? The company had relied totally on the statistics provided by the Forestry Service, because they were the only ones available. And here was a major miscalculation that could threaten the financial viability of the entire project.

JC fired a letter straight back. He wanted to know urgently the Government's view on providing substitute sawlogs to compensate. And, if there was going to be a 'serious reduction' in log deliveries, would the Government recognise that fact in the contracts? 'Will it be the Government's intention to reduce the stumpage rate to a figure that will permit economic production on the inevitably reduced output?' As it happened, the sirex infestation proved a blessing in disguise. The voracious beetles acted like unpaid thinning crews and had greatly improved the quality of parts of the forest.

The problem of the forest's unevenness, however, continued to create despair among even the imported technicians and caused havoc in the paper-making process. But, steadily and doggedly, Tasman got on top of the technical problems. By 1957, it had taken over Reed's tonnages. By 1960, Tasman's newsprint exports alone totalled 20 percent of New Zealand's total exports. By then, it had become the largest exporter of locally manufactured goods, and it remains so today.

New Zealand had become proficient at producing newsprint. Despite the vicissitudes with the forest, with commissioning the plant, with the management, with cycles in world prices, Tasman had by the late fifties and early sixties more than fulfilled the ambitions of the Government. It was exporting over half of its production and earning Australian dollars and other foreign currencies for a grateful Government.

Fletchers' flirtation with the Spencers, fabulously wealthy by New Zealand standards, grew out of Tasman. The Spencers had cornered the New Zealand market for toilet paper and made an immense fortune out of it. Berridge Spencer was the patriarch of the family and was one of the individualists of New Zealand commerce. The family were printing specialists and relentless investors in the latest overseas technology. If their travels and technical reading alerted them to equipment that, for example, printed rolls faster or more efficiently, they brought it to New Zealand and used it to drive out their competitors.

Their *modus operandi* was simple. Using their technological advantage, the Spencers simply undercut the competition until they went out of business. Purse-proud, they extracted tremendous productivity from their thinly staffed businesses. The Caxton company at that time was a notoriously slow payer. Old Berridge was an arch-capitalist whose commercial creed had little to do with the contemporary ethos that big companies should be good corporate citizens. Berridge Spencer believed a company's job was solely to produce profits. Insiders say that any request for a donation for charity quickly ended up in the wastepaper basket.

Berridge was proud of his wealth and he had worked hard to create it. References in newspapers to certain people being 'millionaires' often riled him. He would grumble that he was 'worth far more than that chap'. Secrecy was part of the company culture and only the immediate Spencer family and Berridge's long-serving secretary, a Miss Miller, knew anything about the economics of the Caxton Printing Works. In one respect, Berridge Spencer was far ahead of his time. In an age tolerant of smoking and alcohol, he was violently opposed to both, possibly because he saw both as a waste of money.

Nobody ever accused the Spencers of not being good at their business. They knew the value of investment, productivity and efficiency. As Sir James now says: 'They got there by being the best in the game.'

The Spencers had formed a long-standing relationship with Vancouver-based Westminster Paper and imported from it all their raw material, a lightweight tissue paper. But after many years of importing paper, Berridge decided to build his own mill to manufacture tissue paper. This would then be turned into toilet paper at Caxton's converting plant in Henderson. Westminster's chief executive, Elmer Herb, requested a half-share in the converting plant (where the real money was) as a price for putting money into the new mill. The Spencers refused and Westminster duly pulled out of the plans to build the mill.

Through Dick Sandwell, who had designed the Kawerau mill and had been contracted to do the blueprints for the Caxton mill, JC heard there might be an opportunity here for Fletchers, so he approached Berridge Spencer with an offer of equity. He ended up buying half the shares in the proposed Caxton paper mill for £150,000. It was one of the few businesses that Jim Fletcher bought into rather than starting up.

The deal made a lot of sense. The new Caxton mill would be built alongside the Kawerau plant that produced groundwood pulp, the major raw material for the manufacture of tissue paper. So the plant was built by Fletchers adjacent to the big Tasman complex, despite the initial doubts of the Spencers, who had earlier argued for a Henderson, Auckland, site beside their converting plant.

It opened in 1957, and the toilet paper it produced proved highly acceptable to the nation's posteriors. It's a measure of Berridge Spencer's wily business acumen that in the six months before the New Zealand-made paper appeared he ordered a lower-quality paper from his Vancouver supplier and thus got the public used to an inferior product just in case the locally produced version didn't measure up.

The venture proved so successful that a second machine was soon installed. It was now, however, that Jim Fletcher learned that the deal didn't make total commercial sense, despite the amicable commercial relationship with the Spencers.

Investment in the mill was really only logical and profitable if Fletchers also had a share in the converting operations. 'The gravy was in the converting,' JC recalls. This was because the Caxton Printing Works was virtually the only domestic customer of the Caxton Paper Mills. Had there been other big customers, Fletchers would have picked up some tidy profits from sales to them. But clearly the Spencers weren't paying high margins for the raw material they were processing themselves. *Their* profit came from the finished product. Thus Fletchers was excluded from the returns achieved by the converting plant

Eventually, JC broached the subject of buying into the processing plant and thus securing a slice of the end profits. The fiercely independent Berridge refused point blank. Jim Fletcher, understanding the private culture of the Caxton Printing Works, wasn't surprised, but it was clear to him that the commercial relationship had run its course.

The success of the Kawerau-based Caxton tissue-making plant also became one reason for Fletchers' disappointment with it. The profits for the Spencers were so attractive and the partnership was so obviously productive that Caxton continually wanted to reinvest the returns in additional machines. Thus Fletchers, though excluded from the handsome returns the Caxton company was getting through the Auckland converting plant, was obliged to pour money back in. In effect, Fletchers was subsidising the Caxton Printing Works' profits.

So, in 1964, Jim Fletcher invited Berridge Spencer to buy Fletchers out of the tissue-making plant and old Berridge agreed.

Jim Fletcher was now working at a furious pace. He would leave home before the rest of the house was up, bearing the briefcases of papers he had brought home the night before. His golden rule of management was to clear his desk each night, and that often meant the desk at home, too. Each morning he went through the mail long before normal working hours, having made special arrangements to have the mail picked up and put on his desk early. 'It allowed me to concentrate on the main developments of the day,' he explains.

But he had to find moments to relax. His physical recreation remained riding, and he would sometimes walk. He liked to read but after spending his working hours reading commercial documents, the last thing he wanted was heavy material for relaxation. So he read light novels — Georgette Heyer and the classic western writers such as Louis L'Amour and Luke Short, on which he's quite an authority, or thriller writers like Peter Cheney and Edgar Wallace. Like his father, he learned to switch off from office problems. On planes, Jim soon figured out that falling asleep was the best way to combat airsickness, and he could drop off almost before the aircraft left the ground. When he got back to New Zealand after a long flight, he was thus fresh enough to go straight to the office from the airport — and he usually did.

The fifties had been an absorbing and gruelling decade. It had been a decade dominated by Tasman, the giant manufacturing operation. But all this time Fletcher Construction, the division that had fuelled the company's expansion into manufacturing, had been taking on some of the most challenging jobs in Australia and New Zealand, mostly with success but sometimes with failure.

Chapter 4

Acquisitive Years

The fifties and sixties were restless, formative, challenging, driving years for Jim Fletcher, for the company and for New Zealand. The fifties began with the staging of the Empire Games in Auckland on a shoestring. Commercial life was much simpler then — a handful of businessmen got together and virtually guaranteed overnight the money for the Games, the athletes were happy to be put up at Papakura camp, which Fletchers had built in wartime, and the runners competed on a grass track at Eden Park.

New Zealand sent troops to Korea to fight Communism. At home, the 1951 waterfront strike shocked and polarised a nation. George Fraser was there, marching with the wharfies and their families.

A lantern-jawed, lanky beekeeper called Ed Hillary clawed his way to the top of Mount Everest with Sherpa Tensing on 29 May 1953, and the new Prime Minister, Keith ('Call me Kiwi') Holyoake, who never missed a political opportunity, 'presented' this feat to the Queen on her coronation as a 'gift'. That year, the Wellington–Auckland express tumbled off the buckled bridge at Tangiwai with the loss of 151 lives. In 1955, the Tasman pulp and paper plant marked a milestone in industrial history when it began producing newsprint. A year later, New Zealand's cricket team announced the beginning of the end of its reputation as a second-class cricket country by beating the West Indies in a test by 190 runs, its first test victory. Television began cautiously, following experimental transmission by Bell Radio and Television Corporation with two hours of programmes on just two nights a week, but soon began to transform the lives of New Zealanders.

Pay-as-you-earn income tax collection made its debut in 1958 in the same year as Arnold Nordmeyer's Black Budget, an austere document from the Presbyterian minister that introduced heavy taxation increases, especially on discretionary spending such as beer and tobacco. Compared with many subsequent budgets, Nordmeyer's was more grey than black but these were the working man's pleasures and he never forgave Prime Minister Nash or Nordmeyer. Labour was thrown out of office in 1960.

There were more international triumphs. A party led by Hillary (now Sir Edmund) half pushed, half drove some converted tractors to the South Pole, thereby infuriating the British half of the expedition, which arrived much later in their purpose-built, considerably more sophisticated and comfortable transport. Yvette Williams won the long-jump gold medal at the Helsinki Olympics on her third and final leap. Murray Halberg, the Aucklander with the withered left arm, and Peter Snell won Olympic gold medals within minutes of each other in 1960 in Rome and Barry Magee, an Auckland grocer, picked up a bronze medal in the marathon. Arthur Lydiard's bunch of local boys from Mount Roskill in Auckland were the brilliant guinea pigs of his endurance-based training methods. In 1962, Peter Snell set a new world mile record of 3:54.4.

Landmark civil engineering projects were going up at a furious rate. The Auckland Harbour Bridge, one of the few big private contracts in which Fletchers didn't play a role, was opened in 1959. That was the year when the Wairakei geothermal power stations began to turn out electricity for the national grid. This was something in which Fletchers had a hand, having helped pioneer geothermal development at Tasman. A year later, in 1960, there was a major gas strike at Kapuni, which would indirectly lead to one of Jim Fletcher's biggest headaches.

It was a confusing period for industrialists. Industrial policy was highly changeable as successive Governments undid each other's work. The new National Government of Keith Holyoake ('ol' Holysmoke', as Jim Fletcher still refers to him with some affection) rejected Labour's scheme in 1962 for the half-finished, licence-protected cotton mill at Nelson (which was, incidentally, being built by Fletchers). New Zealand Steel, with Woolf Fisher at the helm, began producing steel from its Glenbrook mill, albeit very expensively.

We were even considered big enough, or perhaps having enough souls to save, for silver-voiced, silver-haired evangelist Billy Graham to open his Crusade for Christ at Carlaw Park, Auckland, before 60,000 people. America wanted our troops alongside the Marines in Vietnam, and LBJ made a lightning visit to Wellington to cement our military partnership.

Rob Muldoon, an ambitious and pugnacious young politician, steered New Zealand into decimal currency in 1967 and Minhinnick, the *New Zealand Herald's* cartoonist, suggested one coin should be called not a doubloon but a Muldoon. The six-o'clock swill ended with the introduction of ten-o'clock closing in 1967, but not before strong protests from the wowsers.

These were also the golden years of prosperity, but economic storm clouds were building. By 1967, after Britain joined the Common Market, we became less and less its larder and had to find new markets to pay our way in the world.

As Barry Gustafson writes in the *Oxford Illustrated History of New Zealand*: 'For most New Zealanders in the fifties and early sixties, it was simply enough to be with one's family and friends; to own a home or rent a state house; to build a farm or business; to have a secure job; to take advantage or see one's children take advantage of the unprecedented opportunities for education and upward social mobility; to buy from the growing array of material goods available . . .'

Fortunately for Fletchers, which was heavily involved in the retail of building materials, New Zealanders were arguably the world's most enthusiastic handymen. Weekends were times when we washed or repaired our cars, mowed the lawns, laid concrete driveways, painted the house or wallpapered the walls, built our own extensions. To facilitate these handymen, Fletchers had to go to court to obtain dispensation from the trading laws to open its Auckland lumber mart on Saturday mornings. You couldn't buy a bit of four by two unless the civil servants said you could. Fletchers had retained a young lawyer for its case. He was David Beattie, QC, later Governor-General.

After a hard Saturday morning working around the house, we went off to the beach with the family or crammed into cinemas to watch American stars. On Sundays we probably attended church and later stuffed ourselves with a roast and three veg.

It was in the fifties that 'milkbar cowboys' — teenagers with 'duck's arse' haircuts riding BSA and Triumph motorbikes — started to appear. The loquacious Maud Basham, 'Aunt Daisy', chattered away on morning radio to a riveted female audience well into the fifties.

New Zealanders had become infatuated with the American way of life. We treasured Buick and Chevy cars. Our milkbars were the equivalent of the drugstore. Rock 'n' roll shocked parents, teenage girls went in for flouncy stiffened petticoats, and teenage boys adopted the Ivy League look of striped, buttoned-down short-sleeved shirts and light denim trousers.

After doing what had traditionally been men's jobs during the war, the large majority of women retreated to the home and took up domestic skills again — preserving fruit, ironing, feeding the family. Vaughan Fletcher was an exception — she carried on working until her first child was born. However, she was unpaid this time and her husband notes that Fletchers therefore more than recouped the 25 percent pay rise she had won herself that morning at the coffee bar.

For some reason, the struggle for identity is usually expressed in New Zealand in non-commercial terms — in terms of socio-cultural behaviour like drinking, in sports or in writing, but rarely in commercial terms. Yet exactly the same process was occurring in the sixties in the business world. New Zealand's economy was run from Wellington (although Jim Fletcher would often argue — and still does — that Wellington interfered more than it assisted). It was difficult for businesspeople to establish a commercial identity within the structure — some might say straitjacket — established by the bureaucrats and successive Governments.

Industrial firms besides Fletchers were spreading roots — Wattie's, Fisher and Paykel, Alex Harvey and Todd Motors among them. In the future, these firms would earn substantial amounts of foreign exchange, or at least save it through import substitution. Yet the pace of economic diversification was too slow for New Zealand's needs — decisions that should have taken days were taking months and even years as the paperwork piled up in Wellington's in-trays.

Manufacturing was still the poor cousin of farming. In 1961, as the Minister of Finance, Harry Lake, pointed out in his Budget, over 90 percent of our foreign earnings came from farm production. Our exports of manufactured goods in that year were worth only £6 million ($160 million today), and Harry Lake didn't consider them of enough consequence to even mention.

They were also years of heavy construction in which Fletchers would become a major player. Most of the hydro-electric power projects, for example, were built in the fifties and sixties, starting with Maraetai in 1952–54.

Jim Fletcher was congenitally restless. There were always more opportunities to pursue, ideas to explore, projects to develop. He was always far more interested in achieving things than in making a lot of money. In these days, when shareholders require bigger and bigger annual profits, this penchant for starting up companies would be considered a commercial weakness, because typically it's an expensive and risky exercise. A more profit-oriented businessman would have slowed down and consolidated, but JC wanted to go on and do more, to start companies and get them on their feet, to buy others: to build an empire, yes, but also to develop the national pool of manufacturing.

'His attitude was often "what does New Zealand need?"' recalls Jack Smith, one of Fletchers' top construction men. Indeed, JC became so preoccupied with increasing the company's turnover and building things that he forgot about his own salary. He would increase his managing directors' salaries under annual reviews, but the board, which alone had the authority, forgot for five straight years to review Jim Fletcher's salary, and he forgot to remind them. The company just didn't have a mechanism for it and only introduced periodic salary reviews when CSR, with their more formal systems, became more involved in Fletchers. Nor did JC have stock options or other perks. Although he was regularly reading about options and other bonuses for Fortune 500 chief executives in *Fortune,* he never thought to introduce them to Fletchers. His only indulgence remained a company car, and that was a perk other executives also enjoyed. If the boss thought it was good enough for him to have a company car, the same should apply to his colleagues. The result was that Fletcher executives typically drove around in cars far superior to vehicles their salaries could have bought. The myth got around that Fletchers paid its people munificent incomes.

The reality was that contemporaries like Woolf Fisher became far wealthier. What spare cash Jim Fletcher did have went into Alton Lodge, where he bred and ran horses at considerable cost.

In the early fifties, older directors such as Len Stevens and Eric Rhodes would remonstrate with the young man: 'For God's sake, can't you be satisfied with what you've got and just stabilise and get yourself into less debt?' But they were trying to restrain a natural expansionist. 'We always had more ideas than money,' says an unrepentant Jim Fletcher about his long stint at the company helm.

Some of those ideas might be long shots, but if he could see the promise of a new industry, he was intrigued. If he could see a downstream use for plant or equipment, why not go for it? If a big construction project was up for tender, why not bid for it? Building bridges, hospitals, dams, office blocks, houses, tunnels, wharves — that was Fletcher Construction's *raison d'être*.

JC was the opposite of a paper-shuffler, who is typically preoccupied with deal-making rather than with the production of goods and services. Nor was he a company doctor, who focuses on achieving improvements in an existing business. And he certainly wasn't an asset-stripper, who buys a business and then pushes through economies, often by making staff redundant and selling the assets. Fletchers grew mainly by starting things up rather than by acquisition, despite the pain it often had with pioneering manufacturing in, for example, asbestos cement and pulp and paper. It didn't even bid to buy a public company until the seventies.

JC was surrounded by an old guard, long-serving men who knew him, who saw him daily, some of whom had spent their entire working lives at Fletchers, who trusted him and who had earned his trust. They weren't yes men. They had plenty of arguments with the boss. After all, they felt they were custodians of the company, too, and they received a lot of autonomy to pursue its interests as they thought best. This freedom to decide and to act had become embedded within Fletchers' corporate culture and the company's nimble-footedness owed a lot to it. Few big companies could move as fast when they wanted. It was an 'action culture', as Hugh Fletcher much later put it, which promoted a sort of in-house enthusiasm, a joy in doing business.

From quite early on, Jim Fletcher decided to be a leader rather than a manager. Thus he devoted his energies to expansion. 'My role was to travel a great deal, to have a personal contact with all our operating people at a management level, and to try to put a bit of ginger into things,' he explains. 'If we saw there were difficulties, I tried to provide the additional help they needed. Or, if need be, to replace people who couldn't cope.'

JC wasn't a ruthless managing director but he didn't delay when confronted by incompetence or dishonesty — one South Island manager lost his job overnight for fiddling the books. Honesty and openness were values enshrined in the company's official statement of purpose.

More and more, American commercial culture was shaping Fletchers, specifically one example — Kaisers. It was a company that started out as a mere sand and gravel business and then branched out into all manner of industries like construction and shipbuilding, into automobile manufacture (though its Willys plant lost it a lot of money), steel- and aluminium-making, chemicals, communications. 'We came to model ourselves a bit on Kaisers,' Jim Fletcher says. The empathy between the companies remains today. Fletcher Construction still builds hospitals all over the world for the Kaiser Foundation, a charitable body.

By the insular standards of the time, Fletchers was remarkably outward-looking. By the fifties and sixties, Fletchers had become in the eyes of offshore contractors and bankers *the* New Zealand company. A lot of Jim Fletcher's time was taken up in a sort of commercial diplomacy — entertaining bankers and industrialists, introducing them to the Government, briefing businesspeople from all over the world on New Zealand's ways, dropping in to see people whenever he was travelling. Much of it he did out of a sense of duty and a lot of it was lonely work on the road.

Periodically, the inner circle of executives reorganised the company. In 1954, a reshuffling of responsibilities and divisions had created seven subsidiaries — timber, construction, steel, sales and service, the trust company, industries, and plant hire. The new order freed JC to pursue new projects, because he had until then been chairman or managing director of all the subsidiaries.

The inner circle around JC was composed of strong-minded and practical men. They were Bill Bourke, the head of the timber division who had joined Fletchers in 1934 as a measurer in the marble company; company secretary Harry Molony, who had started as a branch accountant in Wellington in 1943 and succeeded the toothbrush-moustached George Hutchinson on his death in 1952 — a job he held for the next twenty years; Joe Craig, who had joined Fletchers as an apprentice carpenter in 1928 and was now managing director of Fletcher Construction; John Fletcher, Jim's brother, in the South Island; Alec Craig, who had signed up with Fletchers as a carpenter three years before his brother Joe and was now running the Fletcher Steel and engineering divisions; and Dr John Watt, scientist and former Rhodes scholar. They were talented operators in their own right — Jim Fletcher's American friend George Ferris had rated Joe Craig, who had managed the building of the Wellington Railway Station at the age of twenty-one, as a brilliant construction man by the best United States standards.

These men didn't have sophisticated management skills because management courses weren't taught in New Zealand at that time, but they were strong on practicality. Jim Fletcher realised his own and his team's lack of business training and, with George Fraser, started in the sixties to bring in professors from Stanford who taught American management practice at seminars in Penrose.

This group of hard-headed operators formed the executive committee, which discussed new developments, and none of them hesitated to tell the boss what they thought. After all, some of them had been on the payroll while JC was still at school. Joe Craig had helped to build the Chateau, to rebuild earthquake-shattered Napier over three years, to kickstart state housing. He might have been a carpenter by training, but he had experience that textbooks can't teach.

It was a highly decentralised style. When Jim Fletcher hired Harry Molony, the latter ventured to his prospective boss that the salary offered wasn't great shakes and what were the real prospects? Molony clearly remembers JC's reply: 'The prospects and what you get are entirely over to you.'

Every successful company has a corporate culture, and Jim Fletcher's basic desire was to give his staff freedom. This stemmed from his view of his own job, which was to chase new industries and new opportunities and not to sit at a desk and run things. He acted as a sort of trouble-shooter and business-development manager at the same time. As Molony puts it: 'He wasn't a manager; he was a leader. His attitude all the way along the line was that a manager should be able to do his job.' But he'd intervene quickly if things weren't going right.

He always knew where the money was going. Arthur Jewell, who would later be Fletchers' chief timber man, remembers how JC wanted full monthly financial reports, including profit, funds employed, capital spent and other data. 'He wasn't slow in coming down on us. He wasn't unfair, but he certainly criticised something that didn't meet his idea of good performance,' explains Jewell.

With Molony, Jim Fletcher devised innovative systems for monitoring cashflow. 'Most companies at that time didn't really know where they were until they drew up the annual report,' he remembers. 'But we monitored cashflow weekly.' They also developed early-warning systems for production, sales, receipts and credit performance. Head office acted as a banker, with all surplus funds being channelled into it.

Appearance and behaviour were — and are — regarded as important at Fletchers. Around the office, Jim Fletcher is still never without a tie. Stationery had to look good and company vehicles spruce. (George Fraser, with his old cardigans, was the sartorial exception.) However, JC's conception of good commercial behaviour went further than image. Fletchers prided itself on quick payment of sub-contractors, on open dealing. Like his father, Jim Fletcher wasn't one for formal meetings. He believed in mixing with people at all levels and absorbing impressions rather than just statistics. Although he was far from careless about small print, he hated to spend too much time poring over numbers. 'I was seat of the pants. Don't bother me with the details,' he says about himself.

JC wanted employees to identify, not with Fletcher Holdings, but with the particular company that had hired them — timber, steel, construction or whatever. Management independence worked both ways. Although the managers earned the freedom they wanted, head office could then apportion responsibility squarely if things went wrong. Within Fletchers, there was no power without responsibility, as several senior executives would discover over the years.

People weren't numbers; they mattered. Arthur Jewell remembers how in the early days Jim Fletcher would often meet executives when they stepped off aircraft after long flights from abroad. If they had come up even from Rotorua, he would set aside time for a cup of coffee and a chat. In the fifties, Fletchers maintained a small flat in Auckland for staff away from home, and a frequent caller to it would be JC, just to say hello and to make sure things were comfortable. He had a natural sense of courtesy, still has.

Jewell, an unabashed admirer of Jim Fletcher after a working life alongside him, remembers how motivating this was: 'It made you want to perform. He didn't do this purposely, but you felt you had an obligation to the man. You were quite happy to work a lot of extra time for him.'

Jim Fletcher illustrated his willingness to explore the unconventional early on. In 1942, Fletchers had bought the Port Chalmers shipyards, the southern-most in the world, but the volume of ship-repair work had slid away steadily over the years following the wartime contracts for minesweepers — straight-bowed ships with a tall smokestack, a mast with a crow's nest to spot floating explosives and a bow-mounted gun. JC didn't want to close those historic gates if he could help it. They had carried out large-scale repair work in the early 1900s, built gold and tin dredges for mining in Australia and New Zealand, even in the Philippines, Borneo and Canada, replaced the rudder of the *Merrick*, the ship of Admiral Byrd's Antarctic expedition in 1947. Century-old Stevenson and Cook had been part of Port Chalmers since its most prosperous days when Union Steam Ship was founded and based there. But the modernisation of the world's merchant fleet had meant a disastrous drop in the yards' staple business of repair work, and there was no longer a reason for them to stay open.

Jim Fletcher's solution was to try to form a joint venture with Park Royal, the British bus-builders (the same company that designed custom bodies for for the Royal family's Rolls-Royces) and with Australian bus-building companies, which would allow Stevenson and Cook to produce their designs under licence. And if buses, why not railway rolling-stock? Post-war New Zealand was critically short of rolling stock of all kinds.

In trips to Britain from as early as 1946 and in frequent visits across the Tasman, JC had pursued the idea and had carried it almost to the stage of implementation when the Labour Government bought the shipyards back and he dropped the scheme. Had the Government not bought back the historic old yards, New Zealand's commuters might still be travelling to work in Fletcher-built buses instead of British Leyland and Mercedes-Benz coaches.

JC enjoyed thinking 'out of the box', which is another commercial expression that did not come into use until the eighties. His idea for making salt comes into that category. By the late fifties, Tasman was approaching the output for which it had been designed and Jim Fletcher, looking at that billion-dollar investment, thought, 'Why not put that expertise and infrastructure to downstream uses?'

JC knew that the thriving dairy industry in the Bay of Plenty was the largest user of salt for butter-making in New Zealand, all of which it had to import and then truck from the nearest port of Mount Maunganui. The pulp and paper industries at Kinleith and Kawerau were also major users. 'The beauty of the idea was that all the major clients were within comfortable distribution distance,' he explains now. Furthermore, he knew that salt was the basis of a chemical industry. Therefore, he reasoned, salt production could form an entirely new industry in New Zealand.

The economics of the enterprise looked viable. Tasman would pipe salt water from the Bay of Plenty into ponds built for the purpose within the Kawerau plant. The ponds would be enclosed in polythene. Steam, of which there was a plentiful supply from the adjacent geothermal fields, would be piped under pressure into the sealed ponds. The water would evaporate rapidly, leaving salt, which Tasman would sell to the dairy and pulp and paper companies.

This was far from a wild notion. A British company called Mertz McLennan was already experimenting with the process and had built a pilot plant in Iceland. JC's plan was to work with the British company and see if the proposal was viable for Tasman. However, he was only one director on the Tasman board and, as he recalls nearly forty years later, 'the other directors were completely uninterested'. Also his relations with Dougal, managing director of Tasman, were frosty because of what were, in Jim Fletcher's view, Tasman's avoidable early problems. Dougal would not entertain the concept and the salt-making venture died. At Kawerau, anyway.

Shortly afterwards, Skellerup opened a sun-dried salt-plant at Grassmere near Marlborough, and JC observed it with regret. 'Our steam-powered system would have been more efficient because it would have speeded the process up,' says Jim Fletcher ruefully. 'And we would have been right in the heart of the commercial market.'

JC continued to chase other import-replacement schemes. He put young Carl Ryan, much later Fletcher Challenge's top man in Canada, onto the huge and diverse import-licensing schedule with instructions to find imported materials or products that were in high demand but short supply because of the regulations and which could be produced locally from domestic resources. Ryan came up with two strong candidates — wallpaper and glass.

By world standards, New Zealanders' love of wallpaper was unusual. At that time, we used enormous quantities of it per capita compared to other countries, and, since it was all imported, this looked to be a promising industry for a local manufacturer. Thus Jim Fletcher went on his travels again, this time to the offices of WPM Ltd, the major manufacturer of wallpaper in Britain, and suggested a joint venture. WPM was politely dismissive, explaining that the New Zealand market was too small.

This reaction served only to fire up JC. The market *was* big enough, he responded, but for only one manufacturer. (In fact, the import-licensing system meant that the licence-holder would be the sole domestic supplier.) When the licences were abolished and the industry opened up, the manufacturer would by that stage be entrenched and permanently profitable. Furthermore, he went on, Tasman could produce the base paper for the fancy wallpaper. To boot, the dairy industry produced casein, which was the essential ingredient of wallpaper glue and sizing. Thus WPM would have a strong case to put before the bureaucrats; it would be an import-substitution producer and a substantial local purchaser.

It was just as well that JC, who had by now been knocking on doors and introducing himself for years to the principals of major offshore companies, was hardened to setbacks. Despite his arguments, the proposal still fell on deaf ears. Then, within months, ICI started up a wallpaper plant in New Zealand, and UEB followed not long after.

Jim Fletcher hoped to have better luck with the manufacture of glass when he tackled Pilkington, the giant British glass-makers, in London. He talked to the British executives enthusiastically about the good silica sand, glass-making's raw material, in New Zealand and the booming house-building market, which was a big buyer of glass. Instead, they replied with the same argument as WPM. Pilkington had just established a plant in Ireland, and the small

New Zealand market was far too big a geographical and financial leap.

Coincidentally, and unknown to JC, local manufacturer George McKendrick was at that very time planning to open a plant at Whangarei, encouraged by the head of the Department of Trade and Industry, Dr Bill Sutch, who had effectively granted McKendrick the glass-manufacturing franchise for New Zealand. The plant opened within a matter of months and, when it failed some years later, Pilkington bought it. It was a failure for Sutch, who had also been behind the abandoned cotton mill in Nelson, as well as for McKendrick.

Many of the civil servants with whom Fletchers had to work either couldn't or wouldn't see the potential of a concept. They repeatedly allowed their imaginations to be inhibited by the anticipation of small difficulties. George Fraser, who had been a civil servant and understood the way bureaucrats thought, used to describe his former colleagues as 'inverted Micawbers, waiting for something to turn down'. Many ministers were dominated by their senior staff, and JC regularly ran up against them.

Wellington was an octopus whose tentacles reached into every corner of life including commerce. 'In all those years I can never remember any of them saying: "That's interesting. Let's have a look at that." Instead it was always something like, "I don't think that's on," or "Have you thought about this?" ' JC says. Although people like Entrican, driven by his own grand design, and Ashwin were big-thinkers, JC regrettably found that too many civil servants were cramped in their thinking.

It was the era of the 'command economy', when Wellington knew best, and industrialists had to spend much of their time in the capital sweet-talking civil servants instead of running their businesses. And quite often, as the case of the Meremere power station shows, having to accept wrong-headed decisions.

The Meremere station near Mercer, alongside the Waikato River at one of its widest parts, is a coal-fired one. It's been mothballed now after an unnecessarily expensive career as part of the national electricity grid. Fletchers' interest in Meremere stemmed, like the stillborn salt-making venture, directly from its experience with Kawerau — specifically, with the Bechtel corporation — and indirectly through its involvement in geothermal power a few years earlier. The path to the Meremere story starts therefore at Kawerau.

When Tasman was under construction, geothermal power was in its pioneering days in New Zealand. Bores had been sunk at Wairakei, but there was a lot still unknown about how to tame this bottled-up steam.

The principle of geothermal power is simple enough. Hot rock heats water deep below the earth's surface. A ceiling of impermeable rock stops the water, now at boiling temperature, from escaping and pressure builds. When the water is exposed to air temperature through drilling, it flashes into scalding-hot steam. As was discovered in Kawerau, tapping the high-pressure steam is one thing, but controlling it is something else.

The new town of Kawerau was right on New Zealand's volcanic region — a strip fifty kilometres wide by 250 kilometres long that stretches from Ruapehu to Taupo and on to White Island, which belches steam off the coast near Whakatane. Maori in the district had for centuries used the steam escaping through fumaroles in practical ways, mainly for cooking and bathing.

Ministry of Works engineers had their own ideas about how to discipline geothermal power and were moving towards the development of their own generating station at Wairakei. But, power being a huge permanent cost in such an energy-devouring complex as a pulp and paper plant, Tasman was always anxious to find cheaper supplements to the local electricity grid. That was why Fletchers teamed up with Bechtel, the United States-based global construction company, in a consortium called Fletcher-Bechtel-Raymond that was hired as consultants to Tasman. In turn, Bechtel had sub-contracted Brown Drilling Company from Long Beach, California, to penetrate the dangerous depths of the Volcanic Plateau.

It was pioneering work. Only the Italians had harnessed geothermal steam to generate electric power, at Larderello, in Tuscany, where a number of bores were turning out more than 250,000 kilowatts of power, or just under the combined installed capacity of the Karapiro and Maraetai hydro schemes. (The Italians based a chemical industry at Larderello, as JC had hoped to do at Kawerau through the salt-making venture.) At that time also, New Zealand's engineers had started to worry about the long-term inability of the hydro-electric schemes to meet all of the country's, and especially the North Island's, energy needs. They were even talking about the need for atomic power in the mid-fifties. One attraction of geothermal power was its cheapness. Like hydro-electric power, but unlike coal and oil, it is a renewable resource.

The equipment Bechtel brought to Kawerau was at the leading edge of technology — for example, a T12 rig with a thirty-metre collapsible mast and capable of drilling to 1,350 metres. It was the best that money could buy.

Drilling started on 16 April 1956. The first well failed to strike steam but the crew drilled two more, both to a depth of 700 metres. On 23 April, the crew shifted the rig to a new site and had got down to 430 metres within seven days without much trouble. Work was going well until the New Zealand crew on the rig went on strike, one of the first of the rogue disputes that would much later become a cancer at Tasman. Five Americans, all of them on productivity bonuses, carried on alone and sometimes worked for forty-eight hours non-stop. They finished the hole at a depth of 620 metres and tapped a steady and gratifying supply of steam power. Things were looking good, and especially so when on 19 May the short-handed crew drilled another hole that also proved to be a good source.

It was on the next hole that the Americans and New Zealanders, by now back to work, ran into trouble. They erected the rig on the east bank of the Tarawera River, about 300 metres south of the Tasman plant. The drill, chewing out layers of rock and pumice, got down to 130 metres. Suddenly, a shower of steam and water burst out of the hole and the crew scattered. Within minutes, more steam and water roared into the sky. Soon the bore was completely out of control.

The Texans pumped in water to try and cool the bore down, but the eruptions blew the water straight out again. Boiling muddy water built up in the cellar floor where the rig was based and conditions were worsening by the hour.

Next, the crew tried to shut down the valve on the main pipe, braving the steam to get at the valve. But it proved impossible to get anywhere near it. Even the Texans, who hated being beaten, had decided it was time to bail out. Before they did, the crew fought to salvage as much gear as they could. They had got everything but the rig itself out when the cellar floor, which had been built over the now-collapsing ground, buckled and subsided. The valuable rig tipped over in slow motion and hit the ground.

There's a tough-minded ethic among construction people: if you possibly can, you don't let the elements beat you. The crews hurriedly got tackle together to try to lift the rig clear with cranes and bulldozers in a quiet moment. These efforts were hastily abandoned when the rogue well started blowing and roaring with renewed violence.

Still the Texans and New Zealanders didn't give up. They slung a drill pipe from a crane located at a safe distance from the rebellious well, skilfully lowered it into the hole and forced water down the pipe at a rate of 1,350 litres a minute. The bore refused to be subdued and continued to spew boiling mud, scalding water and hot rocks. More water was forced down the pipe, but it was too much and the hose broke at the head fitting of the pipe. A higher pressure hose was installed, but to no avail.

It was now impossible to get anywhere near the rogue bore and during the night the ramp and trailer and some other valuable gear was winched away through a tackle system. Finally, having retrieved what equipment they could, the crew withdrew. They knew they had lost.

It was a sobering expression of nature's power, and the bore kept complaining at this undue interference for several months before quietening down. The Texans sensibly gave up on the bore and drank more than their usual share of bourbon that afternoon.

Most of the Brown Drilling people were thirsty, Camel-smoking Texans and it's one of those interesting socio-cultural byproducts of the Tasman project that they were responsible for introducing bourbon and Camels to the then-remote Bay of Plenty. Unable to find either in the area, they put a persuasive case to Fletchers about rectifying this deficiency. Fletchers was not entirely without skills in the art of handling bureaucrats and filed for these exotic imports on the basis of hardship. Soon the local pub had copious supplies of both bourbon and American cigarettes.

There was some tension and jealousy between the Ministry of Works and the Texans, most of it on the bureaucrats' side, and ministry engineers weren't entirely unhappy that the overseas experts had come unstuck. But later they struck their own rogue bore at Wairakei. Kawerau had two good bores, one bad. It was considered a good record. By March 1957, eleven months after sinking the first drill, Tasman started using geothermal power from the productive wells. Pipes from a grid of eight wells fed the steam into the timber-drying kilns and later into the wood-preparation and timber-preservation plants. The experiment with geothermal power had come off, one rogue bore aside, and JC was already looking for other opportunities to work with Bechtel.

Then Sid Holland's Government, having sat for three years on the plans of English consultants to build a new coal-fired power station at Meremere, asked Fletchers to do the job with American partners. JC immediately flew to San Francisco. The matter was urgent, Minister of Works Stan Goosman told Jim Fletcher, because the Government didn't want to enter the next elections in the middle of power shortages. Meremere would be a station for peak demand, he told JC.

The British consultants Preece, Cardew and Rider had reckoned it would take four years to build the station to their own design, using all-British equipment. This was too long, Goosman told Jim Fletcher and asked if he would talk urgently to some of his influential construction contacts.

This was May 1958, not much more than a year after Fletchers had worked with Bechtel at Kawerau. Relations between the two companies were excellent, so JC duly went to America and soon returned with an exciting alternative to the now somewhat dusty English plans. Having talked with Bechtel, who would bid for the construction with Fletchers, and Ebasco, a giant United States power utility, he could guarantee that Meremere could be constructed in half the time. That is, within two years. But, JC told Goosman, he could do even better than that.

The Americans proposed a different but far more efficient coal-fired design than the British one. Ebasco's designers were politely dismissive of Preece, Cardew and Rider's suggested configuration for the plant. The British scheme envisaged six units of 30,000 kilowatts each, which, the Americans said, was old-fashioned, expensive to run and maintain, and not very heat-efficient, as their latest designs were proving each day.

Ebasco's configuration was simpler. It proposed just two 90,000-kilowatt units, which would require a quarter of the staff, would produce

127

more heat and cost about $US500,000 less each year to run. This would be a huge saving for a plant with a life of twenty years or more, equivalent in today's dollars to $14 million a year, or $280 million over the designed life of the plant.

The Americans knew what they were talking about. At that time, Bechtel was successfully building 90,000-kilowatt units in Asia. In a letter that Jim Fletcher passed on to Goosman, Ebasco's engineers argued that 'two 90,000-kilowatt units were very far superior to six 30,000-kilowatt ones'.

Bechtel sent out one of their best engineers and senior executives, Dr Earl English, who had supervised the Kawerau geothermal project and knew New Zealand conditions. In meetings with Goosman, English argued politely and strongly for the modern configuration.

But Stan Goosman had shifted camps, to JC's bafflement, and suddenly seemed determined to defend the British blueprint. 'Our people would find these large boilers difficult to deal with,' Goosman told the American. 'They are trained in hydro power.'

'Not a problem,' English shot back. 'We're training Koreans in America, and they've learned very quickly. Surely you wouldn't rate New Zealanders below Koreans?'

Goosman then argued that a breakdown with a two-unit system would be more serious for the national grid because half the designed output would be then be cut. 'They are designed not to break down,' explained Dr English patiently.

Listening in astonishment to this conversation so soon after being urged to pursue the American plan, Jim Fletcher could hardly believe his ears. He knew that Goosman's argument was false. What mattered was not how much of just one plant like Meremere went down because of a failure of part of it, but how much of the entire electricity-generating system that breakdown represented. And even the loss of 90,000 kilowatts of generation, assuming the worst, was a relatively small part of the entire grid.

To Jim Fletcher's continuing amazement, Goosman finally told them flatly that the Government was now committed to the British configuration. The experienced Bechtel man told the minister: 'Mr Goosman, you are going to have on your hands a very costly power station.' And the pair left Wellington.

Jim Fletcher was furious and embarrassed. He had been sent on a wild goose chase and had brought in, at the Government's request, the best American contractors. Yet the Government had never apparently seriously entertained an alternative to the British scheme. He later learned that Goosman had weeks before deliberately or inadvertently — he never knew which — signed a letter put in front of him by his staff that invited the British designers back to New Zealand to finish the job.

The Meremere plant was duly built with the six 30,000-kilowatt British-designed units. As the Bechtel man had predicted, it proved to be easily the most expensive station in the national grid. Estimates of the high cost of running the station quickly proved correct. 'It was a 1930s style of plant in the 1950s,' JC now says. Others have since confirmed that; years later, the head of the Electricity Department told Jim Fletcher that Bechtel's design would have been far preferable.

Jim Fletcher didn't like to be office-bound. He wanted to get out there, talk to people, see things for himself and sniff out opportunities. Sometimes this led to unexpected results.

In the fifties, Fletchers was trying to expand its quality timber supplies, timber being the raw material of so many of its companies. So when a Frenchman named Jean Rouleau alerted Fletchers in early 1950 to the possible sale of rights to a forest on the remote island of Eromanga in the New Hebrides group, Jim Fletcher and the company's timber man, Lou Hahn, were interested.

Fletchers had been looking for an alternative source of peeler logs — the symmetrical circular logs that provide the best plywoods and veneers — other than native timbers. Two years earlier, they had imported high-quality peelers from Samoa, and they would bring them in from Borneo a few years later. A growing problem with native species like matai, totara and rimu was that much of the best wood had already been processed and, given the high sapwood to hardwood content of inferior indigenous timbers, the real return was coming from a small part of the log. Also, the finished wood from some offshore species commanded higher premiums.

Rouleau said he was prepared to sell the rights, so JC and Hahn made arrangements for what they envisaged as a pleasant site inspection.

They would take the flying boat to Sydney, a scheduled flight in a seaplane into Port Vila in the New Hebrides, and then step aboard a millionaire's yacht that had been chartered for the short voyage to Eromanga.

However, everything that could go wrong, did.

The flying boat was nearly halfway between Auckland and Sydney when engine trouble forced it to return. The pair took off next day but had missed the Port Vila connection and had to wait a further twenty-four hours in Sydney. During a refuelling stop for the seaplane flight from Sydney in Noumea, New Caledonia, they learned from M. Rouleau when he boarded the plane that the chartered yacht had been wrecked two days earlier but — *ne vous inquietez pas* — satisfactory alternative arrangements were already in hand. Since they were flying into the New Hebrides, why not have a look at the Frenchman's forest by air? Jim Fletcher agreed on a fee with the flying-boat captain to buzz the plantation, but just when they glimpsed the island, the weather closed in and they didn't see a single tree for their expense. So far, the expedition had suffered nothing but setbacks.

The replacement yacht turned out to be a scruffy little coaster called the *Pangona*. Unknown to JC and Hahn, who had started to react to their smallpox and yellow-fever injections, the vessel had been laid up at Port Vila for nine months awaiting a new set of diesel engines. Fletcher and Hahn learned much later that the engines hadn't arrived.

The party — Fletcher and Hahn, Rouleau and an English merchant from Port Vila named Reid — boarded the vessel with growing misgivings and set off. The *Pangona* chugged on during the afternoon and evening, then, almost at the moment she reached Eromanga, the diesels coughed a few times and stopped.

By now, the New Zealanders had lost faith in Rouleau, but they still wanted to see the forest, having spent several days getting this far. Eventually, the recalcitrant engines were restored to working order and the ship set off again for the other side of the island where the forest was located. Twice during the night, the engines broke down again. When the *Pangona* reached the bay at the entrance to the forest and ran a passage of rough water into the protective bay, the engines stopped again. Islanders promptly started trading with the skipper, who, the Fletcher pair soon noticed, was making an enormous profit on his unmarked tins of food. A swarm of flies immediately besieged Jim Fletcher and Hahn and never left them. Hahn's arms had now swollen up like footballs and his condition was causing his boss some alarm. Nevertheless, they set off with Rouleau to inspect the forest.

Jim Fletcher takes up the story: 'We'd been led to believe the forest was a veritable paradise, with enormous kauri-type trees starting from the water's edge. We got ashore and everything was absolutely rotten. It was hot and sticky. We fell into streams several times. After we'd been walking for an hour and a half and hadn't seen a tree worth a damn, it was getting pretty obvious that they weren't big enough or well enough shaped to make peeler logs.' They turned back in late afternoon without reaching the heart of the forest after the guide lost his way.

By the time they made it back to the ship, it was dark. The *Pangona's* engines were persuaded to turn over and the coaster chugged through the gap, diesels wheezing reluctantly, and then stopped within minutes of clearing the heads. The engines wouldn't start again.

The stage was now set for an uncomfortable comedy. The Fletcher men were adrift with their hosts, a lot of passengers from Eromanga who cooked dinner in an open 44-gallon drum on deck, plus some pigs and chickens. The skipper was now laying low, counting his profits for all JC knew, while the boat drifted in the opposite direction to Port Vila. Jim Fletcher hastily consulted the charts. 'The only thing between us and Australia is New Caledonia,' he told the sick Hahn.

As they wallowed past the bay where they had stopped earlier, one of the Frenchmen put off in a small boat with two islanders to alert the weather station there to the stricken coaster's predicament.

Next, the weather turned malevolent. A huge waterspout — the first JC had seen — loomed up on the horizon. A local crewman, who subscribed to the theory that bullets could break up the spout, poured a hail of ammunition from a .22 into it but without effect. The waterspout rocked the boat violently but did no damage, except to Jim Fletcher's and Lou Hahn's nerves. 'It frightened the living daylights out of us,' remembers Jim Fletcher.

The voyage had turned into a nightmare. The skipper's charts were hopelessly outdated, and the Fletchers men were convinced his course would miss the next port, which was New Caledonia. At night they would sneak up to the wheelhouse and, in JC's words, 'give the wheel a few twirls to the right'. The *Pangona* had only a tiny sail and the first mate, a magnificent-looking native with a skin like old bark, sat in the bow all day cradling his grandson and whistling for the wind.

The drinking water ran out. For food, there was only the remaining unlabelled cans, some of which the skipper traded with the natives. Jim Fletcher got sick of saveloys in oil for breakfast, lunch and dinner. Hahn, a keen rugby player and a top axeman, was normally of robust health but now he was really ill. The boat drifted on helplessly for two days.

Pondering their predicament on the third morning, Jim Fletcher thought particularly of Vaughan, who was due to have their third child any day, and yet here he was, drifting helplessly over a sea pockmarked with coral reefs and underwater rocks.

Disturbing his reveries, like an angel of mercy, a Catalina seaplane flew over and dropped an air-sea rescue pack with a message asking the *Pangona* to signal confirmation of her identity. It transpired that the dinghy party had made it to the weather station, and a French gunboat was coming to the rescue. The Catalina then disappeared and the *Pangona* resumed its wayward progress towards New Caledonia.

But Jim Fletcher had seen the charts and knew that the rocky islands of the Loyalty group were in their path. Somehow he had to slow the rate of drift. The inventive New Zealanders made an anchor of chains, pots and pans and anything else they could find, and flung this assemblage over the side. The speed of drift slowed satisfactorily during the night.

Daylight found them planning to make a raft from the saloon table lashed to oil drums. They could see land through the mist and had no intention of losing this heaven-sent opportunity to get off the ill-starred *Pangona*. The skipper had come out of his cabin to argue that the boat would drift around the bottom of New Caledonia and manoeuvre itself into Noumea, but the Fletcher executives weren't willing any longer to rely on his judgement.

The gunboat arrived in the late afternoon of the next day and signalled to ask what the ship most urgently required. 'Something to drink,' they replied. The gunboat promptly sent over on a line a case of champagne and some messages in a wicker basket. The crew just as promptly dropped both in the tide as they were manoeuvring them aboard. Thereafter, the disgusted crew of the gunboat sent all messages down the line sealed in a French letter.

But cupidity had come with rescue. 'The next message we got from them was to say they thought this was a clear case of salvage and that a reasonable fee would be £30,000.' JC surmised that somebody must have told them there were two rich businessmen aboard.

'Up to this stage, we thought we'd been prepared to give first, second and third mortgages on our wives and kids if we could only be saved. But once a tow line was aboard, our commercial instincts reasserted themselves. We thought this was clearly nonsense. We were never really in any serious danger and weren't doing so bad by ourselves anyway. We'd almost got to New Caledonia,' JC says.

'So it was decided we would suspend the discussions on what fees or compensation they were entitled to and let the lawyers and the ship's owner and everybody else settle it.'

After some argument about whether Port Vila or Noumea should be their destination, Port Vila got the vote. But Jim Fletcher had to part with most of his spare cash to get off the boat at Port Vila, the skipper having bumped up the charter fees, leaving just enough money to get Hahn, now very ill, and himself to New Caledonia aboard an Air France flight.

Once they had reached Noumea, JC put Hahn to bed and tried unsuccessfully to pawn his watch, binoculars, camera, anything to buy tickets. Finally Jim Fletcher cabled head office: 'MUST REPEAT MUST HAVE TWO HUNDRED POUNDS BY NOON TODAY.' Unfortunately, the cable got garbled in transmission and arrived at Penrose reading: 'MUST EAT MUST HAVE TWO HUNDRED POUNDS TODAY.' His accountants, remembering how much money the pair had taken with them, took a hard line and the money wasn't sent. As Jim Fletcher says, 'They thought, "Those buggers, they've been living it up over there, let 'em starve!"'

After several entreaties, Qantas flew the pair to Sydney where they found all the flights home booked for a week to ten days because of the Commonwealth Games. By this time Hahn was on the mend, but it had been a hard week and Jim Fletcher was losing his equilibrium. He stormed up to the counter of TEAL, the forerunner to Air New Zealand. 'Look!' he said to startled counter staff. 'My wife has had two children and she's about to have a third. I was missing when the first two were born and I have been threatened within an inch of my life as to what will happen if I'm not back for the third, so I just have to get back. You've got to take me on compassionate grounds!' The staff were unmoved. There weren't any seats, they said.

Jim Fletcher isn't normally a man to pull rank, but this time he rang Geoff (later Sir Geoffrey) Roberts, then general manager of TEAL. 'Geoffrey,' he said, 'I don't often ask for favours but this is a real emergency.' The airline found a seat for the exhausted pair and, when Jim Fletcher finally arrived home at Penrose, he told Vaughan: 'If you don't have this child within the next day or two, my credibility is totally gone.' Angus, their third son, obligingly arrived within a few days.

Eromanga's elusive forest haunted JC for years, a ghost that turned up at his elbow at the most unexpected times. The Sydney office of Fletchers was later offered Rouleau's interest in the trees. Later again the Presbyterian Church, which controlled half of the forest that Rouleau didn't, came to Fletchers with a separate offer and company staffers went up again and found the peeler logs that JC's incompetent guide had missed that steaming afternoon. And much later, in the mid-seventies, Jim Fletcher and George Fraser heard of the forests once more in, of all places, Paris. A French company called Rougier et Cie had by then bought Rouleau's interests and offered Fletchers another crack at the logs. This time, Jim Fletcher took up the offer and the logs were shipped to New Zealand.

Trips to Australia were usually much more fruitful. JC was always looking to find industries and processes that Fletchers could copy, and New Zealand's roofs would never look the same again after a 1960 trip to Melbourne.

It was a friend of JC's, Christopher Weatherby, scion of a British family that had kept the British Stud Book for centuries and practically ran British racing, who had suggested to Jim Fletcher on a New Zealand visit that he should drop in on his Melbourne friend John Davies. (Weatherby may have been blue-blooded but he wasn't a stuffed shirt. Having spied during one visit to New Zealand a trampoline at the Fletchers' Penrose house, he removed his shoes and coat and proceeded to give an extempore exhibition of bouncing.) Davies, senior partner in Davies and Dalziel, had just become a director of precision engineers E. T. Brown Ltd, which was producing a new type of roofing — 'a licence to make money,' enthused Davies. The ultimate opportunist, JC immediately got Brown's address in Melbourne.

JC knew that New Zealanders were well used to iron (actually steel) roofs as opposed to tiles and other alternatives. His enthusiasm knew no bounds when he saw that E. T. Brown was making a new type of roofing that could be cut to individually specified sizes because it was 'cold-rolled' as opposed to being cut in standard lengths under heat. Thus there wouldn't be leak-prone overlapping needing lead-capped nails. In a matter of weeks, he had secured the New Zealand licences, because he was confident that Brownbuilt's long-run iron would sell easily to home-owners and builders.

Within a few months, Fletchers had opened a plant in New Zealand in a fifty-fifty partnership with E. T. Brown, and this is still turning out Brownbuilt roofing, though now under the name of Dimond Industries.

Brownbuilt became one of Fletchers' most consistent earners. Later, the factory started using the same cold-forming techniques to produce Armco guardrail for roads and racetracks and many other uses. Even Jim Fletcher couldn't have guessed that he would make a highly profitable contribution to road safety when he brought Brownbuilt to New Zealand.

Easily the biggest purchase of this era was that of the Kauri Timber Company. Overnight, it converted Fletchers from a small player in the New Zealand timber-processing industry into the biggest one. It had started with a cautious overture from the company's Australia-based managing director, Reg Taylor.

The Kauri Timber Company is embedded in New Zealand's early commercial history, but it wasn't a locally based company, despite its name; it was an Australian one, owned by pillars of the Melbourne financial establishment. In fact, Australian businesspeople had owned and stripped the giant kauri forests for eighty years up to that time.

Ironically, the Kauri Timber Company didn't have much kauri left in the sixties, most of the trees having been sold across the Tasman decades before. What was left of the kauri forests was protected.

What KTC did own was a lot of long-established and profitable timber-based businesses in New Zealand, some of which had been on its books since 1888, when Melbourne interests bought hard-up New Zealand sawmills all over the Coromandel and Northland, plus huge tracts of timber. Steamers chartered by KTC used to call in at Kaipara Harbour, on the west coast north of Auckland, and take away a million feet of timber in one load. By the turn of the century, KTC was a giant in New Zealand, employing over 5,000 people and cutting some seventy million feet of kauri every year.

Thus, even though the kauri business had gone, KTC was the major player in the South Island timber industry and one of the biggest in the North Island. Its portfolio of fully owned or part-owned interests included exotic forests in Putaruru, the King Country, Raglan, Te Kauwhata, Morrinsville, sawmills in Otorohanga, Ongarue, Putaruru and Mangapehi, all of these owned by Ellis and Burnand in the central North Island. It owned retail timber yards, sawmills and forests on the West Coast of the South Island through Butler Bros, founded in the 1870s by two enterprising young Englishmen, William and Joseph Butler. It owned another West Coast sawmilling company called Stuart and Chapman, founded in 1901. It owned Kauri Sawmills, based at Edgecumbe, with a major installation at Penrose, comprising a timber yard, drying kilns, joinery factory and pre-cut mill. It also owned the Ellis Veneer plywood mill at Mananui, south of Taumarunui.

Fletchers had long done business and competed with KTC. When James Fletcher built the Auckland city markets in 1916, it was with KTC-supplied kauri. In 1960, the two companies owned half-shares in New Zealand Plywood (South Island), but that wasn't an entirely happy relationship. From Fletchers' viewpoint, the problem lay with the West Coast sawmillers under KTC's umbrella. Butler Bros and Stuart and Chapman were supposed to provide quality peeler logs to NZ Plywood under a 1949 agreement, but were doing so reluctantly or not at all. This was in spite of the premium Fletchers had agreed to pay them for the logs and the half-share KTC had bought in the plywood factory for that express concession. 'Some of the best logs were being lost to us,' Jim Fletcher recalls.

A happier joint venture was Australasia's first particle-board factory, which the two companies started up in New Zealand and which would change the floors New Zealand walked on. Based on a German process in which a mix of wood flakes and glues is compressed, bonded and dried, the factory created durable flooring and wall panels from reconstituted wood, replacing the old tongue-and-groove floors. Though JC hasn't made any attempt to claim recognition for it, particle board is 'green' because it saves natural resources by recycling what would otherwise be waste wood.

For years, JC's restless vision had sought to find the right structure for the timber business. It needed to be consolidated and expanded — a vertical industry, in business parlance, that started with Fletcher-owned trees and proceeded through Fletcher-owned sawmills, then through processing into doors, joinery and other finished products in Fletcher-owned factories, and ended with their sale through Fletcher-owned merchant outlets. In 1961, Fletchers was still a junior player in timber, though a senior user of it, and its relative smallness was a nagging problem for the company.

The difficulty of access to timber worried a company that had a voracious need for the raw material, especially because of the housing division. 'There was little native forest under private ownership that wasn't already tied up,' explains JC. The company didn't own any forests but had contracted to buy the output of several North Island sawmills. That left the Forestry Service-administered forests and the Maori-owned ones. In practice, Fletchers found it could never get a look into the so-called public tenders for Forestry Service trees, some of which were locked up in short-term cosy arrangements between the incumbent contractors and the Forestry Service. 'The public tender system was a farce,' recalls JC now. 'It didn't encourage long-term investment.' So the company had taken the alternative route of buying the output of Maori-owned forests, which JC remembers as 'a terribly tortuous process'.

It involved establishing who were the beneficial owners through the Maori Land Court. Records were often hopelessly dated, sometimes no more recent than the nineteenth century. Although a handful of names might be on the document, fifty or more descendants might legitimately claim ownership through birth. Even if the owners agreed on a contract, a judge might overrule it. And even if the judge approved it, the forestry minister had the full right of veto. Blocked elsewhere from access to timber, Fletchers timber men Lou Hahn and Arthur Jewell had over the fifties and sixties learned how to lobby the Maori owners and work the system; thus Fletchers' main and rather tenuous source of timber supply in the late fifties was Maori-owned trees.

Fletchers was also weakly represented in the highly profitable timber and hardware trade. This was dominated by long-established firms like Briscoes (whose owner had died so stylishly in Christchurch), with Briscoe Mills in Wellington, C. & A. Odlin in Auckland and Wellington, Henderson and Pollard in Auckland, Kauri Timber Company in the South Island, John Edmond in Dunedin, John Burns, Ashby Burgh and Mason Struthers in Christchurch, all of them entrenched and profitable.

Both the millers and merchants were happy for Fletchers, a major customer, to stay out of their business. 'The last thing they wanted,' grins JC, 'was to see an important buyer getting into their trade.'

To consolidate and expand in timber, Fletchers had made various unsuccessful approaches to KTC over the years, and vice versa. The companies were probably too much natural competitors to be able to work alongside each other.

So Reg Taylor's overtures were highly significant. JC flew to Melbourne to see Taylor and KTC's chairman, Rex Bishop, and discussed the offer on April 13 and 14. It transpired that KTC was overborrowed, had big loans maturing shortly and needed cash urgently. The sale of some of KTC's New Zealand interests would shore up the balance sheet nicely.

Next day, Jim Fletcher bumped into Taylor at the Hotel Australia as he was waiting to catch a plane back to New Zealand. Taylor was gloomily 'crying into his beer', JC recalls, and he confided that KTC's problems were somewhat worse than his chairman had let on.

As he flew back on a TEAL DC6, JC made some notes. 'In those days of longer journeys there was plenty of time to think on planes,' he says. Within a few days, he had cabled an offer to KTC in Australia to buy its interests in the South Island plywood factory, Butler Bros and Butler Timber, Stuart and Chapman, Otago Timber Company, Ellis and Burnand, Ellis Veneer and other smaller but valuable part-owned assets.

Fletchers' trump card was a cash offer — a down-payment of £A500,000 as soon as the papers were signed, with the rest following shortly afterwards. KTC needed the money and the cash-based deal would let Fletchers, JC hoped, drive a tough bargain. However, it was a cheeky offer because Fletchers didn't have any of the cash at that stage.

KTC's Melbourne headquarters considered the offer for a week or two and JC advised Molony to be ready to fly to Melbourne at short notice for negotiations. 'I think it's going to blow,' he told Molony.

It did, one Friday night in mid-May 1961. Reg Taylor rang to say that KTC was prepared to sit down and start talking. Molony flew to Melbourne on Saturday morning and haggled with Taylor and KTC through Saturday afternoon, all Sunday, Monday and Tuesday morning.

'We talked all day, around again, backwards and forwards,' Molony remembers. Shrewdly, JC had refused to give Molony a top price, so he was working in the dark. He had called Jim Fletcher on Sunday night, delighted to have screwed the Melbourne team down to £1,250,000 for assets both knew were worth significantly more than that.

'Too much!' retorted JC. 'I won't have a bar of it.'

Wearily, Molony went back to the negotiating table and they haggled some more. By Monday morning, KTC had come down to £950,000 and he rang his boss again.

'Far too high!' shouted Jim Fletcher down the co-axial cable link with its booming echo.

By Tuesday morning, Molony was tired and fed up. He told the KTC negotiators that he was catching the two-thirty flight home, deal or no deal. If they hadn't tied things up, the deal was off. By late morning, with the minutes ticking by, they finally struck a deal on £930,000, or £980,000 if KTC left in the 1960 year's profits. Molony put Reg Taylor on the line to JC.

'Reg, the most we can do is £930,000,' insisted JC. The hard-pressed KTC team agreed, to Molony's relief, and he caught his plane. But he went only as far as Sydney, where he saw the CSR shareholders. 'We're going to need £430,000 quick,' he told them.

The CSR general manager got the board's approval that day. By Thursday, Fletchers had the money and some of KTC's plum assets at a firesale price. The offer went unconditional on 3 May. The entire exercise had taken less than a month.

For JC, that might have been enough. But within a few weeks, KTC told a surprised Jim Fletcher that now it was prepared to sell its remaining New Zealand operations, lock, stock and barrel. Clearly their financial problems were deteriorating. For Fletchers, this was a tempting proposition and JC went to Melbourne again to discuss it, with Molony following later to scrap over the price. This last deal was eventually struck for £850,000.

As it happened, on the same visit Jim Fletcher dropped in on an old friend in Sydney, Jack Armstrong, who was general manager of the giant Commonwealth Trading Bank. The bank wasn't Fletchers' banker in Australia, but JC would routinely visit him, Woolf Fisher-style. The impromptu call turned out to be one of the most productive he would ever make. JC explained the KTC deal and added that Fletchers would have to raise the money. Although JC was sure the Fletchers board would agree to an issue of shares to raise the capital, which at that stage looked like a further £750,000 or so, there was still the Reserve Bank's foreign currency regulations to get past. With foreign exchange so short, the central bankers regarded practically every dollar leaving New Zealand as a treasonable transaction.

The Commonwealth Bank man had a suggestion. 'Why don't you get CSR to subscribe for a block of shares?' he said. 'If you can get them to do that, I'll put it to the bank board at a meeting today that they lend you the money meantime.' Simply put, Armstrong was proposing a form of bridging finance. All Armstrong wanted in exchange was that Fletchers channel all its Australian business through Commonwealth Trading Bank accounts, which suited Jim Fletcher anyway.

The schedule was tight. The bank board was meeting at eleven that very morning, which meant Jim Fletcher had to get down to CSR and back with an answer by ten so the necessary proposal could be prepared for the bank directors.

It was nine o'clock. Jim Fletcher left Armstrong immediately and walked down the street to general manager Jim Vernon's office in CSR's headquarters and explained the situation. CSR was not noted for its decisiveness, but this time it moved with uncharacteristic speed. Vernon agreed that CSR would subscribe for the Fletchers' share issue and play its part in financing the KTC purchase. Within an hour, JC was back at the Commonwealth Bank with the necessary approvals. The bank's board approved the proposal soon after eleven and Fletchers had its money.

Within a few days, all the contracts with KTC had been signed. In one bound, Fletchers had jumped to the top of the league table in New Zealand in sawmilling, to number two in timber-merchandising, to full ownership of the Christchurch plywood plant (Fletchers now owned three of New Zealand's five plywood mills), to control of its competitor Ellis and Burnand, to a very serious competitor in building merchants stores and to easily the dominant player in the South Island timber industry, where it had previously been a bit player. The deal also brought into Fletcher Timber substantial stands of native timbers, an increasingly scarce commodity. And it moved Fletchers one giant step away from its dependence on income from the construction division. In timber, Fletchers was now bigger than the Kauri Timber Company had been even at its peak.

It was a coup. It had taken just two months from the date of KTC's original letter and JC's chance meeting with Reg Taylor in the Hotel Australia to the signing of the agreement to acquire the balance of KTC's New Zealand interests. It took until Christmas to tidy up the purchase, a little longer to mop up most of the minority shareholders, but a further fifteen years to buy out all the small shareholders in Ellis and Burnand. But the bulk of the purchase deal had been swift, especially given the complexity of the shareholdings in the KTC assets.

Pat Entrican was not pleased. Most of the West Coast purchases from KTC had brought Fletchers cutting rights on state-owned forests, which were the preserve of Entrican's Forestry Service. 'Our arrival was gall and wormwood to them,' recollects Jim Fletcher with some delight.

The sawmillers and merchants were stunned. From New Zealand's early history, timber companies such as Taupo Totara, Bartholomew, Aicken, and Parker Lamb had felled the private and state native forests. Suddenly here was a major threat from Auckland. 'We were irking the Establishment,' remembers Fletcher.

The consternation of the local timber industry was nothing to the reaction of the local management of KTC. They were thunderstruck. All the negotiations right up to the signing had occurred over their heads. They learned of the deal only when Fletchers staff moved in. They were outraged at the price, which they regarded as absurdly cheap.

A few months later, Reg Taylor and his chairman, Rex Bishop, invited Jim Fletcher to a secret meeting in Melbourne and offered him the rest of the business in Australia. KTC's cashflow, consumed by high-priced loans, was now seriously deficient. But after Harry Molony had investigated it carefully, Fletchers declined the offer. 'Too many fishhooks,' Jim Fletcher concludes now. An old Danish company, East Asiatic, later bought KTC, to its permanent regret.

Adding in the second half of the deal that mopped up the New Zealand interests, the entire purchase had cost £1.6 million.

Much, much later, JC would see similarities between Fletcher Challenge's purchase of Canada's Crown Zellerbach, a company that ran into financial trouble through unwise expansion and had to sell its most valuable assets, its Canadian forests and technically superb plant and equipment. The figures look small today, but £1.6 million ($42.5 million in today's dollars) was a huge bite for a company with ordinary shareholders' funds of just £5.9 million. It represented 27 percent of those funds and was, Tasman excepted, Fletcher's biggest single splash to that date.

Although the Kauri Timber Company brought Fletchers into the West Coast in a big way, JC already had plans for the area. A year before, he had conceived a scheme that would, he was convinced, revive the Coast's declining and uncertain economy through co-operation between the Government, especially the Forest Service, and private enterprise.

In mid-1959, Walter Nash's Government had struggled to find a future for the West Coast's ailing economy through a committee of enquiry. The economy certainly needed help. Most of the coal mines had operated at a loss for years. As a *New Zealand Herald* reporter wrote after a visit to Greymouth at that time: 'In blunt terms, coal is a dead loss.'

The committee hadn't got very far when JC brought to it a grand plan. He saw the Coast as ripe for the same regional development that had turned bare land at Kawerau into an enormous industrial complex employing hundreds. Why not, he argued, establish a West Coast Authority along the lines of the Tennessee Valley Authority, which would develop mining, timber and perhaps other industries in a disadvantaged but resource-rich backwater?

After discussing the concept with the Government, Fletchers signed Arthur D. Little and Co., a Massachusetts-based company of consultants, to come to Westland at Fletchers' expense and draw up a report on opportunities for private investment on the Coast.

ADL knew its business. Founded in 1886, it had carried out thousands of assignments all over the world. An American, Peter Stern, headed the team of consultants, which Fletchers dubbed the 'Stern gang'.

Over eight weeks in April and May 1960, the team investigated possibilities for private ventures, ranging from fertiliser production and the mining of minerals to using coal as a base for road-making. Its firm conclusion: forestry presented the 'sole major opportunity' for private commercial development. This was a disappointment for Fletchers, and especially for JC, but at least ADL felt the timber industry looked promising. This was still, remember, before the KTC purchase.

The Stern gang proposed a sophisticated plan for forestry, modern integrated sawmills to cut and process the forests, thereby keeping the added value dollars in Westland.

At that stage, the West Coast's sawmilling industry was what Fletchers privately called the 'robber economy'. There was terrific wastage because a lot of the equipment in the marginally profitable, long-established mills was old. The Stern gang noted the absence of facilities in the existing mills to kiln-dry, treat, prefabricate, peel, pulp or chip the timber. Until then, the wood had left the Coast as rough-sawn timber for processing over the Alps in Christchurch, points south, or even in the North Island. This annoyed Jim Fletcher, who saw the coast's economy being stripped.

ADL believed the Coast's forests could support an industry making pre-cut house frames, timber for farmers, weatherboard, flooring, barrels, mouldings, panel boards, fascias, perhaps even pegs, furniture components, meat skewers and dowels.

The West Coasters were excited about it. 'Timbers will save us,' said one Greymouth man quoted by the *New Zealand Herald*. 'Fletchers is on the right track. Stop sending the rough-sawn stuff through the tunnel. Keep the peelers here.'

The West Coast's forests were a jewel of the indigenous industry, holding the biggest share of the native timbers such as rimu still standing. Scientifically, the trees were known as podocarps — totara, kahikatea, miro and silver pine as well as rimu — and occupied a huge swath west of the alpine fault. The beech forests, for which ADL proposed a smaller integrated mill, flourished in the central and northern West Coast.

The problem in 1960 was that the forests had been neglected and mismanaged. 'The death of matured trees in the podocarp forests constitutes a significant loss of a valuable timber resource,' the consultants wrote. With proper management — they called it 'sustainable yield' — trees could be hauled out of the Coast for a further five generations of growth.

Fletchers quickly seized this opportunity and proposed a new mill based at Ross, which could do practically everything possible to the wood that hadn't been done thus far on the Coast — drying, planing, treating, finger-jointing, end-matching, barrel-making. Fletchers proposed to hire sniggers, who haul out the wood with diesel tractors, carpenters, slipmen, tramwaymen, box mailers, whistlemen, yardmen, saw doctors, sawyers, fiddlers, slabbies, blacksmiths, bushmen and doggers-on. Adding in a veneer plant and related spending, it was a £3 million investment over five years, and Fletchers was ready to put up 60 percent for control. West Coasters and other private interests would put up the rest.

Four related industries were proposed — timber, plywood, fibreboard and, later, pulp and paper. In exchange for investing in the region, Fletchers wanted from the Government guarantees of long-term log supply, which was, of course, the bedrock of the scheme they were proposing. Plus there were the usual requirements — an acceptable stumpage price, roading, state housing and so on.

Most importantly, 350 to 400 people would be employed immediately, and the total payroll would rise to 1,000 later. Indirect employment would, of course, be much higher.

A bold vision. So what happened? Wellington and a change of government killed it. Fletchers had run straight up against the Forestry Service, whose co-operation was critical to the entire enterprise because it owned the forests. Pat Entrican resented the Stern gang, even though Fletchers had explained that the consultants had been brought in only because they would bring objectivity to the research. Entrican and his local conservators on the Coast were highly proprietorial about these forests, the nation's assets. This was their jealously guarded bailiwick. Yet here were these American upstarts, with Fletchers in cahoots, telling the Forest Service its business.

The sawmillers weren't exactly overjoyed either. They feared

Fletchers, probably with good reason, for they could see that an integrated industry would, over the years, undermine their thinly capitalised and old-fashioned mills. They couldn't see that a revived local economy would provide new opportunities. It should be noted, however, that the sawmillers weren't West Coasters — the industry was mainly in the ownership of Canterbury firms.

Hoping to do something for Fletchers and the West Coast, JC ran into misunderstanding, jealousy and flak. 'They said, "Those bastards, Fletchers. They've only been on the West Coast for a haircut and here they are telling us what to do," ' he recalls. 'We could see the commercial logic but we had created antagonisms instead.'

Then Nash's Government lost office. Holyoake's National administration didn't have many supporters on the Labour-voting Coast, and the new Minister of Forests was an east coaster.

Fletchers did build a plywood mill — at the little town of Gladstone, near Greymouth — in April 1965. Governments move slowly — it had taken three years to extract permission to build the plant. True to JC's plan for the Coast, Fletchers had closed some of its processing facilities in its timber yards in Christchurch, Oamaru and Dunedin, and at considerable expense duplicated them on the Coast, because that was where it believed that value should be added.

Holyoake opened the mill in effusively generous terms on a rare sunny day. It was 'a great day for the Coast', he declared to guests, who included Jim Fletcher, his arm in a sling after taking a fall at a fence in the Pakuranga Hunt the previous Saturday. The mill 'highlights the confidence of one of, if not our greatest, industrial enterprises — confidence in the Coast and confidence in the future of New Zealand and a great New Zealand,' Holyoake went on. He offered his congratulations on Fletchers' 'initiative, imagination, vision and drive . . .'

One local paper, the *Grey River Argus*, talked about 'this revitalising shot in the arm' the community of Gladstone had received. The *Greymouth Evening Star* reflected warmly on the faith in the West Coast held 'by an energetic far-sighted organisation'.

Complimentary words, but the grand plan foundered on human frailties. Though the long-term supply of peeler logs was basic to the relocated plywood plant's viability, the Forestry Service refused to grant

Fletchers cutting rights to the state-owned forests on the same basis as the other millers. Instead, Fletchers was told to cut out its own freehold forests first, though no such strictures were put on rival organisations. Many years later, when it had cut out its own trees, the company came back to the Forestry Service, looking for the state trees and quoting the 1964 agreement. To Jim Fletcher's anger, the department reneged on the deal.

Without the Government's whole-hearted co-operation, the same co-operation that had carried through the Tasman project, JC's plan was doomed. Fletchers sold its timber-processing interests in the seventies to Henderson and Pollard, largely because it had been unable to gain access to the forests on the same terms as its competitors. A last-minute change of heart by the Forestry Service came too late, and Henderson and Pollard picked up the rights Fletchers had wanted for nearly a decade. The experience confirmed many of JC's opinions of civil servants.

But Jim Fletcher's grand plan had really died fifteen years before from Wellington's neglect. He is still bewildered by the episode: 'We were the only company to try and make a go on the Coast and here was the Government doing every damn thing to hinder us. They held us to all our conditions but didn't meet theirs. They penalised us and drove us off the Coast.'

Jim Fletcher is not a litigious person, but Fletchers later sued the Forestry Service because, it claimed, the company had not been allowed into the forests on the agreed terms. The case was settled favourably to Fletchers out of court.

Jim Fletcher's try-anything style continually kept his board on their toes. In 1974, he proposed that Fletchers swap tractors for butter with the Soviet Union. This venture came through Edgar Kaiser, by now a good friend, who headed a group of industrialists visiting the Soviet Union. JC was in distinguished company here — Gianni Agnelli of Fiat and Dr Armand Hammer of Occidental Oil among many others. As well as being exposed to the full showcase of Russian culture, Jim Fletcher made some good contacts within the often-impenetrable individual ministries. Having missed out on opportunities in Japan because he had not foreseen how quickly Japan would become an acceptable trading partner after the war, JC returned to New Zealand determined to seize this moment.

'I came back thinking, "Well, we missed the bus in Japan, let's not miss the bus in Russia." ' He knew that the Russians made loyal and reliable traders once a relationship had been established.

He button-holed Joe Walding, an influential voice in Labour politics, and invited him to the Auckland Cup at Ellerslie racecourse. At the time, JC was president of the Auckland Racing Club. He and George Fraser described to Walding the opportunities within the Soviet Union and argued a case for reciprocal trading with it. Would Walding be willing to head a small team to scout the potential? Walding had signed the original trade agreement between New Zealand and the USSR, and seemed highly suited to the job. Walding agreed to go to the Soviet Union, and JC's eldest son, Jim, went with him. The Labour politician had another skill suitable for the peculiar demands of dealing with Soviet bureaucrats — he could drink most of them to a standstill.

The venture started brilliantly. Joe and young Jim Fletcher returned with a 'trade protocol' that had been signed in a restaurant on the back of the menu in the early hours of the morning. In the rough it read: 'I, so and so, the Minister for Trade in the USSR, agree that the USSR will buy meat and dairy produce from Fletchers provided Fletchers buys industrial goods from the USSR.' It was astonishingly informal, and favourable to Fletchers, which had to buy just a fraction in dollar values from the Soviet Union of what it hoped to sell there. In effect, Fletchers would act as a broker for New Zealand goods in barter-trading.

Almost immediately, JC fell foul of the all-powerful producer boards. The USSR wanted butter, and Fletchers informed the Dairy Board but the board was from the outset a reluctant seller. Although the initial shipment went well — the first butter sale to the USSR in half a century — the Dairy Board then told Fletchers it didn't have any more butter to sell. This was in 1975 when New Zealand farmers were panicking about future dairy sales into Europe.

Jim Fletcher was furious. 'You've been jumping up and down for years because you are losing business over the Common Market. You want new markets. Well, here's a huge market ready and willing to buy. They'll even send ships to pick it up,' he told the Dairy Board. In the end the producer board let through a fraction of what the Soviet Union wanted to buy.

In its first year, the trade agreement was wildly successful — selling $40 million in meat and butter. But the other side of the agreement, the buying of Soviet-made industrial goods, was a tougher act. With the New Zealand Co-operative Dairy Company and New Plymouth-based car importers Moller Bros, Fletchers brought Russian Belaurus tractors into New Zealand but with only modest results. New Zealand wanted to sell, but not buy.

New Zealand's involvement in commercial fishing arose directly out of this back-of-the-menu accord. It was Joe Walding who stitched up the deal. The Russians agreed to supply all the trawlers, crews and know-how to fish in the New Zealand economic zone. And, in effect, they put up the seed money, too, because Fletchers' charter fee would come out of what was left from the proceeds of the catch after all expenses and profits had been subtracted.

Fletchers couldn't lose, and it didn't. That venture gave it the experience much later to go into fishing on its own with big British trawlers.

Joe Walding eventually bought Fletchers' interest in the restaurant-menu accord and traded with the Soviet Union entirely on his own.

By the end of the sixties, Jim Fletcher had been in the top job for nearly thirty years. He was in middle age, and had established a record of starting businesses that not only survived but were profitable as well. He had built Fletchers' turnover and profits to levels that astounded even his father, himself a natural expansionist. From the £2.2 million turnover and thin pre-tax profit of £17,477 in 1942, equivalent to $950,000, the year JC had moved into the top job, Fletchers had broken all barriers. By 1950, turnover had more than tripled to £6.7 million, equivalent to $285 million. Five years later, turnover had nearly tripled again to just over £17 million, equivalent to $528 million. By 1961, there was another quantum leap — £21.3 million in turnover, or $568 million. Profit still didn't match the jump in turnover, but Fletcher Holdings' expansion was dramatic by any standards.

In all that time, John Fletcher's old firm of Gilfillan, Gentles did the auditing. Fletchers has always believed in long-term relationships.

In 1965, the company posted its first £1 million profit, on a turnover of £37.7 million. There weren't any celebrations. Jim Fletcher was too busy for that. He and the other staff were doing so much travelling to get around the company's various jobs, such as the Gladstone plywood plant and a hospital in Kaitaia, that the company had bought an aircraft, a little Cessna with the call sign 'Charlie Foxtrot Gulf'.

Old Sir James had turned eighty in 1966 and stepped down as chairman of the board of Tasman. Two years later, though still hale enough, he retired from the chairmanship of Fletcher Holdings and Len Stevens took over. In one way it was the end of an era, but for years now it had been JC's company.

Horses continued to provide Jim Fletcher with his sole relaxation, westerns and romance novels aside. He had started hunting on the cheap with ex-racehorses — Moonfleet first and then King Rod back in the late thirties. When he worked at South British he hadn't been able to afford a reinforced bowler hat so he had borrowed an old street bowler from his dad. It wasn't much protection against a fall or getting kicked in the head, but it satisfied the Pakuranga Hunt's sartorial standards.

He had started racing horses on a shoestring around the same time, while still an impoverished clerk at South British, and would maintain the habit for over half a century. JC's parents didn't approve of horse-racing, which was perhaps an incentive to take it up. 'It really stretched my means,' he recollects. He certainly couldn't afford any other pleasures. 'It meant that I delayed starting to smoke or drink for quite a few years — in fact, I never really took up smoking. I was very shy in those days, so I didn't go to dances or things like that.' And he certainly wasn't chasing girls.

The bugle call of the hunt was a siren song to the young man. He loved the ritual of it, saying good morning to the powerful hunt master with his huntsman and whipper-in, wearing the hunt colours of green with a black velvet collar, watching the excited harrier pack of hounds milling around the horses, observing the protocol of staying behind the hounds and (mainly) jumping over approved fences, clapping when the run's best follower received the traditional hare's paws. Jim Fletcher doesn't hunt any more, but a glint appears in his eyes whenever he talks about it.

149

'It's tremendous fun because, if you have a good hunter, he will know more about the hunt than you. They positively love it. I have had horses on a particularly good day who will be sobbing, they are so damn tired. But they will bloody near fling themselves at a fence — they are going to get over one way or another.

'They can be terribly intelligent. When I first started hunting, there was a great old character, "Bullock" Webster, who founded the Waikato Hunt and was master of Pakuranga for many years. He was well into his seventies when I first started. He had this great horse, Tally Ho, and he used to ride in the old style, back in the saddle. When he was in a big jump, his legs would be stuck out in front of him and his arms would be at full stretch with the reins. He didn't have too much grip by this time and on occasions Tally Ho would jump him off. We would swear that the horse knew "Bullock" was coming off and would swerve in midair and pick the old bloke up as he was on the way down!'

Pakuranga was open country then and some of the best hunts were in and around what is now prime residential real estate. The men and women of the hunt often charged over fences and stone walls near Mangere, East Tamaki, most of it open paddocks then, and near the Auckland international airport, with Webster and Tally Ho in charge. As the sixties drew to a close, suburban Auckland was creeping outwards and encroaching on the hunt's usual territory and the master had to go further out to find open country, to the lovely rolling hills of Ararimu, Karaka and Whitford.

But there was ample consolation for JC. At least he could look at the new housing, the new Fletcher-built Pakuranga shopping centre, the company factories at Penrose. The company he ran was part of that growth.

Jim Fletcher (left) aged eleven, with brother John at Waitaki Junior High.
FLETCHER PRIVATE COLLECTION

John, Ella and Jim Fletcher as teenagers.
FLETCHER PRIVATE COLLECTION

*The dynasty: Managing director JC, chairman Sir James, and John Fletcher,
executive responsible for the South Island.*
FLETCHER CHALLENGE ARCHIVES

Opposite above: *Not a great rider but a fearless one: JC out in front
at the Pakuranga Hunt.*
FLETCHER PRIVATE COLLECTION

Opposite below: *JC with staff at Alton Lodge.*
FLETCHER PRIVATE COLLECTION

JC (right) with Prime Minister Robert Muldoon on a visit to Pacific Steel.

*Proud winner of the Governor-General's award for exports: with son Jim
(left), Governor-General Sir David Beattie and Trade and Industries Minister
Lance Adams-Schneider.*

My three sons: JC with Jim, Angus and Hugh.
FLETCHER PRIVATE COLLECTION

JC and Vaughan celebrate another victory by the Fletcher stable.
NEW ZEALAND HERALD

*JC addresses his last annual general meeting as chairman of Fletcher
Holdings in 1979, shortly before the formation of Fletcher Challenge.*
FLETCHER CHALLENGE ARCHIVES

'Arise, Sir James.' JC is dubbed by Governor-General Sir Keith Holyoake in 1980.
NEW ZEALAND HERALD

President meets King: JC, now in the non-executive job of president of Fletcher Challenge, meets the King of Tonga.
NEW ZEALAND HERALD

JC in 1991, with a trophy won by his outstanding sprinter Mr Tiz.
NEW ZEALAND HERALD

Chapter 5

Dirt and Danger

The construction boys loved challenges and most of the time Jim Fletcher left them alone. The division had amassed an astonishing versatility of expertise over the decades and could build anything. It was run by men who thrived on results — so many floors up per month, so many metres tunnelled per day, so much concrete poured each hour.

It was the construction division that had fuelled Fletchers' move into manufacturing. Fletcher Construction had always been the company's cash cow, the supplier of funds for expansion. Even as late as 1965, twenty-three years after Jim Fletcher had become managing director, construction was the big earner. In that year of the landmark £1 million after-tax profit — £1,019,947 to be exact — construction had contributed easily the lion's share of the turnover. Fletcher Construction had earned £13.2 million. That was £1.7 million more than the timber division (now boosted by the Kauri Timber Company assets), two and a half times more than builders' supplies, nearly three times steel and engineering, and nearly four times manufacturing.

Successively under three different personalities, the wise Joe Craig, the polished Jim Espie and the rugged Jack Smith, the construction team built for the spiritual sector — churches and synagogues, seminaries and convents like St Mary's in Wellington, Auckland's Anglican cathedral and the Methodist central mission. It built places of learning — university buildings in Auckland, Dunedin and Christchurch and secondary school buildings such as the King's College library in Auckland, Edgecumbe College, Crossfield Street in Auckland, St Hilda's College in Dunedin, Seddon Memorial Technical College in Auckland, Morrinsville School, Ngaruawahia School, classrooms for many schools including St Cuthbert's in Auckland

and Turangi High. It built places of healing — hospitals like the Whangarei Base Hospital, Waikari in Dunedin, the Mater Maternity in Auckland, the acute block at Auckland Hospital (which took fifteen years to complete), the clinical services block at Otago Hospital in Dunedin, and the Dunstan Hospital at Clyde, old people's homes everywhere. It tackled daunting civil-engineering jobs including railway and vehicular bridges, hydro schemes, tunnels, pipelines, reservoirs, and wharves such as the Fergusson container complex in Auckland.

It built for the growing tourist industry — Auckland's 332-room Intercontinental Hotel in record time, Takaro Lodge near Te Anau, the thirteen-storey Travelodge in Auckland in a joint venture, Rutherford Hotel in Nelson, the Redwood Motor Hotel in Christchurch, the Sheraton in Dunedin, Lake Hotel in Taupo, Queenstown's Travelodge, Rotorua's Vacation Hotel, the 450-room Sheraton and the 352-room Regent in Auckland.

It won a lot of diverse government work — telephone exchanges, the Christchurch air terminal, the ill-fated cotton mill at Nelson, ambassadorial residences. For industry, agriculture and commerce, it built many factories, Wool House and the Public Service Association building in Wellington, an irrigation canal at Waiau, Canterbury, a security printing factory at Whangarei, Wellington's sixteen-storey CML centre.

It built big and small — the centennial grandstand at Ellerslie, Auckland, innovative and cheap seating arrangements for the Auckland Lawn Tennis Club's Stanley Street courts at $28 a seat construction cost, breweries, museums, the YMCA gymnasium in Auckland, state flats, sewage plants, kiwifruit coolstores and farmers' woolstores, Auckland's Odeon cinema, sports pavilions, the Air New Zealand hangar.

Some big projects never got off the ground, such as JC's grand plan for the reclamation of Hobson Bay, which would have created almost a second city centre. Despite initial enthusiasm, it died through the public's and, ultimately, the city fathers' loss of interest.

These projects represent a fraction of what Fletcher Construction built. They didn't make money on all of the projects — indeed they lost money on some — but they stuck to the advice that old Sir James had given his son many years before about doing work of which he could feel proud: 'Never build something you've got to run past.' The construction division was tireless, enthusiastic, highly capable, sometimes brilliant.

The construction boys thrived on emergencies. Working seven days a week, Fletchers' 180 men raced against the clock and the rain — 6,250 millimetres in twenty-six months, plus the wettest summer in memory — to rebuild the Hermitage Hotel on Mount Cook just eight and a half months after it was razed by fire on 18 May 1958. Ten years later, they did the same for the 120-bedroom Te Anau Hotel after it was also razed by fire. This time the job took ten months.

It's perhaps easier to count the big jobs that Fletcher Construction *didn't* do, like the Auckland Harbour Bridge. Though the company probably wouldn't have bid, it did not have an opportunity because the bridge never went to formal tender. It's interesting that JC thought the bridge was the wrong option for Auckland; he favoured a tunnel and argued for it with Sir John Allum, Auckland's mayor and the unofficial patron of the bridge, and with the Auckland City Council. Fletchers was willing to tackle a tunnel with the American company Merritt-Chapman Scott, which had the necessary expertise, having built a lot of New York city's subways. A tunnel would require less maintenance, among several other virtues, Jim Fletcher argued. However, Allum was wedded to the idea of a bridge and, anyway, relations between Allum and the Fletchers had never fully recovered from some wartime clashes with old Sir James.

Of the hundreds of projects over those hectic years, a handful stand out. These are the Ohakuri diversion project, because it launched Fletchers into civil engineering (what the Americans often call heavy construction); the Lyttelton tunnel, for its size and difficulty; the pioneering Kapuni pipeline, because it worried Jim Fletcher sick and posed unexpected technical and human difficulties; and the multifarious Australian and offshore contracts, because they express Fletchers' aggression and ambition.

The Ohakuri project was let by the Ministry of Works in June 1956. It required a tunnel to be built at Ohakuri, roughly halfway between Rotorua and Taupo, to divert the Waikato River while the Ministry of Works, whose stamp of approval was essential for private companies wanting civil engineering jobs, built the dam almost alongside for the hydro-electric station. The MoW, which was normally proprietorial about these big jobs and liked to do the projects itself, was too hard-pressed to tackle it all.

Joe Craig, then head of Fletcher Construction, reasoned that if the company did a good job at Ohakuri, it might get a foot in the civil-engineering door, because most of the big jobs were state-let. Sir James had been a builder, not a civil engineer. The only previous civil-engineering jobs Fletchers had done were some concrete bridges and roadways in the twenties and thirties, and it had lost money on both. It wasn't a very auspicious beginning.

Normally, an open cut is enough to divert a river. That was what had been done at the other two nearby Waikato River hydro projects at Waipapa and Atiamuri. But at Ohakuri, the river tumbled down a steep gorge and the ultimate waterslide — a 400-metre-long, eight-metre-wide concrete-lined tunnel — was required to control these boiling waters. A vertical shaft thirty-five metres deep and ten metres wide would have to be sunk from the surface into the tunnel. This would house the sliding gate that would be dropped later to bend the river back on course after the MoW's dam was finally built. Deadline for construction was two years. It was a six-days-a-week, round-the-clock project, and Joe Craig put young Jack Smith in charge.

Smith, son of Sir James's cousin who had followed him out from Scotland, had come through the ranks in the company virtually from infancy. 'As a toddler,' he recalls, 'I can remember being carted off in my Sunday best on a tour of all the job sites in Wellington. Dad used to inspect them most Sundays on the way to church.'

A huge-shouldered bloke with big hands, a big laugh and a handshake to make you wince, Smith had been introduced early to American construction attitudes. He had worked on the Auckland wharf with Fletcher Merritt Raymond and after that went to America to learn the ropes with Raymond Concrete Pile. There he soon found out that you did the job as quickly as you could, and got paid well for it. If the company made money, so did you. Mostly, United States construction labour worked like crazy to meet deadlines and earn bonuses. Jack Smith brought that attitude to the Ohakuri tunnel.

Fletcher Construction, though it hadn't previously done tunnelling work, felt it could tackle the tunnel on its own, without entering another joint venture like the Auckland wharf. It was the largest civil engineering job the company had ever undertaken on its own account, but it would hire American know-how instead of sharing the profits with American tunnelling companies. Don Jacobs, a San Francisco-based tunnelling expert, was signed to help Fletchers through this exercise. Jacobs had a hand in organising the hiring of tunnelling experts, most of them from Australia's Snowy Mountains, provided all the specifications for equipment, and kept an eye on the technical details. Jack Smith got on with the job of managing the project.

Tunnelling is filthy work. Throughout that first winter, the men worked in mud up to their calves. In summer, the mud turned to dust. 'You are fighting nature,' explains Smith. 'It was a bit of a hell-hole of a site — mud, slush and the rest of it.' It was also dangerous; one worker was killed on the job.

Paradoxically, Fletchers' inexperience in tunnelling had some advantages. Smith decided to do it his way. He used all-diesel equipment, supported the tunnel walls with steel rather than the usual wooden beams, scooped the tunnel out with lightweight and manoeuvrable drilling equipment, and brought in trucks that had been beefed up for earth-moving. While the other strategies worked well, the last turned out to be a mistake — the trucks couldn't cope with the punishing loads and terrain and there were numerous breakdowns. Long before they had shifted the total of 80,000 cubic metres of rock and earth, many of the trucks had expired from the burden.

Yet the job was a triumph. Smith's team blasted and dug out the tunnel right on schedule. The giant gate, like a portcullis, dropped neatly into its shaft. The job was done on time and on budget. Fletchers turned a handsome profit. Suddenly the company had jumped into the big league of heavy construction.

The job also left Smith with an opinion he never changed — that the MoW was a financial burden on New Zealand. Fletchers had worked practically alongside staff who were building the dam's permanent spillway, and soon saw that a private company like Fletchers could have done the work at a fraction of the cost. Having to account for practically every litre of petrol to head office, he was dismayed at the way all sorts of costs were buried by the MoW people in their final reckoning. Had the true costs of the MoW's civil-engineering projects been known, he guessed there would have been an uproar. 'It was an empire that the politicians didn't have the guts to take on,' he says now. 'Our power stations were never built because there was a need to create power. They were built to keep the MoW's workforce going.'

J ack Smith also landed the Lyttelton tunnel job in 1961. This was Fletchers' second big civil-engineering test, and once again Smith made his own rules. The notion of a tunnel through the Port Hills to link Christchurch with its port of Lyttelton had first been proposed in 1851, but nothing had come of it. More than a hundred years later, Fletchers formed a consortium with Kaisers to do the job, though in practice it was Fletchers that ran the show and Kaisers had only a nominal involvement.

It was much longer and bigger than the Ohakuri diversion tunnel — 2,000 metres long, or nearly three times as long as the Ohakuri, eight metres wide with an excavation height, including ventilation area, of ten metres. It was another job that often proceeded in grim weather, with the workers, from Smith down, sloshing around in gumboots through lakes of surface water.

The MoW had designed the tunnel and it supervised its construction under the umbrella of a local authority. The latter was Fletchers' client, and Jack Smith enjoyed being at arms-length from the ministry's people. He bought heavy earth-moving equipment this time — 'We'd learned our lesson with second-hand gear at Ohakuri,' he says.

With the assistance of Don Jacobs once again, Smith's people employed a jumbo-sized, United States-made drilling platform to bite into the rock and earth. Smith had the giant, rock-chewing drills mounted in six pairs. Normally, even the labour-saving Americans would have run at least fifteen-man crews per shift — two per drill and the balance to drive the earth-moving equipment. 'Instead, we had one man on each pair of drills and the same man driving the truck,' recalls Smith. In hindsight, he was probably lucky to get away with this but it worked brilliantly.

There was a special spirit about the Lyttelton tunnel job. The public wanted it badly, and the workers knew that. It took 250,000 kilograms of explosives and the shifting of 150,000 cubic metres of rock before they pierced the hill on 15 June 1962. Even before ships in the harbour sounded sirens and the official party walked the tunnel from both ends and met in the middle, the sweat- and dust-stained tunnellers, grinning widely, scrambled through an opening barely a metre in diameter to shake hands with their mates from the other side. The rest of the job, roading, tiling, concreting, went to schedule, and Sir Bernard Fergusson, the Governor-General, cut the ribbon on 27 February 1964.

Smith was the very model of a construction man on site in his khaki shirt and trousers, often stained with mud, tucked into heavy boots. It was probably inevitable that he would end up with the toughest project the civil-engineering division had taken on: the Kapuni natural-gas pipeline. He and Fletchers would come to wish they hadn't.

Think of putting a drain in the backyard. You figure out the best and straightest route, dig a trench, lay the sections of the drain in the bottom of the trench, join the sections, cover it all up, and then throw on some grass seed. In a couple of months, nobody would know a new drain lay underneath the grass.

The difference with the Kapuni pipeline was that it was 640 kilometres long, ran through some of the most rugged back country in the North Island, not to mention over the land of hundreds of farmers, crossed twenty-six rivers where it had to be laid on the riverbed, and involved technology never seen in New Zealand before.

Fletchers, highly confident of its civil-engineering skills after Jack Smith had managed the construction of the Marsden Point power station near Whangarei, bid for the job against some of the biggest international names in pipeline technology. It was competing against three New Zealand firms that had linked with United States pipeline experts, a full American tender and two Italian ones. In early 1969, Fletchers' bid of $9 million was accepted. 'We underbid the job,' says Jack Smith bluntly.

For New Zealand homes and industry, the pipeline was to be a lifeline of energy. It would transport natural gas north and south from the just-discovered Kapuni field, near New Plymouth. The pipes would snake south through Hawera, Wanganui (and across the Wanganui River), Palmerston North, Levin, Hutt Valley and into Tawa, which was the official gateway to Wellington for the purpose of the exercise. Its northern route took the pipeline through cruel terrain, goat country that can be fully appreciated only by flying over it. It wound through the Waikato to Hamilton and then on to Takanini, Auckland's gateway. Additionally, Fletchers contracted to put in a line to move the condensate from the gas field to New Plymouth for processing into petroleum.

Old Fletcher hands from JC to Jack Smith readily admit now that their run of successes in civil engineering had gone to their heads a bit. After all, their reasoning went, we didn't know anything about tunnelling, but achieved two highly successful and profitable tunnelling jobs, so why not a pipeline? It didn't sound too difficult. 'We should have heeded George Ferris's advice about overconfidence,' recalls Jim Fletcher philosophically. 'He used to say it's infinitely better to lose your shirt on the first tunnelling job, because that makes you more cautious for later ones.'

Head office, which was always looking ahead, believed in pipelines as the transport of the future. *Arrowhead,* the staff magazine, noted wide-eyed in the 1969 spring issue that pipelines could mean to the late twentieth century what railways had been to the eighteenth and nineteenth centuries. There was plenty of evidence for this view, because pipelines around the world at that time were shifting a diverse range of products from liquids such as beer and milk, semi-solids like cement, coal and woodchips, and even tea.

Fletchers ran into trouble even before a ditch had been dug. The Government insisted on an earlier completion date than Fletchers had planned. The contract, which was signed with due pomp in Parliament Buildings, required tight deadlines. The condensate line had to be hooked up by 1 July 1969, the line south three months later, by 1 October and, under the original arrangement, the Auckland line by the end of summer 1970. When Fletchers bid for the contract, Jim Espie, then in charge of Fletcher Construction, and Jack Smith knew that bad weather would be the mortal enemy of the job and had agreed to save the difficult part of the contract through the Waikato until early summer. However, the Government, for technical reasons, subsequently insisted on simultaneous completion dates at Auckland and Wellington. Fletchers protested, pointing out that this would knock profits off an already-low bid. It would still do the job but sought adequate compensation.

The Government's response was to send a team from Treasury to examine Fletchers' case. When it reported, Treasury largely agreed with the company but urged the Government not to raise the contract because Fletchers, being Fletchers, could afford to carry a bit less profit. The civil-engineering division had no alternative but to swallow hard, complain bitterly and tackle the Waikato in winter. The results were predictable. 'We got bogged down,' laments Jack Smith.

Pressure pipelines carrying such a volatile substance as natural gas require absolute engineering integrity. They have to be safe and permanent. Laying the 640 kilometres required heavy manpower — 500 in all — unique equipment, expert American welders, and much heartache.

First, bulldozers cut a swath through the countryside as a rough form of roadway, often plunging down almost impossibly steep slopes. An imported wheel-type ditcher digs the trench on reasonably level country, but a conventional back-hoe excavator has to do the job in hilly or rocky terrain. Welders seal and join the sections of pipe. A tractor lays the pipe from a sideboom. A hydraulic bending machine, also imported, shapes the pipes for the curves in the terrain. The trench is filled in. Finally, the land is made good.

Hardly had the first section been joined than the American welders, all of them contracted on high hourly rates, ran into conflict with their much-lower-paid New Zealand counterparts. Don Jacobs had recruited the American welders because of their expertise in argon arc welding, the quality of the welds being crucial.

Jim Espie explains the niceties of the technique: 'They had to go around the pipe in a continuous pass. The ends of the pipes were bevelled in a V shape and they had to fill in the V with several passes.'

The job required thousands of perfect welds, but the New Zealanders thought they could do the job just as well. Tensions ran so high that finally the Americans issued a challenge. 'If you think you can do it as good as us, do it,' they said. It came down to a race — Kiwis versus Americans — and the Americans turned out to be better and faster. End of argument. By the time the pipeline was through, however, the New Zealanders' skills had improved dramatically.

As Fletchers had feared, the weather was turning out to be a major problem and the Waikato terrain was also causing serious delays. Worse than that, the company was facing horrendous losses. Sitting in his office in Penrose, Jim Fletcher began to worry.

The true measure of progress was the number of welds achieved in a day, because it indicated distance covered. In the early months, the pipeline fell a long way behind schedule as the workers battled rocky river crossings, irate farmers whose land was being carved up and fences pulled down and temporarily replaced, and the occasional industrial dispute.

At one stage, the pipeline was so far behind schedule that the Ministry of Works threatened to cancel Fletchers' contract and hand the job over to another contractor to finish. A provision for damages had also been written into the contract because, the Ministry of Works said, it was critical that the pipeline be hooked up on the agreed dates.

In his office down the corridor from Jim Fletcher's office Jim Espie had drawn up a chart that showed the pipeline's progress, and JC would trot down there daily to see how much money the company stood to make or lose on the basis of the previous day's progress.

'Each day I would do a calculation,' he remembers. 'I had a series of guidelines [that told me] the magnitude of the losses.' It was nervy stuff. On many days, especially in the early days of the job, the losses were so considerable they threatened the company's viability.

As the pipeline progressed kilometre by painful kilometre, tumbling down gorges, being floated over rivers then sunk, being held up by rock that had to be hacked out and replaced with earth because rock would damage the pipes, being delayed by angry farmers who demanded compensation for disturbance to their land and disruption to their stock (some even claimed their cattle had suffered the welders' occupational disease, arc eye), and also being delayed because of late delivery of pipes and other essential materials, JC sweated.

Jim Espie's chart was nearly two metres high and showed both north and south routes. Others beside JC would drop by the office to note progress. After a time, it became quite a thing, senior staff congregating in the office to talk about how yesterday's pipeline-laying had gone. Occasionally JC inspected the site from a helicopter. Some of the pipeline-workers reckoned that even if the job was at a standstill because of, say, problems with the tide in a river-crossing or delays in materials arriving, they would leap to their feet at the sound of the helicopter and be apparently fully engaged by the time it appeared overhead.

Day by day, week by week, Fletchers caught up with the timetable. The workers from New Zealand, America, Canada and Britain were on the job from dawn until dusk. The Kapuni pipeline got there on time and great was the rejoicing in Penrose, even though Fletchers didn't make any money from the contract. At best, it broke even.

A disaster? Not from Jim Espie's viewpoint. Fletchers took pride in doing the job. 'It was the most challenging project of the times. We knew our reputations would stand or fall on it. I'm sure a lot of companies, given the difficulties, would have pulled out. I'm quite sure of that.'

In the long run, it was worth it. There might be profits on the next contract that would compensate for losses on the last one. In the long term, it's reputation that counts.

New Zealand was never big enough for Jim Fletcher. In 1946, he had launched Fletchers offshore in Western Samoa through a subsidiary, Fletchers South Seas Ltd. When Jim Espie took over as manager of this pioneering outpost, it was his wife, Thelma, who did the books. Materials arrived once a month on the old Island trader *Matua,* and sometimes the boat would turn up without vital materials like concrete through some clerk's forgetfulness. 'We were at the extreme end of a long line of communication,' chuckles the now-retired Espie.

Fletcher South Seas' first job was to shore up the collapsing foundations of a general store in Suva for a long-established trader, Maurice Hedstrom. Compared with some of the big-ticket contracts Fletcher Construction had undertaken in New Zealand, it doesn't sound like much, but the job was a minor feat of engineering contrived by Bob Fallek, a clever European who had immigrated to New Zealand during the war.

Two years later, in 1948, Fletcher South Seas built a new store for Hedstrom in Samoa. Made of reinforced concrete, it was Fletchers' first major overseas construction project.

Fletchers aside, there weren't any contracting companies in Samoa, and the local administration had hinted strongly to Jim Fletcher that there would be a lot of work for many years to come. After the store, Fletchers moved on to other jobs — an arched reinforced-concrete bridge, a joinery factory and several churches. For a time, Fletchers

South Seas even had a monopoly on coffins in Western Samoa, turned out by the joinery factory and ranging from the cheapest casket made of rough timber and calico to a de luxe model with brass handles.

Espie found that running a major job like the construction of Apia's Methodist Mission, Western Samoa's major church, wasn't quite what the textbooks recommended. Need labour? No trouble, said the church elders and promptly issued a decree for 200 able-bodied young men to turn up on Monday morning, ready to work. It was a reinforced-concrete church and Espie didn't have 200 wheelbarrows. No problem, the wet concrete was conveyed by muscular Samoans on banana leaves. These 'volunteers' got only their lunch and dinner, but no wages, from the church elders.

By 1950, New Zealand's mandate to Samoa under the League of Nations having expired, it was clear that Western Samoa's Public Works Department wanted to take over much of the work and Fletchers' orders were drying up. Fortunately, this occurred at the same time as the New South Wales Housing Commission wanted Fletchers to build state houses in Sydney. Espie was thus posted across the Pacific to Australia as, briefly, assistant manager and then manager of the company's fast-developing construction interests there.

In later years, Fletchers went back to Samoa and even further into the Pacific. In the sixties, seventies and eighties, it took on much bigger jobs such as wharves, hotels and factories in Western Samoa, hotels in the Caroline Islands, banks, warehouses and other projects in Fiji, Papua New Guinea's Parliament Buildings, a hospital in the Cook Islands, silos in Sabah, a steam transmission building in West Java, the New Zealand High Commission in Tonga. That concrete general store in Apia was the progenitor of all these plum Pacific jobs.

Like Joe Craig, Jack Smith and nearly all senior Fletchers appointments, Espie was a company man. He had joined Fletchers not long after JC, in 1941, straight from Auckland Grammar. He started in the drawing office in Nelson Street and then qualified as a quantity surveyor. His career survived one disaster that might have ended it in a less forgiving company. He crashed the boss's car.

At that time, the teenage Espie worked under the formidable William Fletcher and had been told to deliver a skill-saw to a job site at the Milne and Choyce department store, where Fletchers was building an air-raid shelter. Coming back, he was horrified when the rear door burst open, smashed into a council garbage truck and fell off. Fearfully, Espie knocked on William's office door, was summoned in, but became so tongue-tied with fright that he couldn't get the words out.

'It was a rather cheeky gesture, I suppose, but I just hooked my finger at him and summoned him over to the window overlooking Nelson Street,' Espie says fifty years after the incident. 'I just pointed down at his car with the back door completely ripped off.'

Instead of sacking him on the spot (this was long before the days of wrongful dismissal tribunals), William Fletcher just grunted. 'Right, this afternoon you go out to Lucerne Road [his home], pick up my Mercury and bring it in,' he ordered. It was a gruff way of giving the lad back his confidence, and Espie, driving at a painfully slow speed, manoeuvred the beautiful Mercury back into Nelson Street. There can't be many senior executives who started their career by removing the door from the car of the man whose job they would later fill.

Fletchers started fast in Australia. It built hundreds of low-cost houses, with then-new timber-frame construction, mainly in Sydney's northern suburbs like Dee Why, Collaroy. But business slowed down sharply during a recession in 1952–53 and the company, having on its payroll a workforce of British migrant tradesmen for whom it was obliged to find work, had to scramble for jobs. It built numerous factories and warehouses, department stores for chains like G. J. Coles. It took on huge projects like the the 3.8-kilometre-long pier at the Kurnell refinery, and small ones like farmers' homesteads. It did innovative work on an RSA hall at Walget, deep in northern New South Wales, where the black-soil plain was a builder's nightmare because it constantly contracted and expanded, cracking foundations and buildings. Fletchers built a civic centre there with a buffer of concrete, like a moat, around the foundations, to absorb the stresses. 'We had to take on any work we could find,' JC remembers.

Business expanded rapidly after 1954 when Fletchers bought Howie Moffatt, a long-established construction company. The acquisition opened several useful doors for the parvenu from New Zealand.

The company made a mistake or two in Australia, the biggest being joining a consortium to build a railroad at Mount Isa. The countryside was hostile and the Australian partners incompetent. Fletchers lost a lot of money and learned a valuable lesson. Namely, in a construction joint venture it's a fact of commercial protocol that the joint venturers are at the mercy of the sponsor of the project. It's the sponsor who lines up the partners in the project, who manages it, and who can make or break it.

The Mount Isa job was losing so much money and was so far behind schedule that JC tackled Edgar Kaiser. It had been Kaiser who had invited Fletchers to joint-venture jobs in Australia and had brought it into the Mount Isa debacle. 'We've got to do something about this,' JC warned him, but Kaiser simply lectured him on commercial diplomacy. Unless the sponsor turns out to be a rogue and a cheat, you stick together to the bitter end.

Right through the busy fifties and sixties, Jim Fletcher had great difficulty tearing himself away from business. When he did, he usually went to Alton Lodge, the family stud, named after an uncle's farm outside Glasgow that old Sir James used to visit as a lad.

JC and his father had bought the property in 1939 as a run-down dairy farm with some handsome stands of kahikatea trees at Waerenga, just inland from Te Kauwhata on the main road south between Auckland and Hamilton.

They ignored advice to run the farm as a hobby and carry only mares, and bought stallions too. This inevitably turned it into a commercial enterprise that involved marketing the stallions' services. They — or rather JC, because he was racing-mad — initially made a success of the stud with the help of manager Jack Lindsay, from North Canterbury, and a Scottish vet named Murray Bain, who introduced manual testing for pregnancy, and with the shrewd eye of Charlie Robertson, head of Wright Stephenson's bloodstock department.

The success of Alton Lodge reflected JC's enthusiasm for learning from abroad, and especially from America. It was developed according to advice he got in the late forties from one of America's great breeders, Arthur B. Hancock, who owned Kentucky's famous Claiborne Stud, where JC sent Bain for training. Hancock ran a strictly commercial operation, which JC and Vaughan saw for themselves in 1947. 'At that time most of the other studs were rich men's toys,' Jim Fletcher observes.

And he resolved that Claiborne, whose fences were left unpainted out of economy, should provide the model for Alton Lodge's growth in New Zealand, where, Seton Otway and a handful of others apart, the studs were hobbies rather than businesses.

As he acknowledges, Jim Fletcher didn't quite stick to the fully commercial concept. He later had the fences, for example, painted white, a concession to appearance that required five tonnes of paint every time the place was redone.

JC also pinched good ideas from *The Bloodhorse*, the American bible of the breeding industry, to which he had subscribed for years. A string of top sires came from Britain.

JC wasn't afraid to be unconventional either — he upset some of the more staid figures in a conservative industry by running regular full-page advertisements for his stallions and details of the winning form of their progeny in a 'Stop Press' teaser on the cover page of the *New Zealand Racing Calendar*. Alton Lodge also introduced the clever marketing idea of guaranteeing a live foal.

Old King Rod, JC's mettlesome mount at the Pakuranga Hunt, had whetted his appetite for racing. Thus, while his father pottered about Alton Lodge because he was fascinated by fertilisers and pasture development, JC's passion was the livestock.

Alton Lodge's first great sire was Balloch, one of the most potent sires ever stood in New Zealand and father of Melbourne Cup winner Dalray. Even after fifteen years at stud, Balloch's fertility exceeded 80 percent. Next came Gold Nib, then Revelation, Knock Out II, Mid-Day Sun, who had won the English Derby, Fair's Fair and Chatsworth II.

The Fletcher colours were also doing well in racing through Rustler, who won the Wellington Cup in 1973, fillies Blyton and Ganymede, a mare called Estimate, and several other notable racehorses. JC's horses performed well in Australia, too, especially throughout the fifties and sixties with Randwick trainer Frank Dalton. The successes started with Taressa's victory in the 1952 Tattersall's Gold Cup.

Some of New Zealand's finest broodmares stood at Alton Lodge, which also became one of the biggest studs in New Zealand, particularly after some top-class mares were imported from Australia. Then, suddenly, the Fletchers wound it all down. In 1957, they held a deplenishing sale, and closed Alton Lodge as a public stud. By 1962, they had sold the remaining horses and thereafter just farmed the land until 1967. Then they sold it lock, stock and barrel — the cattle, white-painted fences, lovely stands of kahikatea, stables, homestead.

Ironically, the reason Jim Fletcher got out of an activity he apparently loved was that Alton Lodge had become too much of a business. He was almost frenetically occupied in Fletcher Holdings' affairs, and the last thing he wanted at weekends was to have to manage the stud, which had started to experience problems. 'Our business interests were continually expanding and we simply didn't have time to devote to overseeing Alton Lodge,' he says.

Had he been able to devote more time to running it in the professional way that Patrick Hogan, whom Jim Fletcher much admires, manages Cambridge Stud, it might have been different. 'It was a rare year that we made money at Alton Lodge, mainly because we were doing things in a much more expensive way and, I am ashamed to say now, because we were "half-pie". We thought of it as a hobby and would never have run one of our businesses without the concentration that Alton Lodge's capital justified. I was putting more money into it and getting nothing out of it,' he says ruefully. 'It beggared me.'

Doing things 'half-pie' also offended his natural sense of precision. 'The catalyst [to selling it] was that the quality of the management had deteriorated. We felt we no longer had the best-presented yearlings at the sales. The farm was not being kept up to a high standard. I used to go down there and paint rails and cut thistles. But a lot of things the staff were supposed to do weren't being done.'

There were also the demands of a growing family. The three boys were growing up and didn't want to spend weekends at Te Kauwhata. 'It was a late realisation on my part that I was being selfish by denying the family opportunities to do other things with them because I was so committed to the farm in time and money.' A substantial overdraft hung over the farm and, JC reasoned, the family would be stuck with it if something happened to him.

Friction had also developed among the staff, and Jim Fletcher was forced to spend time at weekends easing tensions. The last straw came when the latest manager was convicted of a drink-driving charge. It was time to sell.

Chapter 6

Scrap over Steel

The vast black deposits of ironsands on New Zealand's west coast have been a siren song for industrialists since the middle of the nineteenth century. Up to the 1950s, they had launched many a project to convert them into steel. Most of them had ended in failure or bankruptcy and much bitterness. By the mid-fifties, JC and his father felt the time was ripe for another try. Both would cheerfully admit that they didn't know much about the highly technical and difficult job of converting enormous wastes of heavy titanomagnetite ironsand into iron and steel. But they hadn't known much about the manufacture of pulp and paper either. 'You buy in the expertise,' JC would always say. Thus, in 1956, father and son joined an informal syndicate of just four people, not as the appointed representatives of Fletcher Holdings but as private individuals. It was run on a shoestring with each member putting up about £200 each.

The syndicate was named TIFE, Ti being the chemical symbol for titanium and Fe that for iron. Later the irreverent George Fraser would dub it the 'STRIFE' syndicate after its original members fell out with each other. Besides the two Fletchers, TIFE comprised Bob Law, retired general manager of ICI New Zealand and a director of Tasman, and Bill Martin, a chemical engineer and research fellow at Victoria University who was a missionary for the conversion of the ironsands into a full-blown industry. 'Wiggy' Martin, so called because of his toupee, had done early work on the problem of separating the high levels of titanium dioxide, of 7 to 8 percent, out of the ore. This had proved the critical difficulty with the ironsands for a century or more.

The titanium dioxide produces slag, which clogs the blast furnaces. Martin had researched a different process to overcome the problem. His experiments from 1950 had shown that if the ore was smelted in

167

an electric-arc furnace instead of a blast furnace, it produced a nice fluid slag, which could then be separated out from the molten iron.

But like Entrican's early American experiments with the conversion of radiata pine to newsprint, Martin's were done on a small scale. They only demonstrated possibilities, and he hadn't produced any actual steel. There were, once again, no guarantees that the process would work in a full-scale, continuous steelworks, just as there had been no certainty about the economic production of newsprint from sappy radiata pine.

The Fletchers found quite quickly that Martin was something of a dreamer who wanted to push far beyond the bounds of practicality. He proposed to recover titanium pigment, thorium and vanadium from the slag, establish a nitrogenous fertiliser and chemical industry based on the carbon gases discharged from the arc furnace, and explore other possibilities including gold, which JC and his father soon came to realise were commercially impractical or just plain impossible.

'Bill was an impractical cuss,' JC remembers, though with some affection. 'He wanted to get all the "iums" out of it.' Even in scientific, let alone commercial, terms, some of Martin's ideas were highly speculative.

Dr John Watt, a Rhodes Scholar and chemical engineer who became Fletchers' resident boffin, recalls: 'Even for the best brains and facilities in the world, the extraction of titanium from ironsands is a long and difficult process.'

The Fletchers, father and son, were not, however, completely ignorant about steel. The company had been steel merchants since the 1930s, and not long after the Second World War, when foreign exchange was desperately short, Fletchers' laboratory staff in Dunedin had thoroughly investigated the possibility of converting the ironsands into ore.

Fletchers in Dunedin had sent samples of the ironsand for further analysis to Krupps in Germany, which would, of course, become Hitler's major armaments-maker. Unfortunately, somebody sent the sand in honey tins. Since honey was nearly as scarce as foreign exchange, only a few of the tins arrived at the Krupps laboratories. Krupps duly reported back, describing their difficulties because of the inadequate number of samples they had to work with, but concluding firmly that it was feasible but uneconomic to convert the ironsands into ore.

Years later, when Joe Craig visited Krupps on another matter, they offered to do more tests if they could be given more ironsand samples, preferably not in honey tins. But by then Fletchers was relying on Kaisers' expertise. Fletchers, which prides itself on maintaining its archives, had uncharacteristically lost Krupps' report. In any event, Fletchers had plenty of other things to achieve, and forgot about the matter. Until 1956, that is, when the TIFE group got together. Sammy Cory-Wright, of the engineering equipment importers Cory-Wright and Salmon, later joined as a fifth member.

This small group would be the spark that fired New Zealand's steel-making industry. It didn't happen, however, without interminable and unnecessary delays, without the often heavy-footed intervention of civil servants, some acrimony among the original members and among various companies later promoting their own interests in the industry, without technical problems of nearly insurmountable and cripplingly expensive difficulties, and constant politicking. And nor did it happen in the way that JC and his father had hoped.

The billions of tonnes of ironsand came in two main varieties — the titanomagnetite variety sometimes known as 'Taranaki ironsands' and found almost exclusively on the west coast of the North Island, and the ilmenite variety, spread down the west coast of the South Island. The titanomagnetite sands contain enough iron, roughly 50 to 60 percent, for commercial exploitation. The ilmenite type has about 33 percent iron, which isn't sufficient.

The earliest settlers didn't need chemical engineering degrees to see that the black sands contained iron, and the first attempt to extract iron ore from them came as early as 1848, when J. Parry built a small blast furnace in New Plymouth, made some iron, but failed 'for technical reasons'. In 1886, engineering merchant John Chambers, who had established an Auckland retailing landmark called John Chambers and Sons, set up a furnace at Onehunga, near Auckland, as far as can be told from scanty records.

Chambers deserved more success than he got. He kept at it for twenty years, visiting England and America as early as 1876 with parcels of ironsands. He even made contact with Sir Henry Bessemer, inventor of the blast furnace. But he never got his enterprise, known as New

Zealand Iron and Steel, off the ground. It didn't help that his steelmaker, a Mr Jones, who had been brought in from America early on, went to jail for ten years after shooting an employee, a bricklayer, dead in Queen Street, Onehunga's main road, after a dispute. Jones had apparently made some iron bars before his incarceration.

Jones's replacement died soon after, and the next replacement in turn broke down in health. Chambers's Iron and Steel Company seemed to have a genie bedevilling it. It closed down after he had spent the huge sum, for those days, of £58,000.

The Onekaka Iron and Steel Company didn't fare much better. It was established in 1920 and closed in 1931. A venture called Pacific Steel was registered in London in 1933 but never proceeded. The Government became involved in the late thirties when the pre-war Labour administration established an Iron and Steel Commission to take over the ore leases at Onekaka, engaged Brassaerts, the British consultants, and decided to push ahead with a plant of just on 100,000 tonnes capacity. Then war came and the project was mothballed. When it was re-examined after the war by a British consultant, John Miles (father of the actress Sarah Miles), the ore deposits at Onekaka turned out to be inadequate.

The National Government in 1949 took a different tack by deciding that the development of an iron and steel industry was best left to private enterprise, which was the position at the time TIFE came together in 1956.

JC, by now a seasoned industrialist with a record of successful industry start-ups including Tasman, had strong views formed by his own experience and he put them to the committee. He proposed that the Government should be involved initially, at least to the extent of taking over the ironsands in the name of the Crown to pre-empt speculation in a natural resource, and that a reputable overseas steel-maker should be hired to provide a feasibility study based on the latest techniques.

Fletchers' American connections paid off again. JC's hand-pumping, joke-playing American mentor Mac Gilmore had years before introduced him to the industrialist Edgar Kaiser and one of his brilliant engineers, George Havas, head of Kaiser Engineers, of Oakland, California. Kaisers had conducted similar feasibility studies and had been indirectly involved in steel-making through their associated company, Kaiser Steel, in Fontana, California.

After JC wrote to him in late May 1956, Havas himself came to New Zealand and looked at the ironsands. When he returned, Havas sent two of his best men, which is how Kaiser Engineers arrived in New Zealand in late 1956 with the reluctant agreement of the other three members. It's fair to say that Martin, the chemical engineer, was the least happy about the arrival of the Americans. By now, old Sir James had an admiration for his son's judgment and backed the introduction of Kaisers.

Fletchers provided the transport and drilling equipment, some manpower, and the money to pay for it all. Bill Martin swallowed his pride and enthusiastically gave his time and earlier research, and Kaisers subsequently drew up their report. The committee thought it politic to inform Eric Halstead (nicknamed 'the Senator' for his formal bearing), then Minister of Industries and Commerce in the National Government, of developments and received his enthusiastic approval. It was agreed all round that a lid should be kept on all publicity.

However, JC realised that he and his father were in a potentially embarrassing position that could present a conflict of interest. Here they were, two of New Zealand's biggest industrialists, who were also members of an informal and private committee that might obtain rights over vast native raw materials, which ultimately could offer enormous returns. Thus he pushed harder for the Government to take over the ironsands in the name of the Queen. But this was clearly a legislative process that would take a lot of time and discussion in Parliament, so meantime the syndicate, urged on by Bill Martin, who saw vast potential in the ironsands at Lake Taharoa, north of Hamilton, applied for certain mineral rights there.

At a formal gathering one day in May 1957, the committee, represented by a local solicitor, Bryan O'Shea, confronted the fiercely independent Maoris of the area before the Maori Land Court. Although nobody knew what it might cost to process the area's titanomagnetite ironsands, or to transport them from what was a remote site, the committee offered a royalty of sixpence a ton. This was almost certainly far too high, but the Maoris held out for more. George Fraser suspected they pushed for a higher rate solely because they wanted to price the ironsands out of the market and be left alone. This was the same tribe whose members had many years before been imprisoned for ripping up and throwing away surveyors' roading pegs, and indeed there were still no roads into Taharoa.

The speeches were long, passionate and against the proposal. JC and George Fraser sat through several interminable addresses. One elderly Maori woman talked at length condemning the proposal, and was followed by another woman elder who went on for the same period of time. After she had sat down, the TIFE people enquired what she had said. 'She just endorsed what the earlier speaker said,' was the reply.

Quite correctly in JC's and Fraser's view, Judge Brook's judgment essentially refused to grant the rights and suggested the matter was one for the Crown.

The three-centimetre-thick Kaiser report, the most comprehensive one so far on the potential of the New Zealand steel industry, arrived in the committee's mail at about the same time. The Government, which gave it serious consideration, must have been stunned by the Americans' estimates. A steel mill, based on ironsands and producing the basic flat products and pipe would cost around $US90 million, and up to $US150 million for the more complex manufacture of merchant—the steel used in building construction—bars and wires. But the figures were academic because conventional blast-furnace techniques would not do the job, Kaisers confirmed, and electric arc technology was not then sufficiently advanced to do the job either. For the moment, the ironsands would have to lie where they had for millions of years.

Their other prime conclusion was that large amounts of electrical power and coal would be needed, something that wasn't available in the North Island with its power shortages. Dunedin was seriously proposed as a site for the steel industry because the South Island had plenty of power and coal reserves but Aramoana was the prime choice, the same spot Fletchers would later propose as the site for an aluminium industry. As far as Fletchers was concerned, the South Island was an impossibly uneconomic location for a mill whose customers would be mainly in the North Island.

However, in general, the Government remained in favour of establishing an iron and steel industry, but not at the taxpayers' expense.

The powerful Cabinet committee on economic and financial policy wrote to Fletchers encouraging them to establish an iron and steel industry and, power being a critical factor in the whole issue, adding that it would favourably consider granting Fletchers a licence to develop geothermal power in the North Island.

TIFE was soon to fall apart. Bill Martin was no longer enthusiastic about Kaiser's involvement, some of his wilder ideas having failed to be accepted by the Americans. Martin could see his dream slipping out of his grasp. He had already approached Halstead on his own account, telling him he had come to the conclusion that he had 'a heavy responsibility in this matter', and he urged the Government to take over the industry. His letter of 19 June 1957 also contained an expression of confidence that 'valuable by-products' such as titanium slag, furnace gases for large-scale production of nitrogenous fertilisers and vanadium values could also be obtained.

Quite contrary to the findings of the Kaiser people, who were much more experienced, Martin maintained that the Lake Taharoa titano-magnetite sands and the ilmenite sands at Westport would prove the ideal deposits. 'A soundly based industry could be founded on them,' stated Martin with astonishing confidence. Although Martin had encouraged the idea that the Kaiser report was mainly based on his own work, this was not strictly, or even loosely, correct.

By now the position of JC and his father had become impossible. They were individuals staring at investments of perhaps hundreds of millions in today's dollars. It was clearly time for the corporates to enter, and the Fletchers left TIFE.

The disintegration of TIFE was inevitable. 'What really dismembered TIFE,' remembers Jim Fletcher, 'was that its members had no money. The only way investigations could be pursued further was with quite a lot of money. The others weren't prepared to put in money and nor did they represent organisations that were prepared to do so.'

So, split by the weight of the job ahead of it, by the conflicting strategies among members about how to handle it, and by the essential differences between the hard-headed industrialists and the hopeful boffin, the syndicate collapsed. But hardly had it broken up — though not before the Fletchers had suggested alternative structures, which included Martin — than TIFE reformed in a different guise. This time, however, Fletchers weren't part of it, and it had a different name.

The new business was called the New Zealand Development Corporation, and its declared job was to investigate the possibility of an iron and steel industry based at Dunedin, which was Bill Martin's preferred site because it was close to the Ohai coal fields. The chairman was Wellington businessman Bill Scollay. Also in the new company were Martin and Sammy Cory-Wright. The corporation made a bit of a blue early on when it blithely claimed rights to the disputed Lake Taharoa deposits, which had been the subject of the long speeches earlier. Bryan O'Shea, of Ngaruawahia, spokesman for the local Maori, politely rapped the corporation over the knuckles for 'anticipating a little', because the Maoris still held the rights.

Martin remained the enthusiastic boffin. He kept up correspondence with Halstead, having now firmly aligned himself with Scollay. He told the minister that his work and 'special technical knowledge' were the backbone of the new corporation's plans. He decried the 'much narrower Fletcher proposals', which now inclined to a more modest start to the steel industry and took issue with some of the figures produced by Kaiser.

So there were now, in the late fifties, basically two camps — Fletchers and Scollay's New Zealand Development Corporation — with others waiting in the wings, not necessarily to take the initiative in promoting a steel industry but to take an interest if something happened. Looking back, it's reasonable to say that the differences between the two main promoters were based on the industrialists' practicality and concern about the huge risks and costs involved in what was without doubt a massive experiment, and the corporation's wide-eyed enthusiasm.

A good example of the differences is revealed in the sites each camp favoured. Scollay and Martin wanted Aramoana on the Otago peninsula, which would have involved shipping ironsands from the Auckland region down to the South Island for processing and then shipping the iron and steel back to the main markets in the North Island. Fletchers favoured a site on the inner Manukau Harbour near Westfield, in Auckland, which was handy to the raw material. It would involve dredging, upgrading of the Onehunga port, and the building of a high-level Mangere bridge to allow barges to pass underneath.

But the great imponderable remained: what was the most suitable smelting process? Nothing could happen without that, and at that time nobody in the world knew how to turn ironsands into steel on a big or small scale.

Enter Dr John Watt, Rhodes Scholar, a scientist who had worked under Ernest Rutherford, athlete and friend of Jack Lovelock at Oxford, and industrialist. An engaging, almost self-effacing man with a wry grin, Dr Watt is now in his late eighties, long since retired after a largely anonymous but brilliant career as Fletchers' technical troubleshooter.

As head of all of Fletchers' manufacturing industries, Watt had a quite profound effect in many ways, big and small, on New Zealand's housing. His early research on bituminous coatings stopped the leaks in what is now called butynol coverings for decks and other uses. He helped develop particle board in New Zealand by adapting German techniques for glueing together waste woods such as chips, and even sawdust. Particle board made house construction dramatically quicker and saved for other uses the expensive strip wood then used for tongue-and-groove flooring, walls and furniture.

But if Bill Martin was the catalyst behind steel-making in New Zealand, and JC was the main promoter, it was John Watt who made it technically possible. Over the years, say company insiders, JC learned to trust Watt's judgment to such an extent that he would make decisions involving millions of pounds on the strength of a scribbled note.

To help solve this huge technical problem, Jim Fletcher sent Watt to North America to look at steel-making first hand. Watt, who had already worked for ICI in three different countries, soon found himself, notebook in hand, touring steel mills in North America. He quickly made up his mind — 'It was essential to get rolling [steel-shaping] experience ahead of ironsand smelting.'

His reasoning was commonsensical. Rolling mills produce from scrap or billets of steel different forms such as reinforcing rod for concrete. This is obviously a lot easier than producing the steel first and then rolling it. And it was especially true when dealing with so problematical a material as raw ironsands.

Watt's constant questioning of overseas technicians and his natural scientific scepticism had also shown him that none of the three direct-reduction, or electric-arc furnace, processes in various stages of development at that time offered any guarantees. 'None is sufficiently advanced to be other than experimental,' he advised. Kaisers, after undertaking the report on New Zealand, had engaged the Batelle Memorial Institute of Columbus, Ohio, to pursue some independent research but hadn't got much further than concluding that direct-reduction methods still weren't commercially viable.

Mac Gilmore, owner with his brother of the Gilmore steel mill in Portland, Oregon, had influenced Watt's decision. 'Keep it simple,' Gilmore had told Watt when he was in America. 'Don't try to do too much.' Gilmore's own merchant bar mill had been converting scrap into steel for years at great profit.

The simplicity and relative cheapness of the process is highly attractive. The process melts the scrap into ingots in an electric-arc furnace. These are then converted or rolled into merchant bars for the construction industry — reinforcing steel rounds, light structural sections and the like. Watt had done his own sums and figured that a New Zealand mill would have to work from local scrap, because the cost of importing ingots would make the enterprise instantly uneconomic. The mill should not attempt anything too ambitious, and should attempt to produce only rolled products — merchant bars and rod for the manufacture of wire.

For Watt, the evidence pointed overwhelmingly to the simpler rolling mill strategy. JC agreed, and that's why Fletcher Holdings moved away from the risks of an ironsands-based industry to one that started somewhere in the middle with the processing of scrap. British steel-makers such as Stewarts and Lloyds, who sent out their own experts, later came independently to the same conclusion.

This sort of halfway house solution was far from the end of the full ironsands-based industry, though. As far as the Fletchers, father and son, were concerned, a steel mill based on scrap metal was just a form of apprenticeship, a starting point for a full-scale ironsands-based industry. It would enable them to learn essential skills, and they were confident there was plenty of scrap available.

Thus, on 16 May 1958, Jim Fletcher went to the new Labour Government of Walter Nash with the proposal. Fletchers had to start again with a new set of ministers, and JC talked to his old friend Arnold Nordmeyer, whom he had always admired for his conscientiousness, intelligence and honesty. As he explained to Nordmeyer, Fletchers would establish the Titan Iron and Steel Company to melt scrap and produce steel in a merchant bar mill while also continuing vital research into an industry based on ironsands.

JC asked for a quick decision, which turned out a forlorn hope.

Meantime, the jockeying had started in earnest for the leadership of the steel industry. The inside view of how the game was played in the regulated command economy that prevailed at that time is both revealing and dismaying.

Scollay, as evidence in the form of memoranda and other official papers later revealed, lobbied the Government vigorously. That was fair enough. Jim Fletcher was doing the same thing, but Scollay's New Zealand Development Corporation was making claims about Fletcher Holdings' proposal behind its back that were just plain wrong. He also made wildly optimistic claims for his corporation.

In an epic-sounding letter to Prime Minister Keith Holyoake on 30 September 1957, which talked of the 'great task that lies ahead', the future 'great rewards for the people' and the country's economy, Scollay practically accused the Fletchers of absconding from TIFE with briefcases full of secret data. 'Having obtained all the information and data produced and collected by the syndicate and having enjoyed full access to the engineering and scientific knowledge of Martin . . . Sir James Fletcher and Mr J. C. Fletcher accordingly withdrew from TIFE and invited other members to abandon their interest and go with them on a venture to combine or hand over to — for no consideration — a joint Fletcher-Kaiser grouping,' Scollay wrote. He also referred to 'the Fletcher hand' being shown, as though father and son had been conniving in some conspiracy. He further claimed that the Kaiser report had been 'largely based on Martin's work'. These accusations were pure fiction on several grounds.

First, Fletchers had little or no use for Martin's work. It had been public for years, and any commercial interest could pick it up if they had wanted. Second, they had also paid for the Kaiser work, which was substantially more advanced than Martin's. They had not formed a joint venture with Kaiser other than a contract to build any steel mill, if it went ahead.

The politicking continued into 1958 and 1959. Scollay and some of his team called on senior civil servants from time to time, arguing for the Aramoana proposal and criticising Fletcher's scrap-based steel-mill proposition. The general tenor of their lobbying was that it wouldn't be economic, there wasn't enough scrap to keep it going; and even if there was, it would cost too much to deliver the stuff.

Scollay wrote to Phil Holloway, the new Minister of Industries and Commerce, on 29 August 1958, attacking the Fletchers' rolling mill as a 'hazardous business enterprise' and 'quite unrealistic for this country'. Scollay had, however, backed off from his original full ironsands proposal and had come close to Fletchers' idea. He now argued for a scrap rolling mill, but one that was 'properly integrated into the major ironsand scheme'.

By late 1958, the corporation was assiduously cultivating Bill Sutch, the Secretary of the Department of Industries and Commerce and a former acquaintance of Jim Fletcher. A 17 October letter to Sutch from corporation deputy chairman Chas Taylor in Scollay's absence overseas was fairly typical. It reiterated Bill Martin's many years' devotion to research work and the corporation's unshakeable conviction that the steel industry should not be 'allowed to get into the hands of any one group', before going into a diatribe against the Fletchers.

It was clear to the New Zealand Development Corporation, Chas Taylor insisted, that Fletchers only wanted the construction job in a steel mill and wasn't interested in steel production for its own sake (quite untrue), wanted to gain control of the steel-production industry (quite true), and would end up with 'a stranglehold on a key construction material' that would result in complete domination of the industry by overseas interests through Fletchers (untrue, since British interests were minority shareholders). For JC, the parallels with the preliminaries before the establishment of Tasman ten years earlier were marked.

The corporation put blind faith in Martin's optimism about by-products. It continued to tell the Government that titaniferous slag would make so much money that the steel could be sold 'at a comparatively low price'. This was despite the fact that nobody had ever extracted the by-product anywhere in the world at that time.

In short, the corporation was blithely overconfident about the staggering difficulties inherent in setting up a steel industry. It had surprisingly little substance behind even its strongest assertions, in particular its certainty that a separate and independent scrap steel mill 'would most certainly result in dearer steel to consumers', and that there wasn't enough scrap to keep a rolling mill going.

It also believed that the South Island was the best place to base the industry because of cheap power, and that the Norwegians held the key to unlocking the wealth from the ironsands with their Electrokemisk process.

Unfortunately, the corporation had very limited financial resources in an industry that required a lot.

The politicking was hotting up. On 5 November 1958, Scollay triumphantly cabled Holloway from Europe practically promising that the success of an ironsands-based steel industry was a *fait accompli*. He had information of 'transcendent importance' that would show that no further New Zealand research was needed and that iron, titanium and vanadium could be produced 'without delay'.

Scollay had formed an alliance with Norwegian steel-makers and returned highly optimistic about costs. Something 'under £10 million' should do it, Scollay wrote to Walter Nash. Even £6 million could be enough, he estimated, based on advice from his consultants Christian Spigerverk of Norway.

Fletchers had always held that £25 million was a minimum amount, and £30 million was probably more realistic. Fletchers' estimate was based on a 1958 study it had commissioned from Dr Tom Colclough, one of the international steel industry's roving experts (who, incidentally, was convinced that a scrap-based mill was the only way to start).

Australian mining interests reckoned £12 million for a plant with limited production, followed by an extra £20–25 million over the following five years, plus a further £15 million over the next ten years to cope with growing domestic demand. That gives a total of £53 million at the higher estimate. Thus the range of estimates started at £6 million and peaked at £53 million.

B y late 1958, Fletchers had won approval in principle to go ahead with the scrap-based mill, greatly annoying the New Zealand Development Corporation. The Government had worked in a subtle way. A senior civil servant, helping to wash the dishes after a Sunday lunch at George Fraser's house in Titirangi, Auckland, hinted that

Fletchers might get the franchise if it got together with New Zealand's biggest scrap merchant, which also had a scrap-mill proposal before the Government.

Next day, Fraser passed the hint on to his boss. JC immediately rang Wellington, agreeing to form the desired alliance. Not long after came the letter of approval.

At first, JC regarded this as a tremendous coup because, as the Government had insisted that there would only be one steel company, it meant Pacific Steel would thus be pre-eminent in the industry.

Holloway had given the green light in a letter of 21 October 1958, but only after Fletchers had agreed to go in with Ron Macdonald, of Industrial Metals, New Zealand's biggest scrap merchant, who had himself put up a similar proposal for a mill. It was a shotgun marriage brokered by the Government, but it came at Fletcher Holdings' expense because the deal involved Fletchers buying Industrial Metals. It was a compromise. Macdonald had the expertise in scrap, Fletchers the financial and manufacturing base. For Macdonald, of course, it was a cheap way of expanding his business and of buying into Pacific Steel.

However, when the final and formal approval arrived nearly a year later in response to Fletchers' full and detailed proposal, there was a sting in the tail. In a four-page missive, which, Fraser noted sardonically, 'set out everything except the price of paper clips if Pacific decided to make them', Holloway gave the franchise to Pacific Steel but denied Fletchers the right to push on with ironsands research, which was, Holloway insisted, 'a separate proposition'. Holloway was, of course, under a lot of pressure from other claimants, but Jim Fletcher was stunned. Pacific Steel was proposed as only a first step in a fully integrated, ironsands-up industry. 'We were not in it just for Pacific Steel. We were in it for the ironsands,' he says now. His worst fears — that New Zealand would end up with a fragmented steel industry — were being realised.

Jim Fletcher felt like somebody who had been thrown a lifeboat and then found it wouldn't inflate. Nevertheless, Fletchers went out and bought twenty-two hectares of industrial land in Otahuhu, adjoining the Manukau Harbour. That was the easy bit.

The hard part was the full year spent by executives trying to educate Wellington about the niceties of the steel industry while the civil servants, who would regulate it, tried to set price controls. Their ignorance of an industry they sought to police was a daily problem. 'They were clerks,' snorts Dr John Watt. Sometimes negotiations resembled the much earlier ones over pricing policy for state houses.

The civil servants were highly suspicious that something might be put across them; at other times they just didn't know what they were talking about. On one occasion, told that the mill would produce what is known in the trade as a 'deformed bar' — a length of reinforcing steel with a spiral edge that grips the concrete better — the civil servants objected sharply. This sort of second-rate product would not be acceptable, they told Fletchers.

If Jim Fletcher came to believe over the years that civil servants' main job in life was to throw a spanner in the works of enterprises that would employ a lot of New Zealanders at the company's expense and, to boot, provide payroll and corporate tax for the state, it's hardly surprising.

Fletchers found negotiations with New Zealand Railways particularly troublesome. NZR wanted to set such a high freight rate for handling the steel, both scrap and finished product, that JC bought a ship to do the job instead. She was the 1,200-tonne MV *Onehunga*, and her purchase shook NZR so much that it began bargaining more realistically. When negotiations were concluded satisfactorily, Fletchers had a spare ship but solved the problem by leasing her to the Northern Steam Ship Company.

JC's overseas connections, the support of established local steel interests such as Steel and Tube, Cable Price and others, and the company's long history proved invaluable at this point. After many months of to-ing and fro-ing, Scottish steel giant Colvilles, Britain's Stewarts and Lloyds, and Guest Keen and Nettlefold (GKN), who later established a wire-drawing facility with Fletchers and Pacific Steel, signed up for minority shareholdings. They were the blue chips in the British steel industry and it was a coup for Fletchers to have their expertise and knowledge on their side.

It also resolved a diplomatic issue — other existing New Zealand steel interests were thus brought on board through their British parents or in their own right. Shares were offered to Winstones, Gerry Gowan's Northern Steel, Cable Price, Mason Bros, and Steel and Tube.

Additionally, they were all committed to an ironsands-based industry when it became technically possible. As JC cabled from London after signing up the British steel-makers: 'All parties now confirm that if the smelting of the ironsands is proved economically feasible, it is their firm intention that Pacific should play its full share in the establishment and operation of the major industry.' At his request, the telegram was passed on to the Department of Industries and Commerce.

All the more reason for JC to be baffled later when the Government gave little or no credence to these impeccable connections in deciding the ironsands issue. 'We thought that having three internationally recognised steel-makers as our partners would give us credentials which were unimpeachable,' he says.

But where was BHP in all of this? Both Bill Scollay and JC had ardently wooed the Australian giant. It was on New Zealand's doorstep, had immense expertise as well as the capital, and owned the lion's share of the domestic steel market. The big Aussie looked a natural fit, even without other ties. Back in the twenties, Fletchers had become BHP's first New Zealand customer for Australian-made steel and got itself on the direct-buying list, which meant favourable prices, much to the local agents' chagrin.

JC's father had long been friendly with the legendary Essington Lewis, the chief at BHP at that time. They had worked together during the war on defence projects and shipbuilding and had even successfully raced a horse, Mid Point, in partnership. Sir James had the colours for this partnership registered and made in New Zealand, and it fell to JC in the fifties to bring them to BHP's dingy Melbourne offices. Lewis wasn't there, but JC handed them over to BHP's company secretary, Reg Newton, a man of gargantuan girth. He donned the jockey's cap, draped the colours over his enormous frame and executed an impromptu canter around the office.

Thus it was inevitable and sensible for JC to approach Norman Jones, Lewis's successor as general manager. In several trips to Melbourne, JC almost pleaded for BHP's participation, but to no avail. As Fraser, who attended two meetings with Jones, recalled: 'We received the politest of noes.'

BHP was simply far too busy to get involved, though it was prepared to put in some expertise if it was wanted. The company was developing a new complex at Kwinana, in Western Australia, and New Zealand seemed pretty small in comparison. Also, the high risks inherent in the raw material were apparent. As Fraser put it: 'They were not fired up with the prospect of developing the ironsands.' So, over thirty years ago, BHP decided to stay aloof from New Zealand's burgeoning steel industry.

Fletchers began constructing the £3.6 million scrap-based mill in 1960, and it started production on schedule two years later. Pacific Steel had an initial capacity of 50,000 tonnes and employed 250 people from the outset. It quickly disproved its critics and, after the early teething troubles of staff learning how to be steel-makers, soon made money. There turned out to be a continuous and ample supply of scrap, despite Scollay's claims to the contrary. Still, Fletchers had taken the precaution of buying locally 50,000 tonnes of scrap, a year's supply, before starting production. Pacific Steel saved New Zealand a lot of foreign exchange, has paid the wages of thousands of people over the years, and still functions today with the same electric arc furnace that John Watt bought for Fletchers in 1960. Fletchers later bought out the British partners, who had not, as Sutch feared, used their shareholding in Pacific Steel to shut down the development of a domestic steel industry. In fact they had been helpful.

By 1993, Pacific Steel had produced its three millionth tonne of steel, almost all of it from local scrap.

The ironsands remained the lure, however, for Fletchers as it did for the others. Holloway got everybody together in Wellington's Parliament Buildings on 20 May 1959 and declared the Government's hand. It was the first time all the hopeful participants in the industry had come together and they were able to size each other up. Among the sixty present, Fletchers and Scollay were surprised to see E. R. Hudson, who represented 'Australian mining interests'. 'Who on earth were they?' JC wondered.

Holloway outlined the Government's viewpoint. New Zealand couldn't support two steel industries, he told the interested parties, so whichever company finally got the licence would have a monopoly. The Government wasn't convinced that existing processes worked, which was a bit of a slap in the faces of Scollay and Martin. And the

Government planned to set up an investigating company, which it would control through owning 51 percent of the shares.

This last was a shock, a reversal of the Government's earlier decision to leave the industry to private interests. Up to this point, the various contenders had been jockeying for a licence to start an industry according to their different strategies, subject of course to some government controls and input. Now, suddenly, they were being thrown together into a committee in which the Government would have the ultimate say-so. To boot, the parties noticed, they were being asked to put up money for the investigation without any tax concessions. If the committee's investigations came out against an ironsands industry, they would have spent their money with no opportunity to write it off against taxes. Nobody was happy about that, and a group of them talked about it later with Bill Sutch, who was sympathetic to their overtures. Jim Fletcher was always against the idea of an investigating committee because he felt it was unworkable, but he had to accept it.

The big questions now were who would join the Government's new company and how would the shares be parcelled out. Because participation in the eventual steel-making company would be based on the individual shareholdings in the investigating company, and because the Government had announced its intention practically to withdraw from the planned operating company bar a small shareholding, it was vitally important who got what slice of the action. After the meeting, the lobbying intensified, and no more intensely than from Melbourne.

Hudson was now prepared to reveal exactly who were his 'Australian mining interests'. He did so in a confidential letter to Holloway, which also promised that his associates would spend £32 million in capital, the huge sum in today's dollars of $876 million, within five years of the operating company's being formed.

His associates turned out to be the Kormans, of Holeproof fame. Hilel Korman was New Zealand-based and his brother Stan, from Melbourne, was essentially a financier and property developer who had founded a finance company, Factors Ltd. They didn't disguise the fact that they had no previous involvement in the steel industry. However, Jim Fletcher didn't know their identities at this time although he had tried unsuccessfully through Anglo-Australian Corporation to find out.

Hudson himself turned out to be a lawyer from the town of Broken Hill, who later became something of a pioneer in Australia's iron-ore export trade through the Savage River project.

Scollay's New Zealand Development Corporation, probably seeing the prize slipping from its grasp, was very put out. It complained to Sutch that it had put in a lot of effort, time and money, and it asked the Government to buy its research.

By the deadline of 19 June, everybody who wanted to participate had declared themselves — Hudson for the Kormans; Fletcher Holdings, which hoped that other New Zealand interests might get involved through their planned Pacific Steel scrap-based mill (the name Titan Steel had been rejected by the Companies Office as it had already been registered by another company); Ron Macdonald's Industrial Metals; A. M. Satterthwaite, who was New Zealand agent for US Steel; Joseph Nathan, which represented a British mill; Cementation New Zealand; Northern Steel Supplies; John Lysaght New Zealand; Dr W. F. Chubb, William Cable Holdings; a minor union, the New Zealand Engineers and Related Trades; and, astonishingly, Ron Brierley, who wanted to invest just a fiver.

To this day, Jim Fletcher doesn't know why Brierley wanted to get involved but surmises that he only wanted access to the documents for future investment plays. The man who later won the nickname of 'master raider' certainly had no plans to produce steel. Brierley, JC knew, had once worked as an accountant for Fletcher Merchants, at Kaiwharawhara, near Wellington, while quietly producing *New Zealand Stocks and Shares*, a sharemarket tipsheet. By now, though, the man who would become known as a feared company predator was out on his own. He described himself in his application as 'company director and publisher'.

Bill Sutch and Holloway now called the crucial meeting at which the various shareholdings in the investigating committee would be divvied up. It would turn out to be a farce. After several postponements, it was set for 30 March 1960 in the boardroom of the Department of Industries and Commerce, room 123, first floor, Stout Street, Wellington.

By this time, the Kormans had made public their ambitious plan for the manufacture of steel rod, black, bright and galvanised wire, nails, wire netting and various types of piping. Thus the Kormans were proposing to move quickly through several stages of steel production. A site at Takanini, south of Auckland, had already been fixed.

Among themselves, JC's team didn't think the Australian proposal had much of a chance, especially given Sutch's and apparently Holloway's determination to keep the industry firmly in New Zealand hands. Both JC and Fraser knew Hil Korman but not Stan. In fact, Fletchers' construction people didn't think much of the Takanini site, which, given its soft, peat-based land, is highly suitable for the horse-training industry based there but equally inappropriate for the foundations of a heavy industry like steel manufacture.

The hopefuls duly filed in at 10 a.m. The New Zealanders were dumbstruck to find alongside each placename a piece of paper describing the precise allocation of the shares. With mounting disbelief, JC read it. He quickly did some sums. The Korman interests — Factors Ltd, Holeproof (NZ), H. Korman, J. A. Gentles, who was a business associate of the Kormans and chairman of Holeproof (NZ) — had practically scooped the pool.

Of the 122,500 non-government shares available, Korman interests had been allocated no less than 62,500, or 51 percent of the private interests. Other documents made it clear that these shareholdings would translate into the future operating company, if it was formed. Factors Ltd, Korman's wholly Australian-owned finance company, had alone picked up 40,000 shares, which was as many as Pacific Steel. Other New Zealand interests had been granted derisory amounts — poor Scollay's Development Corporation had just 7,500.

Jim Fletcher was thunderstruck. It was an Aussie coup, and by people who didn't have a track record in the steel industry. As Fraser later recalled: 'After all of Sutch's principles of New Zealand ownership, the New Zealand steel industry was on offer to Australians.'

Everybody started shouting, except the Kormans, of course. The New Zealanders were vociferous. Sutch tried to restore order, but he, too, ended up screaming and shouting. The Kormans, who probably hadn't expected this, waited nervously. An incensed Fraser made a comment out of order and was dismissed by Sutch from the room like a naughty schoolboy. Soon after, so was JC.

It was verbal riot and Sutch was shocked. He ordered a lunch break prematurely. JC quickly got the New Zealand interests together and drafted a statement urging a meeting with Holloway 'at the earliest opportunity'. Sutch decided they couldn't.

After some more fruitless argument, everybody filed out. Needless to say, because of the uproar, nobody subscribed for the shares, as they were supposed to do, and the department officials, in a side room waiting to sign everybody up, went home without taking orders. As a curtain-raiser to the establishment of a national steel industry, it was an unqualified disaster.

The New Zealanders got together later in the afternoon in Cable Price's office in town and again asked for an interview with Holloway, which was again refused. Although Jim Fletcher was the angriest — in fact, furious and offended that the Kormans from the rag trade should be preferred to Pacific Steel with its blue-chip British shareholding — the local steel interests were also upset.

A formal protest, explaining how they were 'disturbed at the allocation of the non-government sector of the capital', next went to Holloway. The letter, drafted by Fraser and Northern Steel's Gerry Gowan, pointed out that those who had been practically shut out were 'the leading steel users in New Zealand and overseas steel companies with a long experience in the New Zealand market'. It added that the Korman group was 'entirely Australian controlled, and to the best of our knowledge they have no background . . . in the iron and steel industry'.

But the letter bore an olive branch, too. The New Zealand steel interests said they would accept the shareholdings provided that the number of Korman directors was reduced to just one, that Pacific Steel got one, and the other New Zealand interests one. Also, they wanted the Government to set the shareholdings for any operating company at a later date.

It was such a mess that the only option was to let things wind down. Next day, Sutch hastily wrote a long note to Holloway trying to calm these turbulent waters and blaming most of the unseemly fracas on the Pacific Steel group. 'Mr J.C. Fletcher . . . appeared to lose command of himself and spoke wildly,' Sutch claimed. He had 'made some very unbalanced and objectionable statements'.

Certainly, Sutch believed that it was Jim Fletcher who had organised the New Zealand interests' objections. All this group wanted, Sutch told Holloway, was 'to secure for themselves an overwhelming balance of the private shareholdings'.

That was probably true, but Sutch had failed to grasp the reason for the New Zealanders' barely suppressed fury — that the steel industry was being sold to Australians despite everything they had been encouraged to believe.

Jim Fletcher now pleads guilty to Sutch's first count, that he had lost command of himself. 'Yes, I did. I blew my top. The whole thing was so absurd.' But he pleads innocent to the second count, that he had fired up the other New Zealanders. 'They were all mad,' he explains.

Sutch's note, written with the tone of a headmaster ticking off a pupil for daring to ask a question, went on to say the Government had several courses. It could 'give in to the group of interests now represented by Mr Fletcher', hand the shares the New Zealanders had refused to take over to 'those who have already accepted' (the Korman interests), to 'tell Pacific Steel, and Mr Fletcher particularly, that they have not been straightforward with the Government and that their attempt to apply pressure to dictate a dominant role for themselves will not be tolerated', or finally to drop the whole approach and set up a public company or some other structure instead.

Sutch rounded off his comments by saying: 'In conclusion, I feel that a few days' delay in which Mr Fletcher's group can cool would be desirable.' In later internal correspondence, he referred to Pacific Steel and the rest of the New Zealand interests as 'malcontents'.

Even now, thirty-five years later, Jim Fletcher cannot understand Sutch's unshakeable faith in the Kormans and his distrust of Fletchers and its British partners. Sutch seemed unable to accept JC's repeated statements that the UK steel-makers were ready and willing 'to play their full share' in any ironsands industry if it was shown to be economically feasible. Sutch's correspondence with Holloway throughout 1959 shows a growing antipathy towards Fletchers, however, and a warmth towards the Kormans, for whatever reason.

Perhaps it was Sutch's native suspicion. In his memos, he kept on referring to the British steel companies and their assumed desire to dominate the fledgling New Zealand industry through their alleged financial clout. They could stultify it, he feared. This, Sutch wrote in late 1959, 'could possibly lead to an attempt by them to stifle the industry before its birth so that their export markets — at least for billets and wire rod — can be maintained'. He was also confident that they would block any future exports from New Zealand to Britain, even though the possibility of steel sales to Europe was quite fantastic. The Kormans were also implacably opposed to the British involvement, and perhaps Sutch picked up their antipathy.

Sutch was commercially naive, a public service economist who was clearly out of his depth in big business. The blind credence he gave to the Hudson–Korman proposals shows that. Sutch glossed over their lack of experience — 'Mr Hudson's associates have full access to technical knowledge on mining and ore processing (particularly uranium in recent years),' he told his minister. There was no reason 'why they cannot buy all the technical advice and skills required'. He failed to pick up the disquiet in business circles in Melbourne about Stan Korman's property and financial interests, though he visited there. Soon after, within weeks in fact, the highly leveraged empire collapsed and Stan went to jail after a public enquiry. (Hil was completely vindicated and remained in Auckland.) The Kormans' failure must have deeply embarrassed Sutch with his minister after so enthusiastically espousing their cause. Fletchers' own enquiries had revealed that this Australian-based empire was tottering.

Sutch also seemed to accept the Kormans' conspiracy theory. Stan Korman claimed in a letter of 11 April 1960 to him that Fletchers was so weakly capitalised that its 'financial weakness . . . had left the door open for English interests to come in, initially on the finance angle which, when the time comes to increase capitalisation, will give them control and freeze out any possibility of our or any other independent organisation's interest'.

Sutch's views certainly affected the department's Assistant Secretary, Jack Lewin, who treated Jim Fletcher and the company staffers, JC remembers, 'like a lot of drongos who knew nothing about the steel industry'. Lewin's internal correspondence is indeed surprisingly demeaning of the Fletchers, with its many references to how he 'was able to persuade them' and 'to make them understand' and so on.

Perhaps Sutch, an Eastern European, felt a bond with the Jewish Kormans, who had fled from Poland and had meteoric commercial careers in Australia. Whatever the reasons for blunders like the attempted allocation of shares in the investigating committee, it showed a serious failure of judgment and a baffling inconsistency.

Sutch's reputation as the architect of New Zealand's industrial development has grown after his death, perhaps because of his books, and despite much evidence to the contrary. It was Sutch, for example, who was behind the abortive glass factory and undoubtedly the abandoned cotton mill among other attempts at economic self-sufficiency. Fletcher Holdings' experience with him substantially contradicts his reputation.

His problem, surmised Fraser in the mid-eighties after many years of dealing with Sutch both before and during his job at Fletcher Holdings, was that he was brilliant but commercially inexperienced. Unfortunately, he had an arrogance that tripped him up repeatedly. 'Bill got all his knowledge out of books,' Fraser wrote. 'He had no experience of practical shop-floor management or marketing, but rarely would admit to ignorance of any important subject.'

Dr John Watt still holds the same opinion. 'It makes one shudder,' he comments, 'to think that the decision on such an important matter as the establishment of a major industry is in the hands of people apparently so naive.'

In any event, the screaming and shouting of 20 May killed the idea of the Government and private interests holding hands while they explored what they might do with the ironsands. It let Woolf Fisher in by the back door.

The Government was now forced to take a different tack. In June 1960, Fisher became the head of a Government-appointed investigating committee to do the job. With unwittingly prophetic words in view of the enormous burden that New Zealand Steel later made on the nation's capital, Holloway said in a public statement that 'an iron and steel industry would have a profound effect on our economy' and it was therefore essential to complete 'a thorough and impartial examination of all aspects'.

JC still believed that it made sense for the further development of the industry to work around Pacific Steel, which was about to become New Zealand's sole steel-maker. But he also retained considerable doubts about existing technology to convert the ironsands economically into steel. He remembered the words of his American engineer friend George Ferris that 'anything is possible but it just might cost too much'.

Scollay's Development Corporation soon faded away and the chairman went on to other business interests, though not before Scollay had put out feelers to Jim Fletcher to form an alliance. JC felt, however, that the corporation was not a suitable partner and politely rejected the overtures. Clearly, the corporation hadn't impressed Holloway, who had made public remarks about those interests that had got the most publicity not having the most to offer. Bill Martin took an academic job in Australia. Titanium slag has never been extracted from the smelting of ironsands, though New Zealand Steel managed by the late eighties to extract vanadium.

Woolf Fisher quickly became a convert to the full ironsands grand plan, and thereafter the two old friends Fisher and Fletcher were rivals. Some of the rivalry was petty and demeaning. When John Watt went to Europe to talk about the latest developments in direct-reduction processes with steel companies and to the Batelle Memorial Institute, by then consultants to New Zealand Steel, he courteously informed Fisher what he was doing. New Zealand Steel's papers now show that Fisher promptly wrote to Batelle forbidding it to divulge anything to the Fletcher boffin and to tell the steel companies to do the same. At that time, Bill Sutch was also on New Zealand Steel's board. A small incident perhaps, but it was hurtful to JC, who had introduced Fisher to Batelle in the first place and handed over to New Zealand Steel all its files from Batelle plus all the other relevant research it had.

The tension simmered for years, including over later Fletcher Holdings attempts to buy into New Zealand Steel after it had become a publicly listed company. Jim Fletcher still wanted to integrate the industry and remained convinced, rightly or wrongly, that Pacific Steel should have some part in New Zealand Steel when it went into production. It was good business to have a foot in the New Zealand Steel camp anyway. But the board and the Government, at New Zealand Steel's behest, repeatedly rewrote the rules of its shareholdings and effectively kept Fletchers out of the action. When Fletchers moved to over 10 percent of New Zealand Steel, pursuing through the sharemarket its strategy for a single integrated industry, the stock exchange authorities were persuaded to accept new articles of association that prohibited anybody other than the Government having more than 10 percent. Later, a bizarre rule was introduced that was clearly aimed at Fletchers — no one with any connections to the steel industry was allowed to be a director on the New Zealand Steel board! 'A marvellous thing for a steel company to have on its books,' JC notes drily.

New Zealand Steel's later troubles are not the subject of this book. Suffice to say that it spent years trying to perfect a process for the efficient and profitable conversion of ironsands to steel. John Watt remains convinced that New Zealand Steel started with the wrong process. The task was eventually achieved, but it required brilliant, if time-consuming and costly, original work before it could be done.

Fletcher accepts that New Zealand Steel was bound to face difficulties because it was a pioneer. After all, Fletchers had been through the same hoops with Tasman and, on a much smaller scale, with Pacific Steel, and he had plenty of sympathy for New Zealand Steel. But the price, especially after the Think Big expansion approved by Muldoon, was enormous in terms of taxpayer dollars, so high in fact that David Lange's Labour Government sold the money-gobbling company to the Equiticorp group, which collapsed later partly from the weight of the investment.

To complete the irony, Equiticorp's receivers then sold New Zealand Steel to BHP. The price was a snip in terms of New Zealand Steel's capital cost. Thus the wisdom of BHP in staying out of the ironsands industry in its expensive development phase was entirely and ultimately vindicated.

History shows that Jim Fletcher's insistence thirty-five years ago that New Zealand could not afford a fragmented steel industry is similarly vindicated. 'It was the greatest disaster for New Zealand when Sutch went for the investigating company and refused to involve Pacific Steel in it,' JC insists. 'Sutch set up a situation that deliberately fragmented the industry. It was a situation that has carried through to this day.'

He believes that Pacific Steel would probably have gone on to produce iron from those tantalising titanomagnetite sands within about five years. His friend Mac Gilmore had already started doing so with a steel company in South America, and the necessary technology was being developed. It could have been done.

Chapter 7

Exit

B y 1960, five years after starting production, the Tasman pulp and paper mill had proved its worth by any commercial and economic standard. Conceived as a partnership between commerce and Government, it had clearly been a success. Tasman's machines had trained a new generation of skilled workers. The plant was producing 85,000 tonnes a year of newsprint of high quality — 10,000 tonnes above the machine's 'nameplate' capacity — for New Zealand and Australian newspapers. The entire operation, though fully exposed to imported competition, was saving New Zealand giant sums each year in foreign exchange.

The fortress economy was at its most impregnable at that time, and most contemporary manufacturers expected and usually got full protection from imports under the huge umbrella of the licensing system. Normally, a manufacturer was guaranteed protection to the full value of their own production. But Tasman had not sought protection in such a crucial commodity as newsprint, especially as it had only one machine. Any interruption to newsprint supply would have left the local users, the newspaper publishers, exposed. In effect, import protection would have meant that newspaper publishers would be tied to one domestic producer. As it was, locally produced newsprint represented a complete break with the publishers' traditional supplies. Tasman actually interceded to help the newspaper publishers acquire licences to buy newsprint offshore if they needed it. Additionally, Bowaters and Reed agreed to underwrite newsprint supply and act as a backstop.

It was time to move Tasman up a gear, to a second newsprint-making machine. The decision to spend £16.4 million — $424 million in today's money — on the No. 2 machine and related expansion, such as an increase in bleaching capacity and water treatment facilities, was logical enough. The markets were there. So was the raw material, the trees. The Government wanted it. The finance was available.

Yet this expansion would set in train a series of commercial and political events that nobody could have predicted but that would have far-reaching results, not only for Jim Fletcher but for Fletcher Holdings.

In JC's two decades at the helm, business had changed dramatically. Even though it was still protected, New Zealand manufacturing and commerce in general had become more international, more professional, more confident. New Zealand no longer depended so heavily on the sheep's back. Those were the lucky days when, at most, a few hundred were out of work at any one time and, as Keith Sinclair wrote in *A History of New Zealand* at the start of the sixties, 'It was jokingly said that they were all known by name to the Prime Minister.' New Zealand was a prosperous country of two and a half million, even though its wealth might be founded on sand — foreign exchange crises would continue to bedevil both Labour and National Governments.

The country's culture had changed too. We were opening up ourselves to the larger world — the Beatles toured in 1964 and Auckland's Mayor, Dove-Myer Robinson, sang at a civic reception for the pop group in what a local paper described as a 'fearlessly flat baritone' (and that probably praised Robbie's voice). We were talking to the outside world — our ability to make long-distance phone calls improved dramatically when the Compac cable linked New Zealand to Australia, Britain and Canada. Lyndon Baines Johnson — 'LBJ' — made a lightning trip to Wellington, the first by an American president, to drum up support for the war in Indo-China, and we quickly obliged by sending the 'V Force' to Vietnam. When Nixon's Vice-President, Spiro Agnew, who would later resign over a political scandal, arrived five years later for the same purpose, he was greeted by protests.

Town planners were worrying about Auckland's growth — by 1966, its population had exceeded 540,000. An ambitious young politician called Rob Muldoon introduced decimal currency in 1967. New Zealand's ability to tolerate difference and dissent, never very robust, was tested fully when Dr Lloyd Geering dared to question the literal truth of the Resurrection and promptly faced heresy charges. The cultural climate was one of change and challenge, of growth and development.

But it had already been like that for twenty years in Fletcher Holdings. Sometimes the growth might have seemed too quick. In the sixties and seventies, the company was known within the industry as 'the octopus' because its tentacles reached so far and in so many different directions — plywood and doors, sawmilling, financial services, steel, pulp and paper, timber, diverse manufacturing from New Zealand's raw materials, linseed and much later rape seed, even dehydrated lucerne pellets for export to Japan, wire-drawing, concrete, engineering and construction. Fletcher Holdings probably suffered from some of the drawbacks of headlong growth but it was an exciting company based on a culture of action.

The No. 2 expansion at Tasman started off smoothly enough. The £4 million second machine, a gigantic co-production from Walmsley and Beloit, doubled output almost overnight from its commissioning in 1963 and soon Tasman was turning out nearly two kilometres of paper every minute. The commissioning ceremony was practically a state occasion, and speakers used it as a symbol of an emerging prosperous nation.

'Kawerau was an extreme example of the enormous confidence in the future which was apparent everywhere in New Zealand,' announced the Governor-General, Sir Bernard Fergusson, who hadn't seen the Bay of Plenty since he had travelled up and down New Zealand as a lad in 1926. Sir Bernard noted that Kawerau now used more power than Christchurch, and for him the Tasman expansion displayed a panoply of virtues — 'imagination, confidence, foresight, great technical knowledge'. He attributed Tasman's success to its chairman, James Fletcher senior, whose energy had been 'positively thermal', declared Sir Bernard in an allusion to the underground steam in the area.

Everyone in politics who mattered was there on that day in brilliant sunshine at the foot of Mount Edgecumbe. The Prime Minister noted in a typically effusive speech that the enterprise had transformed a farming backwater into a fascinating, prosperous and productive enterprise. 'What an industrial saga it has been! All honour to the men who can build great enterprises and towns such as we see here. All honour to the builders who build them out of dreams.'

Arnold Nordmeyer, who had replaced Nash as Leader of the

Opposition, spoke less floridly but pointed to 'a striking example of co-operation and partnership between state and private enterprise'. Listening from his seat in the front row, Jim Fletcher agreed fully. He didn't get onto the speakers' platform and didn't want to — JC has had a lifelong aversion to making speeches. Instead, his father did the honours, and Sir James, the great optimist and salesman, predicted that New Zealand would soon be as famous for its pulp and paper as it already was for its butter, meat and wool.

Kawerau got star status — a documentary on the mill was screened in prime-time the following Sunday night. The occasion was considered of national importance.

Technically speaking, the spectacular commissioning ceremony probably overplayed the significance of the second machine. Yes, it doubled production. But by now, Tasman had a skilled workforce that knew how to produce pulp and paper. Its markets were well established. Funding arrangements were secure, and Bowaters, who had tried to hijack the entire project in 1952, had come in as managers and sales agents seven years later.

With its North American expansion complete, Bowaters had seen that buying into Tasman was the only way of securing its Down-Under market. There were no hard feelings on Jim Fletcher's part over Sir Eric's stalling tactics in the early fifties. Indeed, JC had made a point of keeping in touch with Bowaters throughout the fifties and the relationship between the two companies was cordial enough. JC had always felt that Tasman needed Bowaters' expertise, especially so because of Reed's disappointing management. In 1954, even before Tasman had been started up, JC had cornered the autocratic Sir Eric in Montreal and explained these convictions. Sir Eric listened and agreed — he was still interested in New Zealand when the time was ripe.

So far, so good. But somehow Bowaters still had to be brought aboard. Here was Reed in the driving seat but steering the Tasman vehicle erratically, as it had done from the start. Somehow, Reed had to be extricated. The Government, the major shareholder, had to approve any deal, which meant the involvement of the Prime Minister, ministers and civil servants from several departments. And Bowaters had to be enticed, for they certainly wouldn't come in cheaply.

In 1959, negotiations over Bowaters' entry began in Wellington but broke down because the Government was unhappy that the new arrangement would give British shareholders — Reed and Bowaters — majority ownership and thus control of Tasman. The various parties could not resolve the stalemate, and the Government was quite happy to leave things as they were.

But JC, unhappy about Tasman's fortunes being left in Reed's hands for the foreseeable future, was still determined to get Bowaters in. First, he had to satisfy the Government's objections. He got together with Ashwin, the Treasury mandarin, and arranged an appointment with the Prime Minister at the Grand Hotel during a visit to Auckland. JC met Nash there and explained a formula that would maintain majority shareholding in New Zealand hands. Nash listened, promised to give the matter some thought, and agreed to discuss it further the next day, a Sunday, at the Fletchers' house in Penrose on the way back from a ceremony at a local marae.

Nash arrived on Sunday as promised and, after some further discussion, agreed to consider the formula. But first he wanted a more detailed proposal. And it had to be delivered that night to the Grand Hotel. Vaughan, working from her husband's execrable handwriting, spent all Sunday and most of that night rewriting the proposal to prime ministerial standard in her immaculate copperplate hand.

It was finished after midnight and JC, after debating whether he should run it into the Grand Hotel, decided this would be discourteous. Anyway, he assumed nobody would be awake at that time. So instead, he and George Fraser delivered the document to Nash's plane at Whenuapai, north-west of Auckland, just before it was to take off the next day.

Nash was furious. He never slept more than four hours a night, he explained tartly, and he had wanted the documents delivered to his hotel the night before as arranged. He had waited up for them. Nash ostentatiously put the proposal at the bottom of a pile of other documents he was carrying.

Somewhat chastened, JC and Fraser got on the plane and watched out of the corner of their eye as Nash methodically worked his way through the pile, from top to bottom. He got to the Tasman document shortly before landing, much to the relief of Fraser and JC.

Later the same day, JC met Finance Minister Nordmeyer in

Parliament Buildings, with Ashwin, Entrican and McKillop present. It was quickly decided to approve JC's proposal. Bowaters would come in under a ten-year management agreement, a fifteen-year marketing agreement, pump in £1 million, and buy out the CDFC shareholding of £500,000. But, most importantly, Bowaters would hand over 70,000 tonnes of its newsprint contracts in Australia and New Zealand. The deal was as clean as JC could hope to make it, given the necessarily complex structure of the shareholdings, but it stirred up some latent resentment.

The Fletchers remained unpopular in some political quarters, notably in the Forestry Service. Papers available now show that Entrican wanted to use Bowaters' arrival to unseat Sir James as chairman of Tasman and he had even written to the powerful Tasman sub-committee of Cabinet, claiming that the Government 'faced a very grave decision in leaving Sir James in the chair, even for two years'. Entrican didn't give reasons for his view, but it is probable that Sir James presented an obstacle to the civil servant's ambitions.

However, it probably wasn't because of personal enmity either. Former colleagues say that Entrican typically got tough with anybody who stood in his way. Despite Entrican's views, Sir James stayed on for another six years and was succeeded by JC for a further thirteen years.

The benefits were immediate when Bowaters moved its North American professionals into the top jobs. 'It was like a fresh breeze,' remembers JC. 'We'd had such a lacklustre performance from Reed.' Reed's long-serving director of operations, Leslie Dougal, who had been there from the start and who had so infuriated JC with his excessively relaxed style, left Kawerau and went back to Britain.

Bowaters put in some of its best technical experts and a dozen people in the key executive jobs — 'the twelve disciples' JC called them. They introduced open American-style management and had technical, operational and management expertise plus extensive back-up. If anything went seriously wrong with the No. 2 machine, Bowaters could always bring in their American troubleshooters.

The No. 2 machine was, however, the Rolls-Royce of paper machines. It was the result of a blend of technologies — designed by the Wisconsin-based works of Beloit Iron Works and built by the same Walmsleys company of Bury, Britain, that had made the first one.

Technically the expansion was therefore straightforward enough. 'The No. 2 machine was nothing like the step of the No. 1,' recalls JC. 'By the time of the No. 2, the technology was well proven. The trend to wider and faster machines was by then universal.' Also, the new machine offered the plant huge economies of scale because much of the existing infrastructure was able to cope with the higher output, without the necessity of heavy additional capital expenditure.

Thus, in most ways, the expansion meant much less risk than maintaining the status quo. Tasman's customers had been understandably nervous of a plant that relied on just one machine. An interruption in production through a prolonged strike or through a severe power breakdown could threaten the supply of newsprint. The second machine didn't guarantee that supply, but it did reduce the risk of interruption through mechanical failures. Ultimately, the most powerful back-up was Bowaters' and Reed's guarantee of supply, because it fully protected the publishers.

Compared with the stress of getting the original project off the ground — raising a total of £18.3 million, or $595 million in today's dollars, sweet-talking the Government, dealing with bureaucrats, heading off Bowaters, building a new town and plant, training a raw workforce, commissioning unfamiliar equipment in an industry totally new to the country, and attempting to manufacture newsprint from a forest of erratic quality — installing a second newsprint machine turned out to be a relative doddle.

After ten years, JC could take stock of Tasman. In 1964, the Government's share of Tasman's revenue was running at £4.5 million a year, and by August that year Tasman had contributed £23 million ($575 million at today's values) in revenue to various government departments such as Railways, Electricity, Forestry and Treasury.

NZ Railways had done well out of Tasman too. Tasman's business amounted to 13 percent of its total freight, and the lines between Murupara and the mill were the most profitable of all of NZR's lines.

In the nine years since start-up, Tasman had earned a gratifying amount of foreign exchange — £73.5 million gross. That sum was made up of export earnings of £49 million and £24.5 million in import savings on newsprint and pulp. All this had been achieved without help from tariff protection, and it's something of which JC remains extremely proud — although a little nettled that Tasman's massive contribution to the balance of payments has gone largely unrecognised. He notes with a gleam in his eye that NZ Forest Products' success was entirely based on a protected market, whereas Tasman had to compete directly with imported newsprint.

By any standards, Tasman was a giant in terms of offshore sales. At that time, it was New Zealand's largest exporter of manufactured goods, shipping no less than 40 percent of all the country's exports to Australia. It was also our first industry that could foot it internationally, not only in size but, more importantly, competitiveness.

The Government's sole purpose with Tasman — and Pat Entrican deserves the credit for pushing the scheme — had been to do something with the Kaingaroa Forest. Judged by that alone, Tasman had even by that stage proved a success. Tasman had paid the Forest Service regular revenue for stumpage and for thinnings (the waste trees). More importantly, the haphazardly planted forest was now much more rigorously managed. It was no longer a botanist's forest, a curiosity with a mixed population of trees; it was a commercially managed and harvested forest with a strong commercial present and future.

Tasman had turned the rosy assumptions of the Green Book into dollars and cents. In 1960, it had achieved the biggest profit in New Zealand at that time — £1.14 million, or nearly $31 million today. Profits had, however, fallen short of what JC considered achievable.

Fletcher isn't one to bear grudges, but he finds it hard to be charitable about Leslie Dougal, Reed's first appointment to run the plant and the man who got rid of most of the experts — Sandwell, Abitibi, the Canadian mill experts, and Hobday — long before the No. 1 machine was up to speed. 'Abitibi people should have been all over the plant,' JC laments now. Despite these early blunders, Tasman had by 1964 extinguished all its heavy early losses and was financially sound.

Technically speaking, this plant, dropped in a virtual wilderness nine years before, had become a winner, creating New Zealand's first internationally competitive industry. In terms of speed, the No. 1 machine had been one of the world's fastest and most productive, and so was the No. 2 machine (out of about 500 newsprint machines worldwide). Even by 1964, the pulp mill's production was nearly twice as high as its designed capacity at 300 tonnes a day. The Australian press barons were happy enough with the product and the regularity of supply; happy enough, in fact, to form a partnership with Tasman. About the time of the advent of the second machine, Tasman and Australian Newsprint Mills swapped a 20 percent shareholding.

Good things had also happened in the wider region. Every time JC drove down to Kawerau and Tauranga, he was excited by the ferment of activity there. Tasman had sparked activity in the port of Tauranga and the wider Bay of Plenty that even he hadn't predicted. It was as though the pool of commerce in the region was growing spontaneously, stirring up concentric rings that rippled outwards. Watching ships pulling in and out of the port, JC, though not much given to introspection, felt that just maybe he had started something.

Storm clouds were mounting, however. Steadily and insidiously, labour troubles were spreading to the Tasman plant. Liverpudlian John Murphy had started work in the plant years earlier, as an operator on the recovery boiler. He had expressed to management his interest in becoming a union man and Tasman had given him an office in the plant and a 'letter of comfort' — a promise that he could always have his old job back. Murphy, who had begun shovelling coal at the age of thirteen, was an interesting and complex man. Although he had left school before his teens, he was highly intelligent, a lover of opera and a self-taught philosopher. Having emerged from a poor background, it was probably natural that he would sympathise with the wage-earning rather than the salaried staff. Over the years he would show what one executive called 'an enormous humanity' for his union members.

Murphy became the head of the Pulp and Paper Workers Federation and started out doing what any good union man is supposed to do — negotiating wage rises. He proved very good at it and held some strong cards, chief of which was the relatively low cost of wages compared with the enormous expense of the equipment.

For years, management, acknowledging that the economics of newsprint manufacture are based on twenty-four-hour operation, had taken the easy route and agreed to all sorts of penalty payments just to keep the equipment running. A lost hour of production could never be recovered. Occasionally, management 'took' a strike rather than bow to the more excessive union claims, but in general it was more profitable to maintain production.

JC acknowledges management's failure, though of course he wasn't involved in the daily administration of Tasman. 'It was much more costly to take a shutdown than to pay these excessive wages and conditions claims,' he says. Anyway, the Tasman plant simply didn't possess the financial resources to withstand a prolonged stand-down.

Murphy began to change throughout the seventies, according to those who dealt with him. His relations with management had always been characterised by a 'them and us' attitude he had brought into New Zealand from his own British background, but he increasingly seemed incapable of co-operation. 'He became driven,' recalls a senior Tasman executive. Tasman also had complex labour relations, with eleven unions on site. Increasingly, the disputes originated from demarcation tussles between the unions rather than through fights with management.

A confrontation was inevitable.

A new and younger executive team was now coming through Fletcher Holdings. By the late sixties, JC was heading towards his third decade in the hot seat and most of the old guard who had kept pace through the dramatic expansion of the fifties and sixties had now retired or were nearing retirement. These included John Watt, John Fletcher, the Craig brothers, and Bill Bourke.

Like their predecessors, the new boys (they were all boys because the female senior executive was a phenomenon still fifteen years away in New Zealand business) had come through the ranks. Barrie Downey had joined in 1966 from the Hutt Timber and Hardware Company, persuaded after a two-hour conversation on a Saturday morning with JC that left him somewhat bewildered. To outsiders, Fletchers then had a reputation for ruthlessness. Instead, here was a benign bantam cock of a man, talking earnestly to Downey about where the company was heading and what role the new recruit might play in it. Downey, then thirty-six, went straight home and cancelled plans to emigrate to Australia. 'That's it. I'm not going to Australia. I'm going to work for Fletchers,' he told his wife. Downey would stay for more than a quarter of a century and would later come to believe, contrary to the prevailing myth, that Fletchers wasn't ruthless enough on incompetent staff.

JC himself certainly shared that view and blamed himself for it. Although during the forties, fifties and sixties money-losing subsidiaries were tolerated so long as the group as a whole turned out acceptable profits, largely because they provided jobs, Jim Fletcher believes he was sometimes kinder than he should have been. 'I don't think I am terribly good at dealing with people,' he says now. 'I certainly found it hard to sack people. In many cases, I didn't face up to individuals' short-comings as quickly as I should have.' Even his sons, Jim, Hugh and Angus, would come to agree after they had joined the business.

Yet still the myth persisted that Fletchers was a roughhouse. Years later, when JC was a director on the Alcan New Zealand board, a discussion arose at one meeting about how to cut costs and lift profits, and he was amazed to hear a prominent Auckland commercial lawyer tell the other directors to take a leaf out of Fletchers' book. 'At Fletchers,' he said, 'you either perform or get out.' This was complete news to the man who was supposed to be the architect of this ruthless policy.

It would, however, be a mistake to paint a picture of JC in the sixties and seventies as a cherub who treated everybody with affection and endless tolerance. The truth is that he could be tough, though tougher on himself than on anybody else. It was his enthusiasm that got the place jumping. JC was still as passionate about business as ever after twenty years in the top job, and he expected others to be the same. Thus he set the pace, but he was also easily irritated, especially by sloppy business practice.

He was good to the performers. He showed a burning loyalty to his colleagues, and still does. When reminiscing about the old days, as he increasingly likes to do, JC never utters a word of criticism about this inner circle. If one of them fell seriously ill, there was never any question that he might have to be replaced. It took one senior staffer two or three years before he was fully fit after a bout of meningitis, but JC always made it clear that his job was there for him when he was up to it.

Little things mattered to him because he wanted, perhaps naively, that everybody in this sprawling, expanding company should feel as though they were part of a family. When senior executives had a birthday, a telegram or card usually turned up, even if they were overseas.

The parties held at Jim and Vaughan's house in Penrose at Christmas and other times were another expression of this desire. Executives and foremen and their wives mingled while the Fletcher boys passed around the sausage rolls. There's a fine line between a company wanting to own its staff — that is, regarding them as pieces of valued property like the company cars — and showing them they are appreciated. Although outsiders might think they saw a measure of paternalism, Jim Fletcher had the gift of winning the loyalty and usually the affection of strong-minded, independent executives, most of whom could have succeeded anywhere.

Jim Fletcher led from the front, usually arriving at the office by 6.30 a.m. He lived and breathed business, and could pick out a flaw in a business proposal like an eagle spotting prey. He wasn't a brilliant strategist, however, more of a doer, and he readily acknowledges this. 'I didn't want to be blinded by the details,' he says self-deprecatingly. He had other commercial weaknesses, for instance in negotiations, where he admits he lacked patience.

A fundamental quality was his stamina, which most of his staff found quite awesome. ('I thought he was made of iron,' recalls one.) Sometimes he would have gone and returned from a business trip to Britain or America within such a short time that staff thought he had never left the office. His memory remains prodigious. Every associate of Jim Fletcher pays tribute to his mastery of significant detail. He also possesses a quality that is often absent among so-called captains of industry — common sense.

JC's style might seem contradictory in some respects. Although he could be fiery in a group, he was a model of compassion and consideration one to one — 'mild, soft-hearted and humble' is how one long-serving executive puts it.

It didn't pay to get on the wrong side of him, however. JC could not tolerate nor understand those who didn't have his driving enthusiasm for business. He was incapable of countenancing incompetence or laziness. Above all, he would not put up with less than perfect honesty. This was — and remains — the secret of working with him. He bestows his trust in return for candidness. Increasingly, openness is now prized in business — 'caring commerce' somebody called it. At Fletcher Holdings, candidness was always essential. It didn't pay, for example, to send a note to Jim Fletcher complaining about another member of the staff, because his habit was to take it straight to the target and say 'Is this true?'

Downey remembers that 'if through error or any other reason you conveyed inaccurate information to him, that was something he couldn't tolerate and you could expect great scrutiny until you re-established your position with him again. He never developed that technique out of books or anything else, he developed it from his own instinct. Yet it's pretty standard and recommended form for chief executives these days.' JC had that old Scots liking for telling the truth. He had learned it from his own father, sometimes painfully.

JC, who has much more humility than he has ego, liked to give his staff autonomy. Although nobody received *carte blanche* to do what they liked, and Fletchers' treasury operations had a Molony-inspired system that was far ahead of its day in monitoring cashflow on a weekly basis (most businesses then ran six-month accounts), the corporate culture was built around executive freedom. But autonomy brought its own obligations, and if JC suspected an executive was putting one across him in order, say, to hide a loss or a problem, that executive would be called forcefully to account and very likely lose any prospect of serious advancement forever. But he would rarely be fired. Of all of Fletchers' long-service staff, half a dozen at most were asked to leave or take demotion.

The memo was JC's preferred means of keeping up to speed. If something could be done now, it was. He could get furious, particularly as he grew tired in the last few years of his long years at the top of the company, and he would leave notes around the office asking why this or that hadn't been done or had gone wrong.

One executive recalls being very upset after receiving a missive from JC following a loss of over $500,000 on an Australian venture, so upset in fact that he seriously considered resigning. When he later confessed this to JC, the author of the note was stricken with remorse and was deeply upset almost to the point of tears. He spent an hour trying to dissuade the executive from resigning and eventually succeeded.

The boss's notes remain the stuff of legend. Right until the mid-seventies, he read every item of correspondence that went out of head office by virtue of the famous pink copy that was taken of every letter. Jim Fletcher's was the pink copy.

If the letter or memo required or stirred some reaction from him, he would start writing on the original pink copy instead of on a fresh piece of paper. JC's difficult upright hand would usually start at the top of the memo, climb back down each side, cover the bottom, then turn over to the back and start all over again. The survivors had to learn, after deciphering these memos, that in them the boss wasn't instructing them what to do, just suggesting a course of action they ought to think about. He didn't want obedience, just effectiveness. Still, you had to watch your step. 'There were literally dozens of these missiles flying around,' recalls Carl Ryan. But the notes helped JC a lot — they meant he never forgot anything. Long-standing business associates recall his meticulousness in doing everything he said he would, even down to the most minor matters.

You could always have your say at Fletchers, provided you didn't mind mixing it and had a loud voice. Meetings of the executive committee could turn into furious, completely unstructured affairs, with people shouting at each other and flying off at tangents dealing with everything from criteria for getting a company car to starting a new industry. For the secretaries who kept the minutes, these meetings were a nightmare. Whenever the boss was away, it was different. Nobody would force things, challenge statements or shoot down opinions the way JC did.

As he entered the last full decade of his career, Jim Fletcher had built up a lot of confidence in his own judgment, which is why he contested everything. He contested common assumptions, he contested the wisdom of so-called experts in the light of common sense, he contested pomposity, he even contested his own brother's opinions.

Fletcher Holdings old hands chuckle at some of the furious arguments JC had with 'brother John', as he was universally known within the company. John had retained for many years all the responsibilities for the South Island in his portfolio. 'They would go hammer and tongs, but then Jim would say, "Let's forget it" — and they would, just like that,' marvels one former senior executive. In fact, the brothers got on famously most of the time. It was one of the more unusual and enduring relationships in New Zealand commerce. John referred to JC as 'brother Jim' and sometimes spoke in awe of him. In return, JC set a lot of store by his much more patient brother's advice and capacity for thinking ahead.

It was the big picture that had always attracted JC. He had an ability to distinguish the detail that mattered from the one that didn't. In this, he hadn't changed at all since the forties. Back then, he had taken over the job of honorary treasurer of the Auckland branch of the Waitaki Old Boys' Association, no doubt because of his accountancy training. Young Jim Fletcher saw his job not primarily as one requiring immaculate books but rather as rustling up new members and dues. He did so with such terrier-like persistence, especially in attracting life memberships, that at the end of his term he proudly handed over the books to the honorary auditor with a record high membership and flush finances.

'I absolutely hounded the old boys,' he says now, but without a shred of remorse. Most of them bought life memberships just to get him off the phone. But the auditor, missing the point, took one look at the scratched-out entries and jagged columns, called JC and said, 'These are the worst set of books I have ever seen.'

JC had gained his vision from his father, who had continually set himself large goals. After all, most house-builders stay house-builders; they don't become major contractors and form public companies. Quite early on, James senior understood that the best opportunities were overseas.

It was old Sir James who had first seen the value of the International Industrial Conferences held every four years in San Francisco. Because the media is barred from them, the conferences never attract much publicity. But their influence is enormous. If you are talking big picture, this is a giant mural. Everybody in international industry was — and is — there.

Attendance, which is by invitation only, is limited to around 500 chief executives and chairpersons. To send a second-ranker is seen as something of an insult, and even government representatives are banned so that the captains of industry can talk frankly.

James senior attended the very first one in 1957, and right through the sixties and seventies JC got to most of them, plus some of the regional conferences in between. By 1969, he was on the policy board with some international heavyweights — J. H. Loudon, chairman of Royal Dutch

Petroleum; Sir Archibald Forbes, chairman of Midland Bank; Edgar Kaiser; and Henry Wingate, chairman of International Nickel, among others.

At the 1969 conference, guests included a young-looking Italian industrialist named Giovanni Agnelli, chairman of the board of Fiat; Leopoldo Pirelli, of the tyre company; Tatsuzo Mizukami, chairman of the board of Mitsui and Co.; Harold Hartog, chairman of Unilever in Rotterdam; Alfred Heineken, of the Dutch brewing giant; the same Dr Marcus Wallenberg who had advised the New Zealand Government on pulp and paper nearly twenty years earlier; Lord Pilkington, of the British glass-makers, who had a few years before turned down JC's proposal for a New Zealand factory; an array of American businessmen including Henry Ford II, Walter Haas and his son, Walter junior, respectively chairman and president of Levi Strauss of jeans-making fame, H. J. Heinz II of the fifty-seven varieties, the banker David Rockefeller. At later conferences, there were emerging industrialists, such as a little-known Japanese electronics-maker called Akio Morita who had founded a company named Sony.

Many of the papers presented dealt with global issues. For example, at the 1969 conference, the major economic problems of the free world were covered by University of Paris Economics Professor Bob Marjolin, and the capital requirements of the developing nations by a former Secretary-General of NATO. Also discussed were subjects such as the future of the international monetary system, the development of manpower and management for industrial growth, closing the management gap (this one by Agnelli), the contribution of technology and communication by the head of ATT, and the role of the chief executive. Of many speakers, Jim Fletcher particularly remembers Sheik Yamani, the urbane representative of OPEC, discussing oil prices shortly before the devastating first oil shock.

He enjoyed the conferences because he was right in the thick of the action. There was a direct return from them for New Zealand and for Fletcher Holdings and its subsidiaries. JC nurtured his relationship there with the Bechtel family, who later sponsored the Marsden Point refinery construction in the Bechtel-Wimpey-Fletcher consortium, with Kaisers, and with bankers who later financed Fletcher Holdings projects. Other New Zealanders, who were invited through JC, came to value the conferences, too. Woolf Fisher often attended after he became chairman of New Zealand Steel.

Coming from the land of 'she'll be right', JC and Vaughan Fletcher were always impressed by the American way of doing things. Prominent San Franciscans would host the international guests at private functions. On one occasion, the New Zealanders attended a black-tie dinner for about 300 at Edgar and Sue Kaiser's residence in Lafayette. The marquee-covered tennis court was converted into a giant bar while another enormous marquee over the Kaiser kids' baseball field 'in back of the house', as the Americans say, was the dinner venue. Beside each place at the table was a silver Argentinian vase with the guest's name engraved on it. Kaiser executives were paired with the guests to drive them home whenever they wanted, whatever the time. Everything went with seamless smoothness, and it was only later JC learned that the Kaisers had done a dummy run earlier in the week, using 300 of their own executive staff.

Vaughan loved the company of the spirited American women. At a dinner thrown by the Haas family, she fell into conversation with the hostess, who turned out to be an expert trout fisherwoman and author of a book on the subject entitled *Take a Step Deeper, Dear.*

The new boys were a lively bunch. Carl Ryan, a hard-nosed manager with a mind like a steel trap, was rocketing through the layers of middle management. After joining the company as a cost accountant on the Fletcher Merritt Raymond import wharf in 1951, he became office manager for Fletcher Construction and Residential Construction at Kawerau, investigating accountant in Molony's Auckland office, secretary of Fletcher Steel, branch manager for Fletcher Steel in Dunedin, then back to Auckland as managing director of Fletcher Steel. By 1970, he was part of the inner circle, managing director of Fletcher Industries, the job that John Watt had held. Later, he would complete practically a straight flush of senior jobs (and be regarded as a contender to replace JC) by being appointed consecutively managing director of Tasman, chief executive of the forest industries section of the new Fletcher Challenge, deputy managing director of Fletcher Challenge and, finally, president of Crown Forest Industries in Canada.

Others, like David Sadler, who would become a much-praised chief of finance, came aboard after ignoring the usual warnings about the ulcerous life that awaited within Fletcher Holdings. Sadler came from Winstones to be company secretary of Fletcher Steel, the merchants, after being interviewed by Alec Craig. It was August 1963. 'Winstones cautioned me about the hard life I was letting myself in for,' Sadler recalls. Craig was typically blunt and from across the desk threw the interviewee the steel company's annual reports: 'Take this home, cut your lawns, read it, and if you don't join on Monday, I'll be bloody disappointed in you.'

He wasn't disappointed. Sadler became company secretary for the entire group in 1971, or rather, JC came puffing down the stairs and *asked* him if he would take on the job. Although by that stage accustomed to his boss's non-autocratic ways, Sadler was still stunned by JC's approach. 'He came down and said, "David, would you be company secretary? I hope you will. Will you do it?" Most chief executives would probably have summoned you up to their office and said, 'Young man, you've got a great opportunity. I don't know if I totally believe you can do it but if you work like hell you might succeed . . ."'

While the second machine was thundering and rattling away, Jim Fletcher was making plans. He knew very well Reginald (later Sir Reginald) Smythe, who became managing director of NZ Forest Products after the death of the quixotic Henry, and had sometimes commiserated with him privately over Smythe's endless difficulties with Henry. In 1967, JC approached Smythe about a merger of the two giants. It wasn't the first time JC had broached the subject with Smythe, but these discussions were the most serious of them all. The possibility of a merger never came closer to succeeding than in 1967.

The negotiations came after Tasman had flirted with a plan to install a kraft liner board machine that would have put the company in direct competition with NZ Forest Products. For numerous reasons, the scheme died. But negotiations about a merger remained very much alive.

To JC, the logic was compelling. With Tasman's huge newsprint machines and Forest Products' forests and strong non-newsprint markets in, for example, kraft liner boards, a merger would create a truly international forestry company. In essence, that was Jim Fletcher's pitch to Smythe, and it was entertained very seriously. In Brian Healy's book *A Hundred Million Trees,* Smythe is surprisingly dismissive of the feasibility of the merger, but in fact it got right through both companies' boards, had been approved by the Government, and was within days of being signed when Tasman's shareholder, Australian Newsprint Mills, suddenly reneged and blocked the deal. On the brink of the knot being tied, the *Melbourne Herald* group had second thoughts and unravelled the deal by persuading Australian Newsprint Mills, a 23 percent shareholder in Tasman whose support for the merger was essential, to pull out. The Aussies feared the combined might of the two New Zealand pulp and paper heavyweights. (It's an irony of history that Fletcher Challenge owns half of ANM and Rupert Murdoch's News Corporation owns the other half.)

It's worth recording that, Australians having blocked the merger, it was an Australian company that in the late eighties bought NZ Forest Products and indirectly delivered it to American ownership in the convoluted way that often occurs in sharemarket wheeling and dealing. Elders-IXL, which also owned the Carlton United Brewing Company of Foster's Lager fame, bought NZ Forest Products before the 1987 sharemarket crash and then, crippled by debt, sold Elders NZFP (as the company became) to Carter Holt Harvey. In turn, Carter Holt Harvey's own mountain of debt provoked a shareholder, Brierley Investments, to engineer the sale of a significant interest of CHH to an American giant, International Paper. Thus NZ Forest Products bounced within four years into the hands of three different companies.

Yes, thinking big. Another cherished dream of Jim Fletcher had already come off. It was called NAFTA — the New Zealand Australia Free Trade Agreement — the forerunner of the present Closer Economic Relations pact. It's no exaggeration to say it was Tasman's commercial strength that powered this landmark economic union. The two governments signed NAFTA into operation on 1 January 1966, and it was designed to redress the trade imbalance that had run permanently against New Zealand.

At the time, New Zealand was buying from Australia four times as much as it was selling across the Tasman. Without Tasman, the imbalance would have been much greater. The basis of NAFTA was that New Zealand should concentrate on exporting from its strong industries, notably Tasman, whose newsprint sales alone in 1966 accounted for a third of total exports.

James senior had prosecuted the case for a similar deal as far back as 1957. With his usual bluff prescience, he argued in Fletcher Holdings' annual report for an Australia New Zealand Economic Union. He had seen the coming of British entry into the EEC — in fact, about ten years before the Government did — and the consequent risks to New Zealand's traditional market. (And ANZEC has a far better ring to it than NAFTA, an acronym invented by a committee of civil servants.)

Sir James and the Tasman board had been thinking about NAFTA for years. They had long before made separate trans-Tasman shipping arrangements for the Kawerau plant. As chairman of Tasman, Sir James had signed an exclusive contract with the P&O-owned Union Steam Ship Company of New Zealand under which they transported the Kawerau products in custom-designed ships. The arrangement kept down freight rates, but in 1970 the P&O Line wanted to sell out to Peter (later Sir Peter) Abeles's Thomas Nationwide Transport, alarming the New Zealand Government.

Holyoake's administration was worried about Australian control of this vital shipping link and insisted on enforcing laws requiring 50 percent New Zealand ownership. But the Government couldn't raise enough local money to buy a half-share in Union Steam Ship, so the Minister of Transport, Peter Gordon, worked hard on the domestic industrialists to stump up the cash.

JC, however, who had taken over in 1966 as chairman of Tasman, didn't have much regard for Union Steam Ship's efficiency and could see no reason why the company should buy into it. He had no trouble resisting Gordon's overtures.

Enter Holyoake with his political charm and the knowledge that Gordon had locked up almost enough funds by this stage and that a guarantee of £1 million from Tasman would do the trick. One night, the Prime Minister rang JC at home. Repeating Gordon's arguments, he urged JC to change his mind. As the receiver of the call remembers, Holyoake was at his most persuasive: 'Look, Jim,' he said. 'We want you to tie up this Union Steam Ship Company. We need you in. Tasman has got to be in for appearance's sake and we need the extra million just to round it off.'

Politely but firmly, JC refused, explaining his doubts about Union Steam Ship's suitability as an investment and Tasman's existing level of indebtedness. 'We talked about it in the board,' he told the Prime Minister. 'None of us can see any merit in it.' After all, JC explained, he was talking about shareholders' funds and, of course, he had a fiduciary duty to invest them as wisely as possible.

'Is there nothing that would make you change your mind?' Holyoake wanted to know.

'Well, there is one thing,' JC said. Tasman would buy into Union Steam Ship but only if the company got the export incentives it had never been granted but that were enjoyed by most manufacturing exporters. It hadn't sought or expected import-licensing protection, but Tasman didn't see why it should be excluded from other subsidies enjoyed by rivals like Caxton and Forest Products. After years of argument, Tasman had got nowhere with the civil servants or the Government, but that night JC saw an opportunity for a little horse-trading.

'Leave it with me,' the Prime Minister responded. 'I'll come back.' He did so within an hour. The proposal was for a partial export incentive, not the full one. JC agreed and that was that. Tasman took £1 million, or a third of the 50 percent, of Union Steam Ship but got back substantially more than this each year in export incentives.

The investment ended ten years later, you could say, over a few centimetres. As Tasman's exports increased rapidly, its management became, in almost direct proportion, unhappy with the line's service. Freight rates had risen rapidly and the holds of the new roll-on, roll-off vessels were no longer purpose-designed for Tasman. They were just a few vital centimetres too low for the company to get in an extra tier of newsprint reels or pulp bales, and the resulting freight losses were considerable. Negotiations failed to satisfy Tasman and it was clear that the old understanding beween Union Steam Ship and Sir James had broken down. Fletchers became convinced that Abeles no longer wanted the business.

Tasman finally ordered two custom-designed ships from a Japanese yard, Union Steam Ship managed them, and these proved money-winners for Tasman as they plied to and fro between Australia and New Zealand. The savings over the original arrangement exceeded the board's expectations, a fact worth noting in view of later government comments that the ships had lost money.

But back to NAFTA. A veteran trans-Tasman traveller, and a believer in some sort of economic union between the two countries, JC lobbied aggressively for the concept, too, and joined a trade delegation to Australia in 1959. Tasman had been founded as a business that had to export or die in completely unprotected markets, and he wasn't afraid for it.

NZ Forest Products had a different view, as official papers show. Forest Products had thrived in a protected domestic market and Reg Smythe lobbied just as doggedly against any trade deal that he feared might open New Zealand to competition in, for example, wallboards and kraft liner boards, in which the company had a monopoly. Most other manufacturers lined up with Smythe — they feared Australian competition, too.

Bill Sutch, who had always argued for a closed and protected economy, firmly occupied the same camp. He didn't want any trans-Tasman deal either, which was an amazing pirouette for somebody who had been prepared to sell the steel industry across the Tasman. Minister of Trade John Marshall, who later briefly joined the Fletcher Holdings board, saw it all clearly enough. He wrote in the second volume of his memoirs that 'it early became apparent that my ideas for a brave new world of freer trade were not being received with much enthusiasm. To begin with, the permanent head of my Department of Industries and Commerce, Dr Sutch, who would normally have led our group of officials, was, to put it mildly, unsympathetic and was dropped from our negotiation team.'

Tasman had always been a massive consumer of trees, its raw material, and dependent on adequate supplies of them. The Kaingaroa Forest was its lifeblood and a seventy-five-year agreement giving Tasman access to the forest had been signed in February 1955. It had been a three-stage deal — a twenty-five-year original term with rights of renewal at two further twenty-five-year intervals. However, as a pulp and paper company, it was nervous about having to rely entirely on a forest owned by somebody else, even if that owner was the Government, which was also a shareholder. This Achilles heel showed when the second newsprint machine had been mooted and Tasman's vulnerability over its raw material became apparent.

Tasman's appetite for trees would massively increase with the arrival of the second machine, and the Forestry Service now wanted a higher stumpage rate of five and a half pence per cubic foot for access to the trees in the Matea Forest, with five-year reviews. The stage was set for a row.

Tasman's management and board knew that even at threepence a cubic foot they had paid a high price for the Kaingaroa Forest, especially given the poor condition of much of it, the different varieties of trees (newsprint-makers almost invariably work with one or two species of tree), and the fact that Tasman had paid for thinning the unwanted trees that the forest-owner — the Crown — would normally have had to clear at its own expense. At the same time as the Forestry Service sought five and a half pence, its other customers were paying as little as a penny a cubic foot.

The Crown — and the Forestry Service — had done well out of Kaingaroa and would continue to do so. From stumpage alone it would collect over $35 million, or $102 million at today's values, between 1955 and 1980. From dividends, share of profits and money banked from its sale of shares, the Crown would pick up a further $31 million in round figures for a grand total of nearly $67 million, or $195 million in today's dollars.

The inaccurate belief that Tasman was based on cut-price trees has long irritated JC. In fact, he points out that the figures show the Crown's total return from Tasman has been a handsome one, both in terms of stumpage and a direct share in Tasman's long stream of profits. Over the years, the forest's worth has soared. Valued then at £2.2 million ($95.5 million today), Forestry Corp now puts a price of $3 billion on Kaingaroa.

After many months of negotiations, which included a supporting appearance by the retired Pat Entrican, who — to JC's pleasure — recommended a rate of just threepence, a deal was struck at exactly that. The rate of threepence would stick until 1 August 1968. After that, the rate would go up by a halfpenny.

But Tasman's dependence on the Government's apparently diminishing goodwill worried Jim Fletcher, especially now that the original promoters of the Tasman scheme were off the scene. Sid Holland had died, Ashwin had retired, and so of course had Entrican. The Forestry Service, under a new chief, had warned Tasman it would have to look beyond Kaingaroa, and Bowaters had made it a condition of its involvement in 1960 that Tasman should set about establishing its own forests. This was a necessarily long process however, and though Tasman bought tracts of forests outright and acquired others through joint ventures, its dependence on Kaingaroa was projected to last until the turn of the century.

By 1970, the company had acquired a long-term supply of trees, but even that wasn't enough to feed the two voracious newsprint machines. Substantial additional supplies would be required before the company could contemplate a third machine. At this point, the whole game changed.

It was in the same year, 1970, after more horse-trading with the Forest Service, that Tasman was offered enough trees to take it up to 1985, provided it installed a third newsprint machine. Tasman needed the trees, but did it need the estimated $88 million price of the expansion that would apparently go with it?

Tasman's management was seriously worried about this dripfeed system of guaranteeing the company's raw material. Here was a huge capital enterprise, of vital importance to the country's foreign exchange, being granted piecemeal areas of trees at inflated prices by current standards. The much smaller but fast-growing rival Carter-Kokosaku joint venture had just won the bulk of the trees in a major tender, known as the South Kaingaroa sale. And, to JC's disbelief, Tasman had been offered from that sale slim pickings not only in terms of volume but also in quality. The species were mainly Corsican pine, not the radiata that was essential to produce world-quality newsprint on which Tasman's profits depended and where its hard-won expertise lay.

By this time, JC knew that the best line to take with civil servants was a direct one. He went straight to the Government in the form of the Cabinet's forestry subcommittee, and a meeting was fixed for 30 September 1970. There, Jim Fletcher forcefully argued his case before an astonished committee. They assured the irate Tasman chairman that the committee had told the Forest Service to supply his company with adequate wood and they couldn't understand why that hadn't happened.

The Forest Service representatives were attempting to argue their case when Jack Marshall, then Deputy Prime Minister, turned up. He promptly overruled the Forestry Service and, in due course, Tasman was promised from the state's forests 'adequate wood supplies to operate three newsprint machines'. The contracts were signed in September 1973.

That's how the No. 3 machine expansion started, at the Government of the day's specific request. It was a quid pro quo: the Crown guaranteed the supply of the raw material and Tasman bought the machine.

Like the Tasman board, the Government saw newsprint as the foundation of the NAFTA agreement, and that was its motivation to push on with a third machine. And Jim Fletcher saw that the company was between a tree and a hard place. If Tasman didn't take up the wood, the forests would be permanently assigned to another company in a period of rising demand for the forests. That's why Tasman's board fully understood that it was now or perhaps never, or certainly for another twenty-five or thirty years, for a third machine. The company was also concerned at burgeoning plans by ANM for newsprint developments and a third machine might head those off. In many ways, therefore, setting up the No. 3 machine was a pre-emptive strike.

So Tasman went ahead with plans to put in the third newsprint machine even though it was aware of the commercial weaknesses of the expansion. As JC says, 'We could see we were taking on risks. There was damn-all in it for Tasman.'

By now, labour problems were becoming serious at Tasman. In the sixties, occasional stoppages had disrupted production — a ten-day one in 1960 shortly after Bowaters had taken over management, another one in 1963, and a major one in November 1966.

But by the seventies, stoppages were common. This was practically normal in most major construction and industrial projects in New Zealand then, a situation fuelled by economic conditions and Government policy. In a wages and prices freeze, workers moved to raise take-home pay through non-wage increases — for example, through higher allowances for travel, dirt money and other items. Demarcation disputes were rife, and not even union secretaries could tame their members. Lifelong union men would tell you privately at the time of their scorn for the 'wreckers' within their labour movement with its long and honourable history.

Inflation was now rampant and labour was scarce. It was a seller's labour market, and Tasman's position was less secure than it had been in the sixties. It was steadily losing a lot of the natural competitive advantages that had nurtured it.

The stoppages weren't so much a Tasman problem as a national one. Jim Fletcher increasingly felt the solution lay primarily with the Government, and he told it so. He would often drop in to see Jack Marshall about it, and then Norman Kirk in the Labour Government. Sometimes at night, he and George Fraser would invite over Tom Skinner, then an absentee president of the Federation of Labour (in the sense that he lived in Auckland rather than in Wellington), and discuss the more serious problems with him. Skinner was nervous of the troublesome Kawerau scene, however, and never went there. Instead, he would send his deputy, the pugnacious Jim Knox, with whom Skinner was not always on the warmest of terms. Knox, who had a capacity for bluster, proved largely ineffectual against the increasingly unco-operative John Murphy. The implacable Liverpudlian was in dispute not so much with management now but with the other unions, usually over demarcation issues, where management was often powerless.

To JC's mind, the most effective union man was the often-maligned communist Bill Andersen. Like Jim Fletcher, who was often dragged into the disputes, Andersen felt that management should keep out of demarcation issues. Over time, the Tasman chairman developed a strong respect for Andersen.

Still, even with the burden of an increasingly unco-operative workforce, Tasman had to push on with the third machine. This was another Beloit-Walmsley monster, even bigger than the No. 2 machine. It would turn out 130,000 tonnes of newsprint a year, pushing up Tasman's overseas earnings by over 130 percent to $65 million a year.

In theory the timing was impeccable.

As planning for the third machine began, Tasman ran into trouble. This time it was over crippling delays to the expansion of the pulp mill. The contractors, Downer Comstock, part of the Morrison Knudsen group, Fletcher Construction's major rivals in heavy projects, ran into dreadful labour problems. By early 1974, the job was a long way over budget and eighteen months over schedule, and still hadn't been completed. Things were so bad that it threatened the viability of the entire Kawerau project, as the Government's director told the Minister of Finance in private memoranda. The board had even considered shutting down the entire job.

Ratcheting was the new word in labour relations — negotiations for every successive construction job started at the final rates paid in the last big project, no matter how high they might have been hiked. The workers got height money, depth money, heat money, dirt money, and even confined-spaces money.

Increasingly worried, JC watched as the pulp-mill contract dragged on. 'They kept on dreaming up reasons for penalty payments,' he recalls. Strike after strike stopped work until finally Tasman was forced to take over the job itself. Tasman had picked up some of the lost months, but by the time the expanded pulp mill came into production in July 1974 the pulp market was already on the way down.

Tasman had missed the boat and lost a lot of money, well over $230 million in today's dollars, in the overrun. It had been forced to go back to its bankers for extra loans. It had also lost some customers, who had been severely inconvenienced by Tasman's inability to supply them, especially during a world shortage of pulp. Tasman had the further embarrassment of invoking *force majeure* clauses in the contract — that is, pleading inability to meet its supply agreements because of conditions over which it had no control.

Things were turning sour in newsprint, too. Production had started to fall in 1973 because of industrial stoppages, and Tasman couldn't supply all its Australian customers. Lost sales through stoppages in that financial year ran at over $4 million, or $30 million now.

The company wasn't making any money in the New Zealand newsprint market either, as the local newspaper publishers resolutely held Tasman to a disastrous fifteen-year agreement. Its terms allowed for a price increase in line with inflation, which had been estimated in the contract at a maximum of 2.5 percent a year. In fact, inflation had gone mad since the contract was signed.

Tasman was clearly running into cashflow problems at the worst possible time, on the eve of the commissioning of the third machine. But there could be no turning back.

After the debacle of the pulp-mill expansion, Fletchers got the job of installing the No. 3 machine. Having helped put in the first machine as part of the Fletcher Merritt Raymond consortium and the second one with the Morrison Downer Fletcher consortium, it was the logical contractor for the job, but ironically it wasn't work Fletchers wanted. The company recognised it would have to be so tough with the most undisciplined unions that the residual ill-feeling would spread over into other Fletchers projects. JC accepted the job with great reluctance and had to pressure his construction people to take it on. No other contractor would touch it, except for Downer Comstock, whose bid the Tasman board found 'completely unacceptable'.

Fletcher Construction got the No. 3 expansion done in a labour climate so hostile that the Tasman board once secretly considered abandoning the entire project. Several major strikes disrupted the job for a total of eight weeks' work lost, or 7 percent of the available working time. The boilermakers were particularly difficult. And within Tasman, Murphy was now seeking wage increases in the high teens for his men and other unions were demanding 20 percent increases to maintain their relativity.

The third machine roared into production in November 1975, nine months late and just in time to catch a worldwide slump. Advertising was down and so was demand for newsprint as newspapers became thinner.

Practically all the figures were unfavourable. Labour problems had caused a loss of revenue of $43 million, equivalent to $250 million now. Exchange rates were moving against Tasman, and in the same year the company booked a huge $15 million loss, some $90 million now, on its overseas loans, the victim of a fluctuating currency. JC felt like Lee Iacocca when he took charge of Chrysler Corporation.

Clearly a fire-fighting job lay ahead for JC and the board. There were serious cashflow problems looming. The third machine had been financed entirely by debt, and the returns from the expansion weren't sufficient for the payments. He had told directors on 8 May 1975 that Tasman faced liquidity problems. It was a genuine crisis, though not a great surprise either to the board or the Government. As Minister of Finance, Rob Muldoon already knew about this. Records from Tasman and Treasury show that he had been regularly advised since early 1974 by the Government's own director and by Tasman's financial controller that the labour problems during the pulp-mill expansion would mean Government support would be required.

The company had to get over the hump of absorbing the twin expansions. The last, slated to cost $82.7 million, had come out at $108 million, in today's dollars nearly $700 million. It was an overrun of $25.3 million, or $147 million today. The losses on the New Zealand newsprint contracts were forcing Tasman to sell below the landed cost of imported newsprint. Annual losses on the contract were running at $20 million a year. Also, forward sales didn't look promising, especially in Australia, where the market was soft. To boot, Australian Newsprint Mills was planning to build its own newsprint plant at Albury, in New South Wales. This alone represented a grave threat to Tasman's long-term markets.

As if that weren't enough, the Government had also imposed hefty increases in power, geothermal steam and railfreight charges on Tasman.

As the major shareholder, the Government was well aware of all these developments. It had, after all, urged the No. 3 expansion on Tasman. Its director on the board always produced a summary of its affairs after each board meeting exclusively for the Finance Minister. The Government had been a party to every decision, major or minor, that the board had taken.

JC took stock of the situation. He had plenty of experience of fire-fighting and quickly mobilised a strategy. Tasman was still trading profitably but, largely because of the latest expansion, would run into danger through its debt-repayment schedule. It had run out of borrowing capacity and was already facing difficulties with the banks. Its forecasts showed a cash blowout climaxing in a negative cashflow of $40.5 million in the 1977/78 financial year, or some $184 million today. It was clearly a major shortfall.

Tasman's only recourse was to go to the Government for back-up finance, the Government being the major shareholder. JC and the board voted that the company should approach Treasury for temporary financial backing, and management duly met the Government's representatives. The date of the meeting is important — 10 March 1977.

Associate Finance Minister Hugh Templeton's account is different. He says that the board came to the Government in *May*, saying, 'We're going bankrupt, help us.' According to Templeton, the position was dire. Tasman was running out of money, wouldn't be able to cover its debt by July, the shareholders' funds (including the Government's) would be lost and the receivers would arrive at a gallop.

In fact, the board never said anything like 'we're going bankrupt, help us'. Tasman had a cashflow problem, not one of profitability. The profit was there but was slow in coming through because of debt commitments. In fact, in the so-called 'bankrupt year' of 1976/77, Tasman returned a profit of nearly $4.6 million, and in the 1977/78 financial year, when JC stepped down, a total profit of nearly $13.5 million. This last was composed of a trading profit of $4.25 million, which is the important one, plus $9.3 million in extraordinary profits.

Initially, the Government was accommodating. By May 1977, Prime Minister Muldoon had promised it would provide the requested backup finance, but only against a report into Tasman and its global business by the Development Finance Corporation. Outwardly, this seemed a sensible precaution on the Prime Minister's part, but it proved to be a disastrous temporising move.

JC was no stranger to Muldoon. He had consulted him in the mid-sixties over a technical issue relating to Marac, the full-scale finance house JC had developed out of a debt-factoring operation and of which he was chairman. Muldoon had been less than accommodating, to the extent of rushing through an order in council to block Marac from expanding into a new line of lending.

The Tasman board moved quickly. It deferred capital expenditure and tightened up its operating costs. JC put Hugh Fletcher, the third generation of the family to work with the Government, on Tasman. Hugh, just into his thirties, had proved especially adept at patient negotiation and was now deputy managing director of Fletcher Holdings under his father.

Hugh and a small team looked at what could be done to lift Tasman out of its crisis. He soon saw that Government backup finance was important, but it wasn't a long-term solution. Hugh's troubleshooters concluded that the most pressing job was to renegotiate the ruinous contract with the newspaper publishers.

Now the crisis moved into the corridors of Government power and got increasingly bitter. In May and June 1977, long before the DFC reports had been produced, Muldoon made it clear that the Government's condition for providing its backup finance was that it would make all the decisions about how to restructure Tasman. But since the Government was only one shareholder among others and was, after all, only being asked for a line of credit, this was unacceptable to the Tasman board, which, of course, included the Australians and Reed.

Jim Fletcher told the Prime Minister's office so on behalf of the non-government directors. A typically blunt reply came back — the Government would make the decisions, whatever the board might say.

While the Government temporised over the provision of its promised backup finance, the cashflow situation grew more critical. The recovery strategy was stalled. As JC had explained to Treasury, which was now deeply involved in Tasman's affairs, Fletchers didn't expect or want a Government bail-out. That was neither necessary nor desirable. Fletchers' board was willing and able to put in money on the same basis as the Crown. All that was needed to get things moving was a decision by the Government. All this delay was making a retrievable situation critical, he pointed out.

The sticking point for the board and chairman was clause 4 of Treasury's plan for restructuring Tasman. This piece of fine print gave all the power to the Crown over Tasman's future, and it simply wasn't acceptable to the Tasman board. Quite clearly, it compromised the non-government directors' own fiduciary duty to shareholders.

Clause 4 had to stay, Muldoon insisted, in a flurry of meetings, memoranda and notes throughout June. When the board refused to comply with what was in commercial terms a highly presumptuous demand, Muldoon promptly ordered the Government to withdraw its promised guarantee of Tasman's overdraft. After months of negotiation, things were back to square one.

JC was shocked. He felt that the Government, a shareholder, was playing with the future of Tasman.

Meetings followed in quick succession. On 30 June, the Tasman chairman met Templeton, who was the executor of Muldoon's strategy and head of the crisis management team the Cabinet had put together. The board intended to argue its objection to the offending clause 4. Templeton replied a few days later, on 4 July, confirming that Muldoon's position hadn't budged. Although the Government did not want to gain complete control of the company, Templeton wrote, there could be a problem with bankers if Tasman's annual general meeting, which was just sixteen days away, heard that the Government was withdrawing its support. This was highly confrontational.

It seemed to JC and the board that the Government was now risking the company's future to gain its objectives. Under duress and with great reluctance, the Tasman directors signed the deed and the offending clause 4 at the next board meeting. The date was 21 September 1977, a full half-year after JC had sought the Government's co-operation.

In spite of this lengthy timetable, Templeton maintains that the Government's performance over Tasman showed 'how remarkably good the Muldoon Government was in a crisis'.

Through Templeton, the Government had actually put Tasman in play, in commercial parlance, in the intervening period. That is, offered it for sale to potential bidders. By any standards, this was an astonishing cheek for one shareholder among others — albeit a dominant one with 34 percent — especially without the knowledge of the board.

Templeton had quietly called on Reginald Smythe of NZ Forest Products in June and asked whether he might be interested in investing in Tasman and what might be done to sort out the company. Smythe, who had impeccable commercial ethics, quickly contacted Jim Fletcher and told him what had transpired. Smythe was as surprised by Templeton's visit as anybody (and, in fact, passed on to JC his notes of these unexpected high-level contacts).

As it happened, Smythe was thinking along the same lines as JC. He didn't want to buy in, but he felt that Tasman's unwieldy board structure — New Zealanders, the Crown, Australians, the British — was the real problem. Fletchers should act to rid Tasman of the albatross of its board structure, Smythe told his old friend and commercial foe.

In the early days of Tasman, the board — including the Government, ANM, Bowater-Reed, Fletchers, the public — had been a compromise necessitated by the vast sums of capital to be raised. But in the 1970s, things had changed and some of the inherent tensions in the structure had appeared. Still, JC looks back warmly on the board's achievements: 'I think Father and I did a bloody good job of getting a potentially difficult and disparate board to work harmoniously together with demonstrable results.'

Much later, JC learned that Templeton had dangled Tasman in front of Carter, at that time head of a company much smaller than Tasman and a most unlikely saviour, to Caxton, and even to Winstones. This last was even more amazing, but Templeton was certainly acting under Muldoon's orders. Caxton's John Spencer, who the DFC people believed had 'the entrepreneurial flair lacking in Tasman', would have sold Tasman offshore. According to a preliminary plan, the Spencers would have put in $7 million cash before folding it into a $14 million joint venture with the Times Publishing Company of Singapore. Tasman would have been the first major Singaporean investment in New Zealand, some fifteen years ahead of the wave of money arriving from the small island state.

The long-awaited DFC report on restructuring options for Tasman had by now arrived and formed the basis for a Cabinet committee meeting on 4 August, chaired by Muldoon. Though the report obviously had direct relevance to all the shareholders, the Government kept all the important information to itself and released only the most general material. JC first saw the report nearly twenty years later, after Fletcher Challenge obtained it under the Official Information Act. Quite apart from the propriety of excluding the other shareholders from seeing the report, much of the document's information was wrong, its conclusions misconceived and the recommendations, especially its more sweeping ones, quite wild. Had the Government brought some of the DFC's findings to the board, it could have been reassured about the more dire ones.

The report didn't have many good things to say about Tasman's performance. But its major assumption, put bluntly, was that Tasman was a basket case and something had to be done. All the report's conclusions and proposals stemmed from that. When he read years later the report's views on whether this huge and largely thriving company should be put into liquidation or receivership, JC could hardly believe his eyes.

The DFC's essential points numbered four. First, the board wasn't working effectively. Jim Fletcher was far too busy to do his job effectively as chairman (he had eight outside directorships at the time, which indeed was probably too many) and the Government hadn't 'exercised the control over the board that could be expected of the dominant shareholder'. (The Crown had four representatives.) The sometimes conflicting nature of the board's structure had to be sorted out. (With this, JC could agree.)

Second, the senior management was not 'a strong team', was 'unco-ordinated in terms of future planning' and lacked direction in matters of marketing, finance and general commercial operations. In fact, Bowaters had fulfilled all of JC's expectations when he had brought its management skills back in from 1960. JC remains completely nonplussed by the DFC's repeated criticism of Tasman's marketing skills. 'How can you sell more than 100 percent of what you produce?' he asks rhetorically. 'Almost alone in the industry, Tasman had been fully sold for the last twenty years.'

Third, a strong senior partner had to be found for Tasman, and this could be (much smaller) companies like Carter-Oji Kokusaku (a joint venture with Japan), Caxton or NZ Forest Products.

Fourth, the Government should be prepared to subsidise its charges to the plant such as those for power.

Jim Fletcher wasn't surprised by the DFC report's mistakes — 'they didn't know the first bloody thing about the pulp and paper industry' — but he was certainly upset at its conclusions. And he was dumbfounded that the Government had, as he puts it, 'happily offered Tasman to NZ Forest Products, which would have created a real monopoly, to Carter, and even to Winstones. It's an abiding mystery.' By the time he got hold of the report, twenty years late, there was of course nothing he could do. And, anyway, it didn't matter by then.

The minutes of that first meeting to discuss the report show some significant misapprehensions. For example, the Cabinet committee was told that 'Fletchers had been involved in the management of the company since its inception and that this had been unsatisfactory to date'. The minutes also noted that concern had been expressed 'at the prospect of Tasman continuing operations under its existing management'.

In fact, Fletchers had never had anything to do with managing Tasman, although it often wished it had. Reed and Bowaters had successively held the management contracts. The powers of a non-executive chairman, as Jim Fletcher and his father were, are limited. And, until the previous two years, Tasman had been a success in terms of earnings, foreign exchange, employment, technical know-how and profits, despite an initial period of indifferent management. The Crown's four directors on the Tasman board had, of course, more influence on Tasman than Fletchers' two directors, but this did not seem to carry any weight with Cabinet.

By this time, Muldoon had clearly decided for his own reasons that Jim Fletcher had to go, and he had been talking to possible replacements for the Tasman chairman. These included Ron Trotter, then chief executive of rural-based Challenge Corporation. By 16 September, Templeton had put to Muldoon the names of three potential replacements for Jim Fletcher — Trotter, John Ingram or Allan Hellaby. But the strong-minded Challenge man was clearly the frontrunner. He had been approached by Templeton and given a full copy of the DFC report, from which the Tasman board and management had been excluded. Things were clearly moving quickly against JC.

On 29 September, Jim Fletcher returned from overseas to meet Templeton. (Muldoon never seemed to be available.) The junior minister explained to the veteran industrialist what was happening and added that the Government had to act in this way 'to ensure the survival of Tasman'.

To JC, this was complete nonsense. Tasman had run into a serious but only temporary cashflow problem. Had the Government moved quickly and maintained its offer of a guarantee for a new line of credit to tide Tasman over, everything would have been fine. He pointed out it had been the Government's insistence on playing the sole hand in the 'restructuring' and then delaying decisions for month after month that had made things far worse than they should have been.

He sought another meeting, this time on 3 October, and he brought Hugh with him. Hugh tackled the Government on clause 4. He told the ministers it was something of an insult for Fletchers to take a back seat to Government-appointed directors, given the company's history and commitment to Tasman.

The Prime Minister, however, was clearly heavily influenced by the Treasury view. According to the mandarins, Jim Fletcher should stay on the board for just one reason: 'Theirs is a New Zealand rather than an overseas shareholding. In other ways they have little to offer,' its officers wrote in one report.

Like the rest of the board, the Australians, who had a far better insight into Tasman's long-term performance, didn't want Jim Fletcher to go as chairman. Bob Falkingham, one of the powers in the huge Fairfax publishing empire in Sydney, told Templeton in a meeting that the chairman's departure would cause problems with the ANM people. JC's business friends went in to bat for him, too, and lobbied Templeton. (The associate minister remembers them 'all saying, "Can't poor old Jim stay, you know, a terrible thing, to oust him from the board." ') Falkingham added that ANM was unhappy with the composition of the proposed new board, which would mean Tasman would be run by the Government and the workers.

Templeton gave the Australian the same answer he had given JC earlier — Tasman's survival required Government dominance. The Government's position was absolutely inflexible.

Finally, Treasury's grand plan went before the board on 5 November. The directors — and especially JC in the chairman's seat — read the plan with mounting disbelief.

The Government, which held 34 percent, would appoint four directors, including the chairman. ANM, which held 20.6 percent, would have two directors. Fletchers, which was negotiating to buy Reed's share and would in all probability end up with a 30.6 percent stake, would have only one director. Authorised capital would be increased by $75 million. The Treasury report called the restructuring a 'rescue'.

It became very clear to Jim Fletcher that the Government held him responsible for the cash crisis and was determined to get both him and Fletcher Holdings out, or reduce them to a practically ornamental role.

The other directors were livid. They unanimously opposed the restructuring, opposed the term 'rescue', opposed the increase in authorised capital, and opposed JC's removal as chairman. It was a standoff. The Government's representative went back, reporting the board's united resentment and adding that 'all groups strongly oppose the replacement of the present chairman'.

Privately, however, Jim Fletcher decided that Tasman was more important than his own ego, so he went to Templeton and indicated that he was willing to have Ron Trotter appointed deputy chairman immediately and have him take over as chairman in a few months. He was offering an olive branch, but the Government didn't want Fletchers in the driving seat any longer than necessary.

There were more meetings, with Hugh Fletcher becoming more prominent. He met Templeton and strongly argued for a more leisurely restructuring. Where was the urgency and where was the benefit of the Government's strategy? he wanted to know. Why not a staggered programme of reorganisation that would address Tasman's acknowledged problems? These would comprise changes in marketing and management, in Bowaters' sales agreements, and in the shareholdings, where Fletchers was trying to buy out Reed. In 1974, Bowaters had sold out of Tasman to the Crown and Fletchers, but the sales contracts they had signed remained in force. Here was the Crown doing an about-face and attempting to distance itself from Tasman. Where was the Government's strategy and sense of continuity?

Hugh also urged Templeton to talk with ANM to slow down or stop its plans for its own mill. After all, he said, the 150,000-tonne newsprint market in Australia was absolutely vital to Tasman. Surely this was of critical long-term importance? Hugh felt he had got nowhere.

Acting for the board, Jim Fletcher now bounced back with a request for Tasman to have time to put its own proposals. It did, after all, know the business much better than Treasury or the DFC. Treasury, however, didn't like this and kept on presenting ultimatums to the board to buy the Government's 'restructuring' strategy or face the withdrawal of all financial Government support.

Unable to penetrate this brick wall, JC finally telexed Templeton on 16 November. Was it not possible, he asked, 'for us to adopt a co-operative rather than an adversary attitude?' He probably meant adversarial, but Templeton got the message and enlisted Trotter's intervention. The Government's preferred choice as chairman promptly telephoned Jim Fletcher and they talked long and hard about the restructuring plans.

And so it went on. Hugh Fletcher got back to Templeton with a proposal that sought a fairer representation on the board but accepted that his father would stand down in favour of Trotter. In putting up these strategies, Hugh accepted Templeton's assurances that he had solved what the young Fletcher regarded as Tasman's biggest headache — the disastrous inflation-proofed agreement with the New Zealand newspaper proprietors. The minister was confident that he had agreed on a timetable with the newspaper proprietors that would soon see them paying world parity, or prevailing world prices, for newsprint. Despite JC's strong reservations about the Government's actions, this was the major reason he finally accepted it. At least Tasman would be rid of this financial albatross.

The Government's subcommittee accepted some of the proposals and put them to Muldoon, who was in San Francisco. He promptly rejected them, obviously on the grounds that there was still too much of Fletchers in them. Muldoon's decision was completely wrong-headed. What had ripped Tasman's short-term earnings apart was near-anarchy in industrial relations during the capital works, runaway underlying inflation, for which a wages and prices freeze was nothing more than a band-aid, and an expansion into a third newsprint machine at the Government's request. It certainly wasn't mismanagement or inadequate financial control, as Muldoon continued to insist (or had been led to believe). Privately, JC was appalled at the Prime Minister's obduracy and arrogance. He must have often regretted the passing of those early, productive years of co-operation with a supportive Government.

By now, the entire Fletcher Holdings board was seriously concerned with the way the Government was playing about with the company. The directors sought and got a meeting with the Prime Minister on 2 December. It was now nine months since JC's original meeting with Muldoon and since the whole saga had begun. In all that time, while the ball lay in the Government's court, none of the essential repair work had been done, even though JC and the board had been eager to get on with the job.

Muldoon outfaced the board. On the substantive issues — that the Government would lead the restructuring and the chairman had to go — he didn't budge. He did, however, make minor concessions, such as extending the date of Trotter's accession to the chairmanship to 1978. But he promised these 'concessions' only provided Fletchers went ahead and bought Reed's shares. Once again, JC's conviction that governments make unreliable long-term commercial partners was confirmed.

The changing of the guard was announced by Muldoon. Having got his way, he produced a graceful statement that recognised Jim Fletcher's long contribution to Tasman and attributed his departure as chairman to his, JC's, own desire. Aged sixty-two, JC stepped down at the 1978 annual general meeting and Trotter took over with the extra power of executive chairman.

There could be no doubt that Muldoon had won, and JC acknowledged it. He wrote a gentleman's letter — on 16 December 1977 — to the Prime Minister in which he acknowledged the 'considerate manner in which the negotiations were concluded and the subsequent announcements handled'.

The letter went on: 'I hope that for my part I've shown I'm not a bad loser. Tasman will now be an even bigger and more crucial investment for Fletchers and you can be assured that we shall continue to do our utmost to promote its prosperity. And have no doubt it is a sound and worthwhile investment for New Zealand.' JC also pleaded for Government recognition of the 'militant, even explosive, labour-relations atmosphere' at Tasman. It was a polite way of reminding Muldoon what was really wrong.

Muldoon's five-line reply was brief to the point of terseness and did not take up any points about good or bad losers. Basically, the letter wished Jim Fletcher a happy and prosperous New Year, and that was that.

Now Jim Fletcher looks back on that period with some resentment. Here were the early days of NAFTA and huge opportunities for Tasman and New Zealand, all of it threatened by industrial troubles, by a procrastinating Government that was unable to co-operate on the guarantee of a $10 million line of credit — essentially just short-term financial assistance — to enable Tasman to stay within its banking covenants. It had meant a six-month battle and a draconian restructuring. 'They completely tied us up because they spent months on that first DFC report that said that Tasman was doomed,' he remembers. 'The result was that the Government put us on the sidelines and got us [Tasman] into real trouble.'

As it happened, the Bank of New Zealand told the Tasman board later that it would have been quite happy to provide the $10 million overdraft even without a Government guarantee. But here's the irony — the money was never needed. A small percentage of it was drawn down, but only to maintain the facility.

JC remains especially perplexed by the Government's refusal to let Fletchers pump money into Tasman in equal proportions to its own. He's since seen a Treasury report that said — on what evidence, he doesn't know — that Fletchers probably couldn't raise the money.

'We were ropable,' Jim Fletcher says with his customary forthrightness. 'Because we had said that if it's a question of additional money, Fletchers will guarantee its share with the Government. We wanted to be part of it.

'Muldoon said, "No. The Government's going to take control," which was a total abuse of its position as a shareholder. They put us in this impossible position themselves by the dilatory way they went about things.'

For his part, Templeton maintains it was inevitable that Jim Fletcher would lose control of the restructuring. 'The problem was that Jim Fletcher expected still to lead the decision-making, but he had given his hand away the moment he and the board came and gave it into the hands of the Government,' he says. 'At that point, the Government's prestige was involved and we had to call the shots.'

Is that a fair way of putting it? Hardly. Jim Fletcher had simply done the chairman's job. He had advised Treasury and the Prime Minister of a cashflow blip that was repairable with Government help. Prestige shouldn't have come into it. A simple yes or no to the provision of the Government guarantee would have done the job. Call the shots? The Government was a shareholder, which is a commercial partnership, nothing more nor less.

Jim Fletcher was disturbed to discover later, as was Hugh and the board, that there was no new agreement with the newspaper proprietors on the ruinously low domestic price of newsprint, as they had been led to believe. In a 1987 interview, Templeton claimed the Tasman board had not tackled the newspaper proprietors — 'nobody had the guts to go to the newspapers'. He claimed Tasman 'should have gone ahead on a *force majeure* basis, taken them to court, anything should have been done, they could have got the Government to help them with that'.

In fact, from the time that inflation took off in the early 1970s, Tasman had put continual pressure on the newspaper proprietors. It had spent hundreds of thousands of dollars on legal fees to try and find a way around a contract that was bleeding the company. The board had also considered invoking *force majeure*, but legal opinion indicated that they would lose heavily in damages by doing so.

Moreover, JC had repeatedly tried to enlist the aid of the Government directors on Tasman to get the Government to help, but to no avail. In fact, everything had been done.

As it happened, Templeton's confidence that he had talked the proprietors around and would get domestic newsprint prices up to world parity within eighteen months proved unfounded. Though the Newspaper Proprietors Association conceded minor increases, mainly in the form of *ex gratia* payments just large enough to keep Tasman afloat, the proprietors refused to budge and held Tasman to the contract. Parity with world prices wouldn't occur until 1983, when the fifteen-year contract ran out. The cumulative losses from Tasman's disastrous deal totalled well over $100 million, even in yesterday's dollars.

Jim Fletcher doesn't absolve himself of blame in Tasman's problems. He knows he should have taken a tougher line with the Tasman management, and especially with the chief executive in 1977, Warwick Olsen, who was ill. 'I was grievously at fault,' is the veteran industrialist's judgment on himself.

He believes he should have fought like an alley cat to force the Government to guarantee the funds much faster than it did, or at least to clear the way for an alternative solution. This would have removed most of the pressure and incidentally the Government's *raison d'être* for interfering in Tasman. He acknowledges he was uncharacteristically subdued in forcing an effective response to the Government's heavy-handed interference.

But neither Jim Fletcher nor Tasman could solve inflation or labour unrest — that was clearly the Government's job. They went together, like terrible twins. In times of double-digit inflation, labour demanded double-digit wage rises. And JC still insists that, together, these were Tasman's undoing in those two hectic years. The irony of the situation Tasman found itself in was that it had been the Government's wish to push on with the No. 3 expansion. Had it been a purely commercial decision, Tasman would probably have turned it down.

In an interview after he had lost office, Muldoon was evasive on the Tasman saga. His principal point was that the Government was 'most reluctant to give Government guarantees'. Tasman's was one of the last. Of the issues of Jim Fletcher's ousting, the dealings with shareholders, the full meeting with the board, the DFC report, the Treasury proposals, he professed complete ignorance. 'I've never heard the slightest suggestion that Sir James should be removed as chairman because he wasn't doing the job or he wasn't doing it in the best interests of all the shareholders. That would be quite wrong,' Muldoon insisted.

There could be no doubt, though, as the *Dominion* newspaper noted in an article, that Jim Fletcher had departed 'by Government edict', not by the vote of his fellow-directors.

Trotter, who still has the fog-horn voice of the stock auctioneer he once was, proved a forceful executive chairman. Throughout the fraught ten months, he had behaved correctly and warmly to Jim Fletcher. He certainly wanted the chairman's job, but it was the Government that had asked him to take it. And it had been Trotter who had argued for the delay in Jim Fletcher's stepping-down. JC quickly learned to respect and get on with his replacement as chairman at Tasman.

Trotter, who lived in Wellington, had the ear of Government. He was on first-name terms with most of the ministers and sometimes went on Sunday morning walks with Templeton.

Tasman's liquidity quickly improved. However, pulp and paper markets being highly cyclical and volatile, the company actually posted an operating loss in his first year as chairman — nearly $6.6 million in red ink before turning around the next year on rising markets. The Government, or rather Treasury, never fully understood how vulnerable a pulp and paper company is to its international markets and how quickly Tasman could swing from losses to profits.

One benefit of the fracas was that the board, which had by now outlived its purpose, was restructured. In any event, the original members had departed, Jim Fletcher excepted, which made decisions much cleaner.

An essential question remains: would Tasman have been restructured without this stormy ten months? Almost definitely. The board had drawn up its plans and had started implementing them even before JC's first meeting with Muldoon.

The new board immediately made a signficant and overdue management change. Carl Ryan, a Fletcher man and Sir Ronald's choice, became chief executive and brought in a series of reforms, especially with productivity-driven labour agreements.

But the new chief could not protect Tasman from endemic labour problems. In 1977, major disputes stopped production thirteen times, knocking $10 million off sales, or $43 million now. The worst stoppage was a forty-three-day strike starting in March 1978, which cost $24 million and helped to plunge Tasman into loss.

Carl Ryan worked hard on improving relations with the unions, all fourteen of them, on the site. Working conditions improved. Housing was upgraded. Communications between management and staff were made smoother.

Business is full of recurring ironies. Eventually, Muldoon's intervention did Fletchers an enormous favour.

In January 1978, Fletchers agreed on a price with Reed and bought out its shareholding. After fifteen years, British expertise wasn't needed any more and had, in fact, become an obstacle to Tasman's growth. The deal, which Treasury had said Fletchers probably couldn't afford to do, made Fletchers into Tasman's main shareholder. This was the very scenario Muldoon had sought to avoid. Next, in December of the same year, ANM sold its shareholding. Now the way was clear for a company of genuine international size and status to be formed.

When the Crown sold its share of a revitalised, cash-rich Tasman in September 1979, for which Ron (later Sir Ronald) Trotter takes the credit after he persuaded Muldoon that the Crown should cash in its profits on the shares, Fletchers bought 81 percent and sold on a third to Challenge Corporation. Tasman was now wholly New Zealand-owned by Fletchers, Challenge and the public.

Chapter 8

Second Son of the Second Son

Hugh had been at his father's side since his mid-twenties but he had joined the company before then. He had started in the executive boondocks in 1969 — as assistant to the operations research officer for Fletcher Industries — and then won a Harkness Scholarship, which took him to Stanford University in California. There could be no doubt that young Hugh, second of the three sons, was bright. At Auckland University he obtained a BSc in mathematics and an MCom with first-class honours in economics, and at Stanford he completed a Master of Business Administration with distinction.

When he came back to Penrose in 1972, he became personal assistant to the managing director, who was, of course, his dad. He also got an executive job as general manager of the company's trust and investment group.

In 1976, aged just twenty-eight, he moved up again, this time to deputy managing director. This was the top executive job in all but name. JC was ready to hand it over — in fact, he had been ready for three or four years. Progressively, young Hugh came to run the company. By 1 January 1980 he was in the top job and his father became non-executive chairman of Fletchers.

Like his father thirty-seven years earlier, who had respected his son's need to establish his own mark on the company, JC moved to another part of the building to give his son the distance and space he needed to plough his own furrow.

For some years it had been obvious that JC was tiring. Whether because of the strain of the labour- and politics-bedevilled expansions at Tasman or just because of the accumulating strain of over a third of a century in the job, of all the travel, of hundreds of board meetings, JC was showing signs of weariness. He could get irascible. He had fallen ill several times, though never seriously He was still going into the office at 6.30 a.m. but when he got home at night he would fall asleep almost immediately. Vaughan and the boys were worried about his health. His blood pressure was high. He didn't look well.

JC wanted to hand power over, preferably to one of his sons. But, mindful of propriety, he felt he shouldn't be the one to raise the subject.

The executives took it into their own hands. It was too important to be let drift. They discussed the subject candidly at a meeting, then one of them, Barrie Downey, was chosen to tell the boss that a decision about a new managing director had to be made as soon as possible and that the appointment should be Hugh. They all felt he had earned his spurs. 'In many ways, he was superior to his father,' notes one executive.

Downey saw JC at the earliest opportunity and explained things in the candid style encouraged at Fletchers. 'Jim, we think you've got to stop stuffing around,' he told the boss in his office. 'Hugh should be made your successor. It should be widely publicised. And he should be effectively operational chief of the company from now on. We'll get in behind. I can assure you that this is what we all want to happen.'

JC listened without a word, then said 'Thank you', and Downey left after the shortest conversation he could ever recall with his boss.

A senior director then approached the executives individually to sound them out. The procedure was impeccable. JC was exceedingly sensitive to any charge of nepotism because he knew a clumsily executed transition of power would impose a burden his son would have to carry for his entire commercial life. Individually, the executives confirmed what Downey had told JC, and Hugh was named in 1976 as his official successor, four years before he became managing director.

Though it was what he had wanted, JC found it tough to hand power over and suffered some withdrawal symptoms. But if he occasionally saw the new team make mistakes, he kept his mouth shut. As Hugh remembers it, his father was 'very generous in his transference of authority'. In time, JC came to be seen as the company's elder statesman.

Though he is shy in manner like his father, Hugh was more reflective, and more calculating in assessing the ramifications of commercial strategy, less blinded by enthusiasm. Their similarities are greater than their differences however. As Hugh put it in a television interview soon after taking over: '[The Fletcher style] is a willingness to take risks, to try new processes, to try new marketing methods . . . It goes with our greater tolerance to admit to and accept failure or mistakes . . . We like to think that we are very informal, that anyone can tell anybody that he thinks [the other's] ideas are stupid, and there is no personal animosity as a result. We do get very open debate out of that. Out of that, we think, comes better decisions . . . [It's] also more fun in the workplace, which, after all, is a lot of people's lives. It's a bit ridiculous unless they also enjoy it.'

At Stanford University, Hugh had been shown how incoming chief executives often feel a need to assert themselves and make their mark by doing things differently from their predecessors. This often produces mistakes, but that didn't happen at Fletchers because the transition was orderly, not the result of political machinations or executive bloodbath.

History had repeated itself. The second son took the top job.

It might be a lesson for all commercial dynasties, however, that Jim, the first-born by three years, felt that the issue of the succession should have been discussed openly within the family. Much later, Jim told his father so.

The Fletcher boys had grown up with the business. As a preoccupied businessman, JC probably wasn't the complete father. As Vaughan puts it, her husband's holidays were dictated by the business rather than by family requirements. All three boys accepted that their father would be away a lot and his all-too-few appearances at home couldn't compensate for the long absences. But there were good times at Penrose nevertheless.

Sometimes all four, father and sons, would play cricket in the backyard. The boys were a rumbustious, noisy, vigorous, demanding, turf-defending, rough-and-tumble threesome. The two youngest used to play almost endless cricket 'tests', in which Hugh would be England and Angus Australia. The rules were inventive and complicated. They would toss a coin to choose who would bat or bowl, and one side mightn't get to bat for a week. They would argue about the score, about whether one of them was out lbw, about how many 'batsmen' were out. You could get caught off the wall, and off the roof as the fielder (also the bowler) would rush around the house trying to guess from which guttering the ball would bounce, but the scores would still run into hundreds.

Both brothers acknowledge that Hugh was a cunning lateral thinker even then. Although Angus claims he 'was an infinitely better batsman than Hugh, a better cricketer', Hugh won more than his fair share of games because he was a smart tactician and would adopt one-day tactics by bowling negatively outside the leg stump.

Not long ago, the father and sons were reminiscing about these epic contests. 'I always remember, Dad,' recalled Angus, 'when you played once you hit the ball off the ground about that high . . .'

'Beautiful shot,' interrupted JC.

'. . . it went off the ground straight through the window of the main room and the glass must have been as old as the house, which would be eighty years old at that time, at least. It left a mark no bigger than the cricket ball. It went clean through, as if the hole was made with a diamond cutter. Remember that?'

Hugh: 'Tremendous.'

Angus: 'Beautiful glass.'

Jim: 'It got us off all sorts of misdemeanours for weeks after that.'

JC: 'It was a complete accident.'

They also played rugby, using the hydrangeas as sidelines and two convenient trees as goalposts, or cricket indoors when it was raining, with miniature bats made up from a shoeduster with a string tied around it.

The boys learned negotiating skills at their parents' knees. Hugh remembers how he drove a hard bargain with his mother by extracting a rate of fifty cents an hour to do the weeding. Usually, JC being away, it was Vaughan who took the tough line, and he is happy to acknowledge it.

'I had long since abdicated all responsibility or authority to Vaughan. I was just an innocent bystander, by and large,' he recalls.

'A Pontius Pilate's approach to management,' jokes Hugh.

The boys crashed the family cars a few times, but without injury to themselves or others. They got regularly ticked off by Vaughan, Angus especially so. He was the most socially assured of the three, the most popular, and the most easy-going. She remembers the time she made Angus catch a bus to university after he had bent his car for the fourth time. Not a new one, incidentally, but one of the very much used ones that the boys typically drove.

'I'll have to borrow your car, Mum,' he announced. 'I'm late for my eleven o'clock lecture.'

'Darling, this time you are going by bus,' she replied.

'But, Mum, I don't know how to catch a bus.'

'Darling, it's time you learned . . .'

'So he caught the bus,' Vaughan recalls. 'He thinks I'm tough.'

The parallels with the previous generation are compelling — conversations with their father would often revolve around his work. The boys would rifle his briefcases and pull out confidential documents and ask him about them. As teenagers, they remember holiday discussions about superannuation schemes!

As boys they often played on Saturdays in little carts in the plywood factory while JC went through papers in the office. Some of the best times were on their two holidays a year, when they would drive down to Wellington in the Bentley, stopping by the roadside to have a picnic by the river, the boys playing with sticks in the stream's current, their parents mixing Scotch with the river water.

They were never groomed for work at Fletcher Holdings, and they were never told there was a job for them there. JC studiously avoided saying 'yes' if the boys ever asked whether he wanted them in the company. Vaughan usually put it this way: 'We'll give you a good education and you do what you like.'

Jim started as an accountant in Fletcher Steel and held several demanding jobs within the company before leaving for the commercial world outside. Jim, the son with the ready smile, died on the last day of 1993, stabbed at his Bay of Plenty holiday home after surprising an intruder. Aged 49, he had just rejoined the company. In May 1993, he had been appointed executive chairman of Fletcher Construction.

Angus, who used to work on construction sites on holidays to boost his spare cash, started well down the ladder, like his brothers, and moved on to management jobs such as chief executive of Residential Construction.

Thus the sons had, in their different ways, become part of the company just as their father was easing himself out.

Chapter 9

A Legacy

JC was knighted in the 1980 New Year's list, the year he retired as managing director. Flattery embarrasses JC but even he was pleased by the telegrams, letters and phone calls he and Vaughan got when the knighthood was announced. They came from governors-general, lords, baronets and knights from Australia to England, from the Bechtels and other American construction mates, from Hobday in England, from the Bowaters, from Evelyn de Rothschild, Japanese captains of industry, the most blue-chip of the City of London's merchant banks, from hunting and horse-racing mates, even from the USSR ambassador to New Zealand (a few days before he was expelled). Some of the communications were formal congratulations, but most rejoiced in the award. Many old friends reckoned it was one of the few knighthoods that had been truly earned. 'No man can have spent more time hard at work at home or more hours in aeroplanes,' wrote one Australian business acquaintance.

The most irreverent note came from Dick Sandwell, the Vancouver-based pulp and paper consultant and collector of the memorabilia of Pacific explorers such as Captain Cook. He advised JC to give Lady Vaughan 'a kiss and pat on the bottom for me'.

In thirty-seven years Sir James had straddled several different styles of economy, dealt with no less than eight New Zealand prime ministers and eleven different governments, done business in economic regimes ranging from the most protected to the laissez-faire, had embraced offshore possibilities when many business contemporaries were frightened of the wider commercial world, had launched two huge new industries — pulp and paper, and steel — and a lot of minor ones.

If you looked back over almost four decades of commerce and related them to what befell most of Fletcher Holdings' contemporaries, you would have to say that survival, let alone such huge turnover, was unlikely. Most big New Zealand manufacturing companies had already fallen into outside or overseas hands, or would do so within the decade: Winstones, Wattie's, Carter Holt, NZ Forest Products, Caxton. Nearly all the major contractors had long since disappeared. One of the few domestic companies to survive and thrive was Wilson and Horton, which also has a tradition of family involvement.

Some of Fletchers' overseas associates over the years had also — or would — run into trouble, oddly enough, for dynastic reasons. The Sydney giant Fairfax and Sons fell to a Canadian publisher after being nearly ruined by a junior member of the dynasty. Even the mighty Kaiser empire got into difficulties and was dismembered. There's no guarantee that family succession will make a company endure and succeed; often it's the reverse. Bowaters, for example, lost its way after the autocratic Sir Eric died.

Fletchers, by contrast, prospered. The removal in 1979 of the Crown and other corporate shareholders in Tasman paved the way for the three-way merger on 5 January 1981 of Fletcher Holdings (of which Hugh was now chief executive), Ron Trotter's Challenge Corporation and Tasman. It created easily New Zealand's biggest company, Fletcher Challenge. It was quickly dubbed 'New Zealand Inc' by the business world.

The merger wasn't without tensions. Although Challenge was the junior partner, Trotter wanted both the chairman's and chief executive's job. But, of course, at this time JC was still at the head of the board and the spiritual parent of the merger, having expanded Fletchers beyond recognition since 1942 and launched and nurtured Tasman. There's no doubt that most people in his position would have refused to step down. But had JC not done so, insiders say the merger would not have proceeded. 'It would have killed the merger,' notes a senior executive. 'So Sir James fell on the sword.'

For the good of the company, JC agreed to move upstairs to the new non-executive job of president. The merger was saved and within seven years Hugh Fletcher was at the helm.

But Tasman still laboured under the unresolved problem of its crippling and antagonistic industrial relations. It was the mid-eighties before that changed. 'A new national attitude toward militant unionism,' as JC puts it, helped bring about reform. On that issue, Ron Trotter was of the same mind.

A bitter and costly showdown in 1986 signalled management's intention to regain control of Tasman. After one wildcat strike after another, all unions on the site understood that something had to be done, except Murphy's Pulp and Paper Workers Union. The town of Kawerau had been brought almost to its knees because of the increasingly erratic pay rates. 'By now, almost everybody was of the same mind,' recalls Garry Mace, who had taken over management of Tasman in 1983. The Federation of Labour had also had its troubles with Murphy, who had been in and out of its membership on ideological grounds.

So Tasman voted to take the stoppage. It lasted three months and cost $25 million. In the middle of it, Murphy quietly left for his native Liverpool and did not return until the confrontation was over. He now lives quietly in a more peaceful and settled Kawerau.

After that, through management mending fences by sharing all company information with its workforce and other modern industrial relations strategies, Tasman returned to international competitiveness through higher productivity, introduction of new technology, and general efficiencies.

JC has outlived nearly all his business contemporaries. His unlikely associate George Fraser, remembered widely as the chairman of the New Zealand Telethon trust, died in 1986 at the age of seventy. Sir Woolf Fisher, Sir Reg Smythe and many others died either in harness or shortly after retiring. His brother John, the frustrated scholar, died in 1984 at the age of seventy-one in the South Island, where he had gone reluctantly so many years earlier but which he had come to love. Sir Robert Muldoon died in 1992, soon after retiring from politics.

To say that JC has retired is probably a misuse of the word. He often arrives at Fletcher Challenge House in Penrose at 6.30 a.m. for a day's work. There's plenty to occupy him, with many people and organisations wanting his time. He chairs the art committee, which oversees the biggest private collection of exclusively New Zealand art outside a public gallery. Its paintings are not confined to a showcase foyer or some exclusive room. Instead, Fletcher Challenge's full-time art curator makes sure that paintings hang in the office of everybody who wants them; they even hang in the canteens.

JC's outside interests have increased dramatically with retirement. With his sons, he runs two deer-farming investments — a herd of purebred Hungarian deer at Mount Hutt in the South Island and a red-deer herd at Raroa, near Broadlands on the Rotorua–Taupo road. In the mid-eighties, JC took on the breeding of Pere David deer, a rare variety, with inverted antlers, originating in the Chinese emperor's own herd, in partnership with the Bedfords of Woburn Abbey. But it's his horses he loves the best.

JC and Vaughan's racing career is catalogued in half a dozen huge scrapbooks scrupulously maintained by her. They have raced horses continuously since the 1940s but have never enjoyed the victories as much as now, because they have time to see their horses run.

Racing in the distinctive colours of the Fletcher tartan, Mr Tiz ran up seven Group One victories between 1989 and 1991 in New Zealand and Australian sprint classics. He turned out to be one of the best New Zealand sprinters since the war, including a sensational last to first win in the Galaxy, an 1100 metre $A250,000 Group One race at Sydney's Randwick track. Javelin and Morar are top gallopers, and other horses are coming through.

It's a wealthy man's sport but difficult to make money from. After the expenses of training, transport and insurance, and fees for veterinarians, jockeys and trainers, what's left is the pleasure. It's not the gambling that appeals to JC — he rarely punts. He likes to talk with people and watch the horses win, preferably his own. 'When you breed a horse, it's very easy to get caught up in following the breed,' he says. These days, the formidably successful O'Sullivan family train the Fletchers' horses.

When somebody retires, it's time to take stock. By 1979, Jim Fletcher had been in commercial harness for thirty-seven years. In all that time he had been a seven-days-a-week businessman, toiling to achieve his father's dream, assiduously justifying his appointment at the age of twenty-seven. In all of JC's actions there's discernible a strong element of filial obligation, of meeting his father's expectations. He clearly felt that he had been *entrusted* with the company, and he went at it as though it were a mission.

James Fletcher senior died in 1974. By then he had had all the evidence he could have needed about the rightness of his decision to appoint his namesake back in 1942. His second son had converted the construction company bequeathed him into the New Zealand equivalent of a Japanese *zaibatsu,* the kind of company that powered Japan into becoming a world economic power. A *zaibatsu* is a commercial combine or conglomerate spanning a multitude of business areas while controlled by one or a few families, and Fletchers had become just about as diversified and big as was possible in a small economy.

Fletcher had expanded into timber, pulp and newsprint, into steel, into the manufacture of particle board, roofing, into offshore construction, into consumer finance through Marac, into tunnelling, into joint ventures with some of the biggest names in world construction. Where his father was a builder, the son had become a full-fledged industrialist.

He pioneered manufacturing with an inexperienced workforce. Asbestos, particle board, newsprint, steel — they were all new, brave experiments that succeeded. In hindsight, a success looks easy. Once something is up and running, you can see how it was possible. As the Americans say, any fool can run a company, but it takes a genius to start one. Jim Fletcher started a lot of them.

Few people fully understand the risks of business. At many points, most of JC's biggest achievements could have turned into expensive flops. Crises are part of the territory in huge industrial enterprises, and it takes nerve, persistence and knowledge to overcome them. Before Tasman became easily New Zealand's biggest manufacturing exporter, it had to triumph over crises in finance, in its shareholding, in the commissioning process, in management. The Pacific Steel story was likewise full of potential disaster — Government bumbling, intense competition, commercial alliances whose own imperatives had first to be recognised and then satisfied, technical difficulties, and what would have been the fatal siren song of an ironsands-based industry. Any one of them could have wrecked the chances of establishing a domestic steel-making industry.

The creation of the pulp and paper and the steel industries illustrates a JC hallmark — a capacity for walking a tightrope, for finding success where lesser businesspeople would have discovered disaster. He was often on the brink of failure, yet always avoided it. Often he would lose to eventually win, as in the way Fletcher Holdings remained aloof from New Zealand Steel's recurring financial difficulties by staying out of the overambitious ironsands-based industry, and in the way he submerged his hurt and ego to allow the merger of Fletchers, Tasman and Challenge. As Carl Ryan, one of JC's longest-serving and most able executives, remembers: 'At Fletchers there was no time for the intrigue or self-aggrandisement that was common in so many other companies.'

In one important way Fletcher Holdings differed from a *zaibatsu*. It wasn't controlled by the Fletchers in terms of shareholdings. After 1942, it was the public and institutions such as insurance companies that owned Fletchers. But somehow the Fletchers retained their decent imprint on it. As the company grew outwards and upwards, it managed against all the odds to remain a family business in terms of its corporate culture. It had its own style, and still does, in head office at least.

The company remains today as open and candid as it ever was. Fletcher Challenge believes that the stock exchange rules on disclosure are there for a reason, and few companies are as open in the amount of information they reveal about their activities. That's one reason why it has still not been visited by scandal.

JC had flaws as a businessman, and he cheerfully concedes them. For example, though he could be as tough as barbed wire in pursuing a business opportunity, he was often too soft in human terms. He never lost his abhorrence of sacking or even kicking sideways incompetent staff. Long-serving executives remember him bursting into tears more than once at the prospect of having to tell somebody to go. Sometimes he would shunt the responsibility onto others.

JC wasn't a cold, bottom-line industrialist. At farewells of long-serving staff he has broken down at the prospect of losing a colleague; at his own farewell it was Vaughan who had to rescue him and finish his speech.

Other flaws? His natural shyness inhibited him as a lobbyist. Although JC would always vigorously argue a viewpoint, and especially so to politicians, it was not his habit to intrigue on the company's behalf, preferring to allow the weight of argument decide the matter. In this, he was often disappointed. Sir Ron Trotter could give lessons to Sir James in lobbying skills.

Perhaps what made the biggest difference was JC's human qualities. Because these are elusive to define as factors in commercial success, they are too easy to ignore. Yet intangible factors can make all the difference, and students of management could usefully study Jim Fletcher's role in the company. JC had a knack of winning loyalty and hard work. His staff repeatedly express their fear of letting him down. They just didn't want to disappoint him and, in trying not to, they achieved commercial feats that in theory were beyond them. They were, after all, almost all rough-handed construction men, not trained managers. Yet this unlikely inner circle, much later buttressed by the hiring of experienced New Zealanders from overseas, occupied the engine-room during those years of hectic growth and success.

Of course, JC tried to do too much, and he says so himself: 'I spread myself too thin. I was trying to run a stud, to race horses, to hunt, to run a business, to travel all the time.' He was clearly driven by the need to fill each moment. Vaughan had, as she recalls, 'to prise him away from business. He never needed relaxation. He was cranky about business.'

He also took on outside directorships and occupied them with the longevity that acknowledges continuing performance. Some of these positions were linked to Fletchers or to its business. He sat on the board of Certified Concrete for an astonishing forty years, from 1939 to 1979. For twelve years he was chairman of South British Insurance, and he still sees the irony of leaving the company prematurely as a glorified clerk and returning as a director and ultimately chairman. He was on the BP (New Zealand) board for twenty-six years, a period when it struck oil and gas finds at Kapuni and Maui and, through the acquisition of the Todd oil interests, leapfrogged over Shell to become New Zealand's biggest oil company. For sixteen years he was a director of Dalgety Loan (later Dalgety New Zealand); for fifteen years a director of Alcan (NZ); for eight years on Nylex (NZ); and he was the chairman of the pioneering consumer finance company Marac, steering it successfully around Muldoon's worries about letting New Zealanders borrow money for consumer durables.

Somehow he also found time to work his way from steward in the

Auckland Racing Club to its president, a period when daughter-in-law Sian Elias, wife of Hugh, gave him such a hard time about the lack of women members that she eventually became the first female member.

Essentially, JC has changed little over the years. Although his confidence has grown with the years of achievement, he is still modest. Unlike many businesspeople who have trodden on too many toes, he has kept his friends. People he likes still matter greatly — he keeps in touch with business colleagues of thirty years' standing.

Being of the Depression generation, he retains the work ethic that drove him. He and Vaughan believed in work. It was a privilege and a right. You didn't complain, and the children weren't allowed to complain either. 'I would never let the boys moan,' remembers Vaughan. 'It was an absolute law in the family. Say what's wrong or shut up.'

For an industrialist who has greatly added to the nation's payroll and taxes, he lives modestly in an apartment above Auckland's Hobson Bay, but retains his long-standing indulgence in high-quality cars. He drives a Mercedes-Benz sports coupe with some panache. He and Vaughan travel a little, often down to country race meetings, and say they enjoy life more now than ever. It seems a fair reward.

It's safe to assume that, if the present Sir James's father were alive, he would be pleased with his second son. The company he bequeathed made plenty of mistakes, but it survived them and grew. The company that his father hoped might one day achieve a turnover of £1 million achieved earnings in 1990, Sir James's final year as a director, of $662 million. Fletcher Challenge now regularly occupies a ranking of around 200 in the *Fortune* 500 compilation, the only definitive list of the world's biggest corporations. It ranks with companies whose names are almost household words — Olivetti, Heinz, Union Carbide, British Coal, Glaxo. It's bigger than Rolls-Royce, Daihatsu, Campbell Soup, Quaker Oats, L'Oréal, Fuji Heavy Industries, even Apple Computer. When JC used to read *Fortune*, he certainly didn't think the company would feature in the magazine.

Even the optimistic former carpenter from Kirkintilloch would not have envisaged such a spectacular growth. Though James senior liked to think big, he could not have envisaged a company like Fletcher Challenge emerging from the storekeeper's house he built in Broad Bay, Dunedin, so many years before.

Index